The Jacobite Threat —
England, Scotland, Ireland, France:
A Source Book.

To an Officer in King George's Army

God bless the King, I mean the Faith's Defender;
God bless — no harm in blessing — the Pretender;
But who Pretender is, or who is King,
God bless us all — that's quite another thing.

John Byrom (1692-1763)

THE JACOBITE THREAT —
ENGLAND, SCOTLAND, IRELAND, FRANCE:
A SOURCE BOOK.

by

Bruce P. Lenman
and John S. Gibson

Scottish Academic Press in association with
The Oxford and Cambridge Schools Examination Board

Edinburgh
1990

Published by
SCOTTISH ACADEMIC PRESS LTD.
139 Leith Walk, Edinburgh EH6 8NS

SBN 7073 0606 X   Cloth Bound
SBN 7073 0607 8   Paper Bound

Typeset by Trinity Typesetting, Edinburgh.
Printed by Martin's of Berwick Ltd.

CONTENTS

Chapter 7:   The '15

Chapter 10: The '45

Chapter 11: The Aftermath of the '45

Chapter 12: Jacobitism's Second Coming

ACKNOWLEDGEMENTS

The authors would like to express their thanks and gratitude to several bodies and individuals who have been of assistance to them. Alice Wemyss helped with to the MS of Lord Elcho's Journal. Dom Mark Dilworth made material from the Scottish Catholic Archives available for study. Frank O'Gorman devoted a good deal of time to discussing the original plan of this volume. The Arts and Divinity Research Fund of the University of St Andrews helped materially with a grant, and a subsequent loan, both of which were essential to keeping the project going. The staff of the Rare Book Room of the Swem Library in the College of William and Mary in Virginia were extremely helpful in making available items from their outstanding and underused collections of material from the late seventeenth and early eighteenth century. The William Andrews Clark Memorial Library in Los Angeles made rare late seventeenth-century pamphlets available, in the middle of a major re-shelving exercise. Without the habitual courtesy and efficiency of the staffs of the National Library of Scotland, the Scottish Room of the Edinburgh Central Public Library, and the Libraries of the Universities of St Andrews and Edinburgh, this book would never have been completed. Lastly, a word of appreciation to Mrs Audrey Inglis for the care she took in processing our script and copying such a diversity of source documents.

Bruce P. Lenman
John S. Gibson

INTRODUCTION

This collection of sources illustrating the role of Jacobitism in British and international politics in the period between 1688 and the latter part of the eighteenth century does not need to be prefaced with a short history of Jacobitism. The bibliography which follows this Introduction provides a guide to the latest surveys of the subject, and the introductions to the major sections of this book, supplemented by the much briefer introductions to the individual documents, are designed to give the systematic reader a selective but broadly adequate set of guide posts along the often tortuous path traced by the Jacobite phenomenon during its century or so of current political significance. Even the dates of that "century" are debateable. There can be no dispute about the point of departure, which was the Glorious Revolution in England late in 1688, which drove James VII of Scotland II of England and Ireland into exile in France, and triggered a series of rather different revolutions in the other parts of the far-flung British world. However, a closing date is very much a matter of taste. For the hard-boiled realist it must be 1759, the "Wonderful year" celebrated in the sea shanty "Hearts of Oak" when among other victories the Royal Navy under Admiral Hawke smashed the French Brest fleet in the battle of Quiberon Bay, and destroyed the last serious invasion plans in which France proposed to use an exiled Stuart as the political figurehead for an invasion of England. On the other hand a precise century is obtained (less a few months) by drawing a line in January 1788, when Charles Edward Stuart, an elderly alcoholic resident in Palazzo Muti in Rome (where he had been born) finally died. Even the nonjuring Scots Episcopalians, the stubbornest of Jacobites, gave up when the former Bonnie Prince Charlie was no more.

Yet even as they expressed their readiness to accept the legitimacy of, and to pray for, their Hanoverian monarch George III, the story of Jacobitism assumed a new twist, as the final section of this collection tries to show. The Hanoverian dynasty itself became neo-Jacobite, and "the Cause", which had for so long involved violence and intrigue against the Westminster government, became an intellectual and emotional symbol or set of symbols, often manipulated so as to encourage support for that government and the social *status-quo* which upheld it. The point of all of this is that it demonstrates a simple fact: to the question "what is or was Jacobitism?" there is not, and never was, just one simple answer. The definition even of its time-span is literally open-ended.

But the problem goes much deeper than that. One of the fundamental questions which any student of Jacobitism has to face is expressed in the opening texts in this collection. They are the product of a set of dramatic events, from the extraordinarily daring and technically very impressive invasion of England by William of Orange, to the consequent civil wars in Scotland and Ireland, but they include a substantial amount of political theory, much of it deeply interwoven with theology. The modern reader is likely to find this material difficult to stomach. He or she will inevitably find the categories of thought alien, and the combination of high passion and ponderous complexity which is typical of much of this writing makes it difficult to read. After all, in the early eighteenth-century Richard Steele and Joseph Addison, most notably in the periodicals the *Tatler* and the *Spectator*, set a standard of urbane clarity for workaday English prose which has never quite lost its authority since. However, it is important to recall Dr Samuel Johnson's remark that the *Tatler* and the *Spectator* were designed "to divert the attention of the people from public discontent". In other words, they presented an edited version of what was in fact a bitterly divided, often viciously partizan society, in which irreconcilable animosity was expressed in snorting fury and clotted prose.

Ideas matter, even if the precise nature of their linkages with motivation, action, and events can be difficult to define. Relatively simple notions of divine hereditary right nerved both James VII and II as he reached out for absolute power on the eve of the Glorious Revolution, and Charles Edward Stuart as he sought to recapture his grandfather's thrones in the high adventure of the '45, a rising which most contemporaries had assumed was beyond the realm of the possible. Both men experienced violent reaction when unpalatable reality broke in. James had a nervous breakdown when it dawned on him that his Anglican subjects were not as passive as he had assumed their political theology must make them. Charles lost all heart for further fighting after the battle of Culloden. Nevertheless, his serene assurance of both right and victory had been perhaps the single most important factor sustaining the rising up to that point. On the scaffold, often facing the hideous and obscene death of a traitor under English law (and after 1708 Scots Law was assimilated to English in this respect), Jacobite martyrs were often visibly sustained by an ideology which combined indefeasible hereditary right with the assumption that ultimately Divine Providence would vindicate it on the stage of human affairs.

However, the political thought of the Jacobites was much more complex than an unflinching exposition of a variety of divine right. That sort of argument was developed with particular zest by clerical Nonjurors (members of the Church of England who refused to take oaths acknowledging William and Mary and their Hanoverian successors), and by Scottish Episcopal clergy, nearly all of whom were strongly Jacobite. The snag was that though fluent and convincing, given their premises, on the right to hold power, they were conspicuously blank on the theory of exercising power, nor could Jacobites easily dodge the issue, given the open hostility of King James when on his thrones to their beloved Anglican church. Here the most eloquent and productive of Nonjuring divines, like the Irishman Charles Leslie, were less important to the development of Jacobite thought than the so-called "Country" tradition of opposition to "Court" tyranny, a tradition mediated to the Jacobites improbably but not inconsistently by some of the most radical Whig supporters of the Glorious Revolution. Men like Robert Ferguson "the Plotter" rapidly reached the conclusion that William of Orange had betrayed the Revolution and broken his pledged word to the British peoples by trying to preserve, in a modified parliamentary form, as much of the secretive and autocratic government style of late Stuart absolutism as he could. It was logical enough for men like Ferguson to turn to the chastened Jacobite camp, especially after 1693 when the exiled James had reluctantly accepted the idea that it was better to return to his thrones on agreed terms than moulder indefinitely in absolutist exile. By 1702 Jacobitism had become an opposition creed, indeed rather a radical one if by radical is meant demanding significant changes both in the central features of government, such as the ruling dynasty, and in major policies, such as an unpopular war or the incorporating Union with Scotland of 1707. Though the "Country" version of

Jacobite rhetoric owed much in origin to radical Whigs, it made eighteenth-century Jacobites, especially after 1714 when Whigs established a permanent grip on office and patronage, natural allies of the other historic party in late seventeenth and early eighteenth-century England, the Tories.

This fact in turn has created a host of difficult problems for historians. There was undoubtedly a linkage between Toryism and Jacobitism. "High-Flying" clergy of the Church of England, invariably Tory in their loyalties, could veer very easily towards Jacobitism. On the other hand this did not mean that all Tories were Jacobites, or that those who at some point adopted Jacobite views did so as a first option in politics. A Whig attempt in 1710 to prosecute a loud-mouthed Tory High Churchman, the Reverend Henry Sacheverell, on the grounds that he was challenging the very foundations of the "Revolution Principles" of 1688 was a spectacularly counter-productive failure. Bishop Francis Atterbury of Rochester undoubtedly engaged in treasonable communication with James Francis Edward Stuart, the Pretender (an anglicization of a French word meaning claimant), but he was probably driven to do so out of despair at the shipwreck of Tory and High Church hopes under the Hanoverian Whig ascendancy, and there is no doubt that Prime Minister Sir Robert Walpole squeezed every possible propaganda advantage out of Atterbury's embarrassment when the correspondence was revealed, and that he was happy to drive him into exile and into the service of the Pretender in 1722. After all, an earlier generation of Whig politicans had played the same game with Henry St John Viscount Bolingbroke, an important Tory leader whom they deliberately frightened into flight with threats of parliamentary impeachment (at its worst a form of judicial murder). Once on the continent Bolingbroke predictably took service under the Pretender.

He soon fell out of love with the exiled dynasty, so he negotiated the right to return to England in 1725, at the price of permanent exclusion from the House of Lords, and was until 1735 active in organizing a fierce propaganda campaign against the much-detested regime of Sir Robert Walpole. Simultaneously a royal favourite and the first over-mighty prime minister, Walpole was a cynical exponent of a combination of electoral manipulation and patronage shading into bribery which enabled a Whig minority to dominate politics and persecute a Tory party which still probably represented the majority of the political nation in

England. It is no accident that Jacobite journalists like Nathaniel Mist, who ran an anti-government journal for over twenty years as *Mist's Weekly Journal* in 1725-28, and *Fog's Weekly Journal* between 1728 and 1737, were prominent conductors of this chorus of abuse. Walpole, who maintained an elaborate spy service to penetrate and report on Jacobite activity, repeatedly argued that all Tories were either Jacobites or crypto-Jacobites. He believed his own propaganda, but then he wanted to, because it was politically so convenient.

The nature and extent of Jacobite support was a contentious matter for contemporaries. During the '45, the Scottish chiefs and officers in the Jacobite army were acutely sensitive to the question of how reliable was the story of Prince Charles that English Tories had assured him in writing that they would flock to his standard as soon as he crossed the Border. In fact he had no such letters, and disillusionment with the minute scale of English support was a major factor in the decision to turn back at Derby. More generally, there is debate about the nature and scale of support for each successive Jacobite rising. Two points are clear. First: they were all very different, as one would expect of complex events spread over a lengthy period of time. Secondly, though many Englishmen, including many English politicians, could talk a good Jacobite game, the vast majority of serious players were always Scotsmen, and in Scotland there was disproportionate representation in the Jacobite ranks from the Gaelic-speaking Highlands and the (Scots-speaking) North-East, composed roughly of the counties of Aberdeenshire and Banffshire. Outwith those areas, active Jacobite support in the Lowlands clearly peaked in the '15, and was at its lowest during the '45, the success of which owed more to apathy verging on hostility to the Westminister regime than to mass participation. Even so the majority of Scots in Highlands and Lowlands would have preferred to have the Stuarts back but were not prepared to pay a heavy price for the doubtful privilege. Within these broad parameters, there is scope for endless debate amongst historians as to the number and motivation of committed Jacobites.

At this point it is easy to use documentation to dive into micro-studies at town or parish level, to work out what kind of person was and who was not an active Jacobite. Another major objective of this selection of documents therefore is to remind the reader that there always was a macro as well as a micro side to the Jacobite phenomenon. In other words, as well as being a matter of, literally, parish politics, it was also always a matter of European significance, inextricably tied up with the highest levels of international power-politics. By the 1720s and 1730s few Jacobites thought that there was any hope of restoring the exiled Stuarts without significant foreign support. James, the Old Pretender, completely agreed with this interpretation, and though the Papacy was of all European powers the one most consistently supportive of the exiled dynasty, he and his followers knew full well that the key state was France. She alone had the financial, military, and naval power to invade England, but she also had a host of other commitments. Spain took an interest in the Jacobites after 1715, though her sponsorship of the largely abortive Jacobite invasion of 1719 was something of a freak. Fortunately for eighteenth-century British governments, relations between France and Spain, despite their common Bourbon dynasties, tended to be difficult and strained.

Jacobites, who had a vested interest in attracting foreign support, tended to cultivate unrealistically optimistic hopes both of the likelihood of risings in Britain and of the willingness of foreign governments to act on their behalf. They cherished hopes of support from Russia and Sweden, for example, which turned out delusive. Indeed Swedish officials almost certainly encouraged these delusions in order to con much-needed money out of Jacobite pockets. The brutal fact was that France did not see Hanoverian Britain as its prime enemy in the Walpole era. Invasion plans were seriously considered by France in 1744-45, and in 1759 after a revolution in European diplomacy in 1756 had radically changed the French view of Britain; but neither set of plans came to anything.

One basic consequence of Jacobitism's international role is that many of our sources on the nature of Jacobite strength have to be read with care, for they are not infrequently written, consciously or unconsciously, with a view to manipulating the mind of an influential foreign reader. Not that this is the only reason for reading Jacobite, or any other documents, with alert scepticism: particularly when dealing with dramatic, violent, and controversial events, all evidence is inevitably deeply-coloured by the experience and prejudices of the person or persons from whom it comes. Some events, like battles, are inherently confusing. A wise historian always prefers to try to reconstruct such episodes from a variety of sources which can be checked against one another.

The argument that Jacobite history can always be written by a judicious selection of contemporary sources, either in a pro-Hanoverian or a pro-Stuart vein, and that there is therefore no clear dividing line between history and propaganda is much too simple. There are as many different varieties of a story as there are informants. The Earl of Mar certainly did not see the battle of Sheriffmuir the same way as his arch-critic the Master of Sinclair. Now we know that the Master of Sinclair was a violently-tempered man who had killed Ensign Schaw in a duel in 1708, and then shot Captain Schaw, the ensign's brother, dead on parade without warning shortly afterwards. Condemned to death by court-martial, the Master escaped from Marlborough's army to Prussia where he skulked until pardoned in 1712. None of this necessarily vitiates his value as a witness. It just means that the evidence of third and fourth parties is essential to judge between the protagonists, and this is true of Prince Charles and his arch-critics on the Jacobite side, after Culloden, Lord George Murray and David Lord Elcho.

A grasp of the mental world of the Jacobite century is, of course, worth having for its own sake and for the way it enables us to appreciate the context of cultural change. It is, for example, no accident that Jeremy Collier, who in 1698 published his *A Short View of the Immorality and Profaneness of the English Stage*, was an English Nonjuror convinced that after the national apostacy of dethroning the Lord's annointed in 1688, the English nation had inevitably plunged into an abyss of moral disintegration. Precisely to demonstrate that this was not so, and that they were righteous as well as rightful rulers, William and Mary had looked favourably on the activities of the Society for the Reformation of Manners established in 1692.

In the last analysis, however, the study of the documentary base of a complex phenomenon like Jacobitism is primarily an education in probing and testing sources, often against one another, before erecting the likeliest working hypothesis. This is the vehicle in which the historian rides, however tentatively, closer to truth, or to an interpretation which, if often not the only one possible, is at least not palpably false. All in all, the critical assessment of that great stretch of past life we call Jacobitism is no bad training for business, not least the business of life.

B.P.L.

SELECT BIBLIOGRAPHY

Apart from one or two indispensable works, this bibliography concentrates on the latest publications, which sum up much older work, and almost all of which contain very helpful bibliographies.

I. *The British Background*

(i) *England*

Jonathan C. D. Clark, *English Society 1688-1832* (Cambridge University Press, Cambridge 1985).

Paul Langford, *A Polite and Commercial People: England 1727-1783* (The New Oxford History of England, London, 1989).

W.A.Speck, *Stability and Strife: England 1714-1760* (The New History of England Vol.6, Edward Arnold, London, 1977).

(ii) *Ireland*

Edith Mary Johnston, *Ireland in the Eighteenth Century* (Gill History of Ireland, Vol.8, Gill and MacMillan, Dublin, 1974).

A New History of Ireland IV Eighteenth-Century Ireland 1691-1800, ed. T.W.Moody and W.E.Vaughan, (Clarendon Press, Oxford 1986).

(iii) *Scotland*

Rosalind Mitchison, *Lordship to Patronage: Scotland 1603-1745* (Edward Arnold, New History of Scotland*, Vol.5, London, 1983).

*The above series was being transferred to the Edinburgh University Press imprint in the course of the late 1980s and early 1990s. The same press has reissued the next title.

William Ferguson, *Scotland 1689 to the Present* The Edinburgh History of Scotland Vol.IV, Oliver and Boyd, Edinburgh 1968).

(iv) *America*

Philip S. Haffenden, *New England in the English Nation 1689-1713* (Clarendon Press, Oxford, 1974).

II. *The European Background*

Derek McKay and H.M.Scott, *The Rise of the Great Power 1648-1815* (Longman, London, 1983).

Jeremy Black, *British Foreign Policy in the Age of Walpole* (John Donald, Edinburgh, 1985).

"Louis XIV and the Jacobites", by Claude Nordmann, in *Louis XIV and Europe,* ed. Ragnhild Hatton (MacMillan, pbk, London, 1976), pp.82-111.

David B. Horn, *Great Britain and Europe in the Eighteenth Century* (Clarendon Press, Oxford, 1967).

III. *The Era of Revolution 1688-92*

(i) *England*

W.A.Speck, *Reluctant Revolutionaries: Englishmen and the Revolution of 1688* (Oxford University Press, Oxford 1989).

(ii) *Ireland*

J.G.Simms, *Jacobite Ireland 1685-91* (Routledge and Kegan Paul, London 1969).

(iii) *Scotland*

Paul Hopkins, *Glencoe and the End of the Highland War* (John Donald, Edinburgh, 1986).

(iv) *America*

David S. Lovejoy, *The Glorious Revolution in America* (Harper and Row, New York, 1972).

IV. *General Surveys*

George H. Jones, *The Main Stream of Jacobitism* (Harvard University Press, Cambridge, Massachusetts, 1954).

George P. Insh, *The Scottish Jacobite Movement: A Study in Economic and Social Forces* (Moray Press, Edinburgh, 1952).

Bruce P. Lenman, *The Jacobite Risings in Britain 1689-1746* (Eyre Methuen, London 1980).

Bruce P. Lenman, *The Jacobite Cause* (Richard Drew Publishing in Association with the National Trust for Scotland, 1986).

Paul K. Monod, *Jacobitism and the English People, 1688-1788* (Cambridge University Press, Cambridge 1989).

V. *Detailed Studies and Collections of Essays*

J.G.Simms, *The Williamite Confiscation in Ireland 1690-1703* (Faber and Faber, London 1956).

Lawrence B. Smith, *Spain and Britain 1715-19: The Jacobite Issue* (Garland Publishing, Inc., New York 1987).

John S. Gibson, *Playing the Scottish Card: The Franco-Jacobite Invasion of 1708* (Edinburgh University Press, Edinburgh 1988).

John S. Gibson, *Ships of the '45* (Hutchinson, London 1967).

F.J.McLynn, *France and the Jacobite Rising of 1745* (Edinburgh University Press, Edinburgh 1981).

Bruce P. Lenman, *The Jacobite Clans of the Great Glen 1650-1784* (Methuen, London 1984).

Alasdair Maclean *A MacDonald for the Prince* (Acair, Stornoway, 1982).

Annette Smith, *Jacobite Estates of the 'Forty-five* (John Donald, Edinburgh, 1982).

The '45: To Gather An Image Whole, ed. Lesley Scott-Moncrieff (The Mercat Press, Edinburgh 1988).

Ideology and Conspiracy: Aspects of Jacobitism 1689-1759 ed. Eveline Cruickshanks (John Donald, Edinburgh, 1982).

Eveline Cruickshanks, Political Untouchables: *The Tories and the '45* (Puckworth, London, 1979).

The Jacobite Challenge, ed. Eveline Cruickshanks and Jeremy Black (John Donald, Edinburgh, 1988).

Jeremy Black, *Culloden and the '45* (Alan Sutton Publishing, Stroud, 1990).

Alasdair Maclean and John S. Gibson, *Summer Hunting a Prince* (Acair, Stornoway, 1990).

VI. *Bibliographies*

Magnus Linklater and Christian Hesketh, *For King and Conscience*: John Graham of Claverhouse, Viscount Dundee (Weidenfeld and Nicolson, London 1989).

Alistair and Henrietta Tayler, *The Old Chevalier: James Francis Stuart* (Cassell, London 1934).

Peter de Polnay, *Death of a Legend: The True Story of Bonny Prince Charlie* (Hamish Hamilton, London 1952).

Margaret Forster, *The Rash Adventurer: The Rise and Fall of Charles Edward Stuart* (Secker and Warburg, London 1973).

Frank McLynn, *Charles Edward Stuart: A Tragedy in Many Acts* (Routledge, London 1988).

Rosalind Marshall, *Bonnie Prince Charlie* (H.M.S.O. 1988).

Katherine Thomson, *The Jacobite General* (Edinburgh, 1958).

CHAPTER 1:

THE AMBIGUOUS HERITAGE OF THE BRITISH REVOLUTIONS OF 1688-90 IN ENGLAND, SCOTLAND, IRELAND, AND AMERICA

I: England's Ambiguous Glorious Revolution

Though England was uniquely fortunate amongst the British realms because its revolution in 1688-9 was truly glorious, in that it was bloodless, the replacement of King James by William and Mary left a heritage of deep confusion there. Originally, almost nobody had thought of changing the person of the monarch. Privately William probably hoped from the outset that James would go away, but any attempt to expel him, let alone claim a right to replace him on his throne, would have been politically suicidal. Conservative opinion in general, and Anglican opinion in particular had invested so much of its hope for political and social stability in the elevation of hereditary monarchy and in the concept of non-resistance to it, that a break in the normal succession to the throne created appalling mental anguish amongst many members of the Anglican ruling class. A selection of the many different responses to this problem follows.

i) *An Ultra-Conservative Williamite*
    One of the few Anglican country gentlemen who could see no great problem here was Edmund Bohun (1645-99), a Suffolk J.P. who detested Papists and Dissenters with equal zest. He had in 1684 shown his support for high-flying patriarchal theories of authority by publishing a *Defence of Sir R. Fulmer against Algernon Sidney*. He had therefore openly attacked the radical Whig position before the Glorious Revolution, and during it he argued in terms which made him an unusual phenomenon, a "non-resisting Williamite", but which were in fact brutally realistic and not without merit as an analysis of the motives of King James. Bohun discounted the second flight of James, which that monarch justified on the grounds of immediate danger to his life, and

1

in *The History of the Desertion, or an Account of all the Publick Affairs in England, from the beginning of September 1688 to the Twelth of February following. with an Answer to a Piece call'd The Desertion Discussed: In a Letter to a Country Gentleman By a Person of Quality* (London, 1689), he expounded his view that King James had wilfully abandoned his Kingdom of England rather than rule it legally. Here is a) an extract from the Preface, which summarizes the argument, followed by b) an excerpt from the text of the pamphlet he is answering, which points out some problems this interpretation creates for the other Stuart kingdoms, with c) Bohun's reply to this latter issue.

[Note the arbitrary use of italics in late seventeenth-century pamphlets.]

a)

TO THE
READER

I am persuaded, that those of the Church of England, *who now seem discontented at the Present State of Affairs in* England, *are mistaken in the matter of Fact; and that they do imagine the Religion, Laws, and Liberties of this Nation might have been secured to us, and our Posterity, by other, and those more legal Methods.*

Now if this Conceit of theirs were true, their Dissatisfaction would not be wholly unreasonable; but to me, who have considered every Step of this Great Revolution with the utmost Attention of Mind, it seems altogether false and groundless.—

I suppose it is not pretended in England, *His late Majesty forfeited his Right to Govern by his Misgovernment; but that the sense of it prevail'd upon him rather to throw up the Government, than to concur with an* English *Free-Parliament in all that was needful to re-establish our* Laws, Liberties *and* Religion; *and this is a proper legal* Abdication, *as it is distinguished from a Voluntary* Resignation *on the one hand, and a Violent* Deposition *on the other.*

He was bound to govern us according to law, and we were not bound to submit to any other than a legal Government; but he would not do the one, and saw he could not force us to submit to the other, and therefore deliberately relinquished the Throne, *and withdrew his Person and Seals, dissolving (as much as he could) the whole Frame of our Government.*

2

The Reader may observe, tho' he give Reasons why he withdrew the second time, he never gave any why he went away at first; nor can any be assigned (as I verily believe) but that which I have expressed.—

There may possibly be some few Men so superlatively Loyal, that rather than they would not still be under the Government of James *the Second, they would throw up all the* English *Liberties and Priviledges, and submit to an absolute and unlimited Soveraignty, either out of Scruple of Conscience, Vanity, or Humour; now to these I have nothing to say, but that if they are willing to be* Slaves, *they may; but it is unreasonable that they should enslave all the rest of the Nation too; and as the Number is not great, so I am persuaded (if Patience and gentle Methods are used) these Men will in a short time be convinced by their own Interest, and acquiesce at least, if they do not heartily joyn with the rest in the Defence of the present Government.* —

April 6th.
1689.

b) The anonymous author of *The Desertion Discussed*, whose views Bohun sought to rebut, had raised the problem of the other two kingdoms in the British Isles. Bohun cited his text as follows before attempting to demolish his adversary's reasoning.

THE
DESERTION
DISCUSS'D.

In a Letter to a Country Gentleman.

SIR,

I Don't wonder to find a Person of your Sense and Integrity so much surprized at the Report of the Throne's being declared Vacant, by the Lower House of the Convention: *For how* (say you) *can the Seat of the Government be Empty, while the King, who all grant had an unquestionable Title, is still Living,* and his Absence forced and involuntary? *I thought our Laws, as well as our Religion, had been against the Deposing Doctrine; therefore I desire you would Expound this State Riddle to me, and give me the Ground of this late extraordinary Revolution.* In answer to your Question, you may please to take notice, That those Gentlemen of the Convention, and

the rest of their Sentiments, who declare a Vacancy in the
Government, lay the main stress of their Opinion upon his Majesties
withdrawing himself.—

—it's not improper to observe, That this pretence of a Demise, if it
signified any thing, cannot affect *Scotland* or *Ireland:* Not the first,
For there his Majesty's Commissioners acted in the usual manner,
till they were disturbed: *Nor the second, For that Kingdom
continues still under the Regular Administration of the Lord
Lieutenant.* Neither is it sufficient to say, *That Ireland is an
Appendage to the Crown of England, and therefore it must follow its
Revolution.* For allowing a Demise was really consequent upon a
Failure of Seals and Representatives; yet there would be no colour to
apply it to a Case where there was no such Omission. For no
Forfeiture ought to be stretched beyond the Reason upon which it is
grounded. But this only by the way. I shall proceed to prove the first
thing propounded, *viz.* That his Majesty, before his withdrawing,
had sufficient Grounds to make him apprehensive of imminent
Danger.

c) Bohun's shrewd retort that James preferred to sulk abroad
rather than rule on any terms not laid down by himself was more
convincing than his response to the problem of Scotland and
Ireland, as the relevant passage on p.155 of his pamphlet shows:

Sect. 4. Our Author has a scruple whether the Kings going away
signifies any thing to *Scotland* and *Ireland*; now all this is no better
than *banter*, for when he left *England* he left them too, tho' the one
was for sometime, and the other still is under the *Regular
Administration* of *The Lord Lieutenant* as he tells us, but those that
have since come from thence assure us there is nothing Regular in
his Administration, but the British Protestants are treated as Enemies
by this Minister of his; so that *Ireland* being an Appendage of
England, and thus treating our Brethren, ought by us to be taken for
a Rebel and an Enemy, let the pretence be what it will; Their
Loyalty to the Late King not excusing but Aggravating their Injuries
to his Country men, who have done nothing to deserve this usage,
but it is to be hoped will find hands enough to revenge it in due
time.

ii) *A Contractual Whig.*

Whigs who argued that there had to be an implicit contract
between government and governed, and that James had fallen
because he broke that contract by ruling artibrarily, could see

4

precious little difference between the views of the most conservative backers of William, and those of the Jacobites. The barrister William Atwood was a voluminous writer on behalf of an aggressively contractual Whig point of view, which emphasized the role of the English Parliament and the concept of the Original Contract. He wrote *The Fundamental Constitution Of The English Government, Proving King William and Queen Mary our Lawful and Rightful King and Queen* (London, 1690) in response to a "Lay-Gentleman" whose writings tried to preserve High-flying Passive Obedience as orthodox Anglican doctrine. Atwood replied:

> Since therefore, neither *the Scriptures, Primitive Antiquity*, nor the *Doctrine of the Church of* England are against them, who embrac'd and assisted in the Deliverance which his present *Majesty* vouchsaf'd us; it became not this *Gentleman*, who takes such pains to purge himself from having any hand in it, to censure those *Worthies* who had, as not behaving themselves like *good Christians* and *good Subjects*.
>
> And to call them *a few*, is almost an equal Reflection upon the honour of the Nation, which has never been backward in freeing it self from Tyrrany; and was ready as a Man to act in this King's Service, before they were so just as to lay the Crown at his Feet; nay, before Success had crown'd his glorious Enterprize —
>
> That the Body of the Nation were thus forward, is manifest in their declaring by their *Representatives* that the late *King* had *broken the Original Contract* —

iii) *The High-Church Anglican Jacobite Position*

The Glorious Revolution could not have been achieved without Anglican support, for William owed his success mainly to the depth of support for him in the English political and social establishment, and that establishment was an Anglican one. King James had tried to forge an alliance of Roman Catholics and Protestant Dissenters against the Church of England, which explains the depths of alarm he raised in the hearts of conservatives like Archbishop Sancroft, who saw a future dominated by the twin terrors of Popery and Puritanism. The assumption on which Sancroft and other High-Churchmen operated until late in 1688 was that it would be possible to keep James on the throne, whilst successfully pressuring him to change his policies. They could thus square their relentless advocacy of hereditary rights and non-resistance with their equally conservative determination to protect the rights and privileges of the Church of England, modified by a measure of toleration which Sancroft and most of the bishops sincerely wished to extend to Protestant Dissenters. William's invasion and subsequent assumption of the crown therefore posed fearful ideological problems for conservative Anglicans. Sancroft, with a group of bishops and a significant number of conservative clergy, found it impossible to take the oaths of allegiance to William III and Mary, and became a Nonjuror. The way in which Nonjuror Jacobites could appeal to the passive obedience and indefeasible hereditary right convictions of Anglicans is well demonstrated by this anonymous pamphlet published in 1688.

The Church of Englands Complaint in Vindication of Her Loyalty

If ever Mother had just reason to Complain of her Children, and expostulate the Case with them, certainly it is I. If ever Children did Dishonour their Parent, or at any time Blast her Reputation, they are now mine.

I who formerly gloried in my stedfast and unshaken Loyalty; I who by many Canons and Ecclesiastical Constitutions established the Regal Authority against all Papal and Popular, Foreign and Domestick Power: I who so often declar'd it Unlawful for any Subject, upon any pretence whatsoever to take up either Offensive or Defensive Arms against their Soveraign. I who Contemned by Sister Churches, as Teaching Doctrines and Positions lessening that Towring Loyalty which I professed; and particularly Her of Rome, for maintaining a Foreign Ecclesiastical Jurisdiction, though only in meer Spiritual matters: Now find my Reputation Tainted, my Loyalty brought in question, and my constant adherence to my own Canons and Constitutions, not only doubted of, but denyed; whilst the Malice of some of my Children bring in a Foreign Power to invade my Soveraign's Rights, under a meer pretence of supporting my Grandure; and raise Popular Tumults for the establishing my Peace; whilst the irregular Zeal of others, makes them draw their Swords against their and my Head and Soveraign in the most unnatural Quarel; and others who should have stood up to support my Honour, not only look on with an affected Silence, but by covert wayes abet Rebellion.—

You know what Articles, Canons and Constitutions have been established by me in your Predecessors Times; and what Obligations

6

all my Children have lain under by them: But you know also how little they have been put in Execution.

You know, that from my first Establishment, I declared in my 37 Article, that, The Kings Majesty hath the chief Power in this Realm of England and other his Dominions, unto whom the chief Government of all Estates of this Realm, whether they be Ecclesiastical or Civil, in all Causes doth appertain, and is not, nor ought not to be subject to any foreign Jurisdiction. And this without any limitation.—

From whence it follows, That the Doctrine of Non-Resistance and Passive Obedience, is what was Taught in the Primitive Church, as necessary to be Practiced even towards Heathens, and their Laws, much more ought it now to be towards Christian Princes.—

And certainly, if it was then my Duty to cry out against any Independent Co-active Power, either Papal or Popular; it is no less my Duty now, to disavow any Foreign or Domestick Power, though Protestant.—

Publish boldly the Abhorrence of this Treacherous Invasion, which is the only way to clear your Innocence, and confute the Invadors Accusation. Move your Brethren to send forth your joynt Injunctions to all the Inferiour Clergy, commanding them to Preach Obedience and Non-Resistance to the People, and by that means quell the fury of the Rabble. Declare all those to be Excommunicated persons, whom the King declares to be Traytors. Pronounce Rebellion to be as the sin of Witchcraft, and that they who curse the King in their Thoughts, shall have a Bird of the Air carry the Voice, and an avenging God to punish the Offence. Stand up now, before it be too late for my Doctrine of Non-Resistance, and then you need not fear the being exercised in that of Passive Obedience. For when our Gracious Sovereign shall by that means, see your Loyalty in practice as well as Doctrine, He will be as constant to His Promises, as you can be to your Principles; and if I maintain the Right of Kings, He will maintain me as by Law Established.

FINIS.

(London, 1688)

iv) *The Man Who Changed His Mind: William Sherlock*

Perhaps the easiest publicist for a modern reader to sympa-thize with is Dr William Sherlock, an Anglican divine who at first could not bring himself to take the oaths to William and Mary, but who then argued himself into a position where he could. He was promptly denounced in a vast library of abusive

7

pamphlets as a turncoat, timeserver, place-hunter, and traitor to his church and monarch. In controversies contemporary Christian divines were seldom charitable. What may have added edge to the abuse heaped on Sherlock, who was Master of the Temple in 1691, and who went on to become in the spring of 1691 Dean of St Paul's, was the fact that he hoist the Nonjurors with their own petard by basing his conversion on *Bishop Overall's Convocation Book*, an early seventeenth-century compilation suppressed by James I, but finally published with the sanction of Archbishop Sancroft, just before he was replaced by the Williamite Archbishop Tillotson. The Nonjurors admired the High Church tone of this work, but Sherlock, like James I, spotted the fact that, on impeccable scriptural grounds, it recognized that it was part of God's mysterious Providence to cast down as well as to raise up kings, and that non-resistance was due to Divine Providence rather than earthly rulers.

If Allegiance be due, not to bare Legal Right, but to the Authority of God.

If God, when he sees fit, and can better serve the ends of his Providence by it, sets up Kings without any regard to Legal Right, or Humane Laws.

If Kings, thus set up by God, are invested with Gods Authority, which must be obeyed, not only for wrath, but also for conscience sake.

If these Principles be true, it is plain, that Subjects are bound to obey, and to pay and swear Allegiance (if it be required) to those Princes whom God hath placed and settled in the Throne, whatever Disputes there may be aboout their legal Right, when they are invested with God's Authority.

—The Church of England has been very careful to instruct Her Children in their Duty to Princes; to obey their Laws, and submit to their Power, and not to resist, though very injuriously oppressed; and those, who renounce these Principles, renounce the Doctrine of the Church of England: But she has withal taught, That all Soveraign Princes receive their Power and Authority from God; and therefore every Prince, who is setled in the Throne, is to be obeyed and reverenced as God's Minister, and not to be resisted; which directs us what to do in all Revolutions of Government, when once they come to a Settlement; and those who refuse to pay and swear Allegiance to such Princes, whom God has placed in the Throne, whatever their legal right be, do as much reject the Doctrine of the Church of England, as those who teach the Resistance of Princes.

8

For the proof of which, I appeal to Bishop Overal's Convocation Book, which contains the Acts and Canons of the Convocation begun in the first Year of King James I. 1603. and continued by Adjournments and Prorogations to 1610. under Archbishop Bancroft, a wise and learned man —

In Can. 28. where this Doctrine is decreed, they take care to condemn all those wicked means whereby such Changes of Governments are made, and yet to assert, That whenever such Changes are made, the Authority is Gods, and must be obeyed—

William Sherlock, D.D., Master of the Temple, *The base of the Allegiance Due to Soveraign Powers, stated and Resolved, according to Scripture and Reason and the Principles of the Church of England.*

(London, 1691))
Preface & pp.1-4.

II: *Scotland's Revolution and the Roots of Scottish Jacobitism*

In Scotland Stuart monarchy had united the Scots-speaking Lowlands, with their many urban settlements and northern Anglo-Saxon dialects, and the Gaelic-speaking Highlands and Western Islands, where a rugged terrain bred a hardy peasantry but no significant urban development outside Inverness. However, both the Highlands and the Lowlands were themselves deeply divided by geography and regional customs. The Southern Uplands, which lie between the great central valley of the Lowlands, and the English border, were very different from the Lowlands proper, and in the remote Northern Isles of Orkney and Shetland immigrant dynasties of Scots merchant-lairds presided over two archipelagic cultures which differed greatly from one another, but which were still unmistakeably Scandinavian rather than Scottish in style.

Apart from the monarchy, the nation of the Scots was held together mainly by the coherence of its aristocracy and to a lesser extent by the framework of its established church, its 'Kirk by Law Established'. The Restoration of 1660 had been as much the restoration of the Scots aristocracy after decades of revolution, civil war, and English occupation, as it had been the restoration of the Stuart dynasty. Even nobles who had fought against the Stuarts in the earlier Covenanting revolution joined in this conservative consensus. James VII (II of England and Ireland), was personally known to many members of the Scottish élite having spent some time in Edinburgh as virtual viceroy in the late 1670s and early 1680s. When the uproar over the alleged Popish Plot and the agitation to cut him out of the succession by the Exclusion Bill made England too hot to hold him as Duke of York, he had moved up to Scotland (where he used his corresponding Scottish title, Duke of Albany) and had made himself very acceptable indeed, partly because he certainly meant to invade England with Scottish and Irish help, to wage a civil war against the English Whigs, should they pass an Exclusion Act.

Religious confusion and arbitrary government had by 1688 gravely shaken the foundations of active loyalism in Scotland. The Kirk by Law Established combined episcopal and presbyterian forms, but it felt betrayed by a king who indulged uncompromising Presbyterians as a necessary evil on the road to toleration for Roman Catholics. The secular elites, who had helped crush Argyll's rebellion in 1685, were shaken by an arbitrary, intrusive style of government which threatened their centuries-old grip on the localities. James had a genius for alienating his own most loyal supporters to the point where an activist Whig minority proved capable of seizing control of Scotland in 1688-89.

i) *The Whig Charge That James VII Was Deliberately Destroying Traditional Monarchy and Reaching for Absolutism*

The following extract is from a pamphlet published while in exile in the Netherlands by the most vocal Scots Whig of the Revolution era, Gilbert Burnet (1643-1715). A former minister of the parish of Saltoun in East Lothian, he had been a professor of divinity in the University of Glasgow. An advocate of compromise between episcopal and presbyterian traditions in the Church of Scotland, he resigned his Glasgow chair and made a career in England as preacher at the Rolls Chapel. On the accession of James to the British thrones in 1685, he retired abroad first to Paris, and then to The Hague whence he issued *Some Reflections On His Majesty's Proclamation Of The Twelfth of February, 1686/7, for a Toleration in Scotland Together with the said Proclamation*. Burnet was ecumenical towards fellow-Protestants, and no persecutor by nature.

II.   The Preamble of a Proclamation is oft writ in haste, and is the flourish of some wanton Pen: but one of such an Extraordinary nature as this is, was probably more severely examined; there is a new Designation of his Majesty's Authority here set forth of his Absolute Power, which is so often repeated, that it deserves to be a little searched into. Prerogative Royal and Sovereign Authority, are Terms already received and known; but for this Absolute Power, as it is a new Term, so those who have coined it, may make it signifie what they will. The Roman Law speaks of *Princeps Legibus solutus*, and Absolute in its natural signification, importing the being without all Ties and Restraints; then the true meaning of this seems to be, that there is an Inherent Power in the King, which can neither be restrained by Laws, Promises, nor Oaths; for nothing less than the being free from all these renders a Power Absolute.—

III.   These being the Grounds upon which this Proclamation is grounded, we ought not only to consider what Consequences are now drawn from them, but what may be drawn from them at any time hereafter: for if they are of force to justifie that which is now inferred from them, it will be full as just to draw from the same Premises an Abolition of the Protestant Religion, of the Rights of the Subjects, not only to Church lands, but to all Property whatsoever. In a word, it asserts a Power to be in the King, to command what he will; and an Obligation in the Subjects, to obey whatsoever he shall command.

IV.   There is also mention made in the Preamble, of the Christian Love and Charity which his Majesty would have established among Neighbours; but another dash of a Pen, founded on this Absolute Power, may declare us all Hereticks; and then in wonderful Charity to us, we must be told, that we are either to obey without Reserve, or to be burnt without Reserve. We know the Charity of that Church pretty well: It is indeed Fervent and Burning; and if we have forgot what has been done in former Ages, France, Savoy, and Hungary, have set before our Eyes very fresh Instances of the Charity of that Religion: While those Examples are so green, it is a little too imposing on us, to talk to us of Christian Love and Charity. No doubt his Majesty means sincerely, and his Exactness to all his Promises, chiefly to those made since he came to the Crown, will not suffer us to think an unbecoming Thought of his Royal Intentions; but yet after all, tho' it seems by this Proclamation, that we are bound to obey without Reserve, it is Hardship upon Hardship to be bound to Believe without Reserve —

Some Reflections on His Majesty's Proclamation
for a Toleration in Scotland, pp.1-15.

11

ii) *The Consensus in the Scottish Political Nation that the Style of Government Practised by James VII was Unacceptable*

It would be quite wrong to think that even future Jacobites were prepared to tolerate the regime which had ruled Scotland in the name of James VII since 1685. By 1688 the Drummond brothers (the Earls of Perth and Melfort) and their cronies and toadies wholly dominated the administration. By a combination of arbitrary and often violent abuse of authority, and sly manipulation of the passionate and at times contradictory prejudices of an absentee monarch, they had feathered their own nests whilst alienating virtually everyone else apart from their own small clique. It is significant that when the Convention of Estates received a letter from King James, it passed a resolution making it clear that nothing in that letter would stop them sorting out the excesses and abuses of his government. More significant still was the list of signatories, which included an archbishop (Glasgow) and six bishops (Dunkeld, Moray, Ross, Dunblane, Sodor i.e. the Hebrides, and Orkney), as well as Viscount Dundee, the future leader of the first Jacobite rebellion.

ACT Declaring the Meeting of the Estates to be a free and Lawful Meeting, March 16, 1689.

Forasmuch, as there is a Letter from King James the seventh, presented to the Meeting of the Estates, they before opening thereof, Declare and Enact, that notwithstanding of any thing that may be contained in that Letter for Dissolving them, or Impeding their Procedure; Yet that they are a Free and Lawful Meeting of the Estates, and will continue undissolved, until they Settle and secure the Protestant Religion, the Government, Laws and Liberties of the Kingdom.

The Clergy and Nobility Subscribed thus,

Jo. Glasgow, John Dunkelden, Will. Moravien, Jo. Roffen, Robert Dumblanen, Arch. Sodoren, And. Orcaden, Hamilton, Douglass, Athole, Crawfurd, Lothian, Mortoun, Linlithgow, Eglingtoun, Forfar, Lovit, Bellanden, Lindores, Newark, Blantyre, Argyll, Southerland, Glencairn, Airly, Leven, Annandale, Tweeddale, Panmure, Tarras, Dundonald, Belcarras, Stormont, Kenmure, Arbuthnot, Tarbat. Dundee, Carmichael, Cardross, Belhaven, Rutherford, Bargany, Ross, Torphichen, Forrester, Rollo, Elphingstoun, Duffus, Ruthven.

The Barons Subscribed thus,

J. Maitland, Robert Sinclair, Ad. Cockburn, Andrew Agnew, Da. Arnot, Wm. Elliot,—

The Burgesses Subscribed thus,

John Hall, Geo. Stirline, Robert Smith, Ja. Fletcher, Jo. Anderson, J. Murray,—

> *The Acts and Orders of the Meeting of the Estates of*
> *the Kingdom of Scotland Holden and Begun at Edinburgh,*
> *the 14th day of March 1689. Called by Circular Letters*
> *from His Highness the Prince of Orange, under His Hand*
> *and Seal.*
> (Edinburgh, Heirs and Successors of Andrew Anderson, 1690).

iii)   *The Withdrawal of Allegiance from James VII*

Though virtually all the Scots ruling class was determined to modify the nature of their government, few, even after the successful invasion by the Prince of Orange, can have expected to see James VII replaced by another sovereign. Indeed, the Revolution would have been far more profound in its long-term implications if James had remained titular sovereign. As it was, the flight of James to France and the determination of William to settle for nothing else but three crowns, made the replacement of James inevitable. This famous declaration by the Estates has been more often cited than understood. It is strictly feudal and conservative in tone. Far from "deposing" James, it raised very valid questions as to the legitimacy of his *de facto* sovereignty, and then used the technical feudal term of forefaulture to argue that by wholly failing to observe his half of the feudal bond, James had forfeited his right to rule through it.

XIII.

The Declaration of the Estates of the Kingdom of Scotland, containing the Claim of Right, and the offer of the Crown to their Majesties King William and Queen Mary.

April 11. 1689.

Whereas King James the Seventh, being a profest Papist, did assume the Regal Power, and acted as King, without ever taking the Oath

13

required by Law, whereby the King at His access to the Government, is obliged to Swear, to Maintain the Protestant Religion, and to rule the People according to the Laudable Laws; and did by the Advice of wicked and evil Counsellers, invade the Fundamental Constitution of this Kingdom, and altered it from a Legal limited Monarchy, to an Arbitrary Despotick Power; And in a publick Proclamation, asserted an Absolute Power, to cass, annul and disable all the Laws, particularly arraigning the Laws, establishing the Protestant Religion, and did exerce that Power, to the Subversion of the Protestant Religion, and to the Violation of the Laws and Liberties of the Kingdom.

By Erecting publick Schools and Societies of the Jesuits; and not only allowing Mass to be publickly said, but also inverting Protestant Chappels and Churches to publick Mass houses, contrary to the express Laws against Saying or Hearing of Mass.—

By imposing exorbitant Fines to the Value of the Parties Estates, Exacting extravagant Bale: and disposing Fines and Forfaultures before any Process or Conviction.

By imprisoning persons without expressing the Reason, and delaying to put them to Tryal.

By causing pursue and forefault several persons upon Stretches of old and obsolete Laws, upon frivolous and weak Pretences, upon Lame and Defective probation; As particularly the late Earl of Argyle to the Scandal and Reproach of the Justice of the Nation.

By subverting the Right of the Royal Burghs, the third Estate of Parliament, imposing upon them not only Magistrats, but also the whole Town-council, and Clerks, contrair to their Liberties, and express Charters, without the pretence either of Sentence, Surrender or Consent; So that the Commissioners to Parliaments being chosen by the Magistrats and Council, the King might in effect als well nominat that entire Estate of Parliament; and many of the saids Magistrats put in by him were avowed Papists, and the Burghs were forced to pay Money for the Letters, imposing these illegal Magistrats and Councils upon them.—

All which are utterly & directly contrary to the known Laws, Statutes and Freedoms of this Realm.

Therefore the Estates of the Kingdom of Scotland, Find and Declare, that King James the Seventh being a profest Papist, did assume the Regal power, and Acted as King, without ever taking the Oath required by Law, and hath by the Advice of Evil and Wicked Counsellers, invaded the Fundamental Constitution of the Kingdom, and altered it from a legal limited Monarchy, to an Arbitrary Despotick Power, and hath exercised the fame, to the subversion of the Protestant Religion, and Violation of the Laws and Liberties of the Kingdom, in inverting all the Ends of Government, whereby he hath forefaulted the Right to the Crown, and the Throne is become vacant.—

The said Estates of the Kingdom of Scotland, Do resolve that WILLIAM & MARY, King and Queen of England, France and Ireland, Be, and be declared King and Queen of Scotland, to hold the Crown and Royal Dignity of the said Kingdom of Scotland, to them the said King and Queen, during their Lives, and the longest Liver of Them, and that the sole and full Exercise of the Royal Power, be only in, and exercised by Him the said King, in the Names of the said King & Queen during their joint Lives; and after their decease, the said Crown and Royal Dignity of the said Kingdom, to be to the Heirs of the Body of the said Queen; which failzing to the Princess Anne of Denmark, and the Heirs of Her Body; which also failing, to the Heirs of the Body of the said WILLIAM King of England.

And they do pray the said King and Queen of England to accept the same accordingly.—

The Acts and Orders of the Meeting of the Estates of the Kingdom of Scotland — 1689
(Edinburgh, 1690) pp.15-19.

iv) *Presbyterianism in the Kirk By Law Established and the Episcopalian Backlash*

a) *The Establishment of Presbyterianism:*

After 1660 the Kirk of the Restoration regime had deliberately tried to incorporate both the presbyterian forms which had been introduced under Andrew Melville's influence in the late sixteenth century, and episcopalian ones. Faced by the intransigent Jacobitism of the representative of the Scots bishop, Bishop Rose of Edinburgh, William of Orange reluctantly accepted the necessity of a purely presbyterian establishment in the Kirk by Law Established. Two problems immediately raised their heads. One was the high proportion of ministers, especially north of the Forth, who refused to accept such a settlement, and the second was the hostility of a significant proportion of the Scots nobility and gentry, who regarded an episcopal order as a desirable shield against ecclesiastical and social radicalism. They were also bound to regard the procedures for replacing disaffected ministers, which were an integral part of the new settlement, as an open challenge to their own local power. Disaffected Episcopalians usually formed a rough three-quarters of the active support for any of the future Jacobite rebellions in Scotland.

ACT Ratefing the Confession of Faith, and settling Presbyterian Church-Government.

June 1690:

Our Soveraign Lord and Lady, the King and Queens Majesties, and three Estates of Parliament, conceiving it to be their bound Duty, after the great Deliverance that God hath lately wrought for this Church and Kingdom, in the first Place to settle and secure therein, the true protestant religion, according to the truth of God's Word, as it hath of a long time been professed within this land. As also, the Government of Christ's Church within this Nation, agreeable to the Word of God, and most conducive to the advancement of true piety and Godliness, and the establishing of Peace & tranquillity within this Realm; And that by an Article of the Claim of Right, it is Declared, That Prelacy, and the Superiority of any Office in the Church above Presbyters, is, and hath been a great and insupportable Grievance & Trouble to this Nation, and contrary to the inclination of the generality of the people ever since the Reformation,—they do Establish, Ratifie, and confirm the Presbyterian Church Government and Discipline: That is to say, the Government of the Church by Kirk-Sessions, Presbytries, provincial-Synods, and General Assemblies, Ratified and Established by the 114 Act, Ja.6. Parl. 12. anno 1592. Entituled, Ratification of the liberty of the true Kirk, &c. and thereafter received by the general Consent of this Nation to be the only Government of Christ's Church within this Kingdom — Their Majesties with Advice and Consent foresaid, Do hereby allow the general Meeting, and Representatives of the foresaid presbyterian Ministers and Elders, in whose hands the exercise of the Church Government is established, either by themselves, or by such Ministers and Elders as shall be appointed and authorized Visitors by them, according to the custom and practice of Presbyterian Government throughout the whole Kingdom, and several parts thereof, to try and purge out all insufficient, negligent, scandalous and erroneous Ministers, by due course of Ecclesiastical Process, and censures; and likeways for redressing all other Church disorders. And further, it is hereby provided, that whatsoever Minister, being conveened before the said General Meeting, and Representatives of the Presbyterian Ministers and Elders, or the Visitors to be appointed by them, shall either prove contumacious in not appearing, or be found guilty, and shall be therefore Censured,

16

whether by Suspension, or Deposition, they shall *ipso facto* be suspended from, or deprived of their Stipends and Benefices.

Printed in *The Laws and Acts Made in the Second Session of the First Parliament of — William and Mary* (Edinburgh, 1690) pp.3-4.

b) *"The best of our owne": Archibald Pitcairne and Jacobite Political Culture*

As hostility to the London-based regime of King William mounted in Scotland, the Episcopalian Jacobite strand in the Scottish heritage provided a natural vehicle for the expression of conservative discontent with what was seen as an alien regime linked with a rabble-rousing Presbyterian Establishment. Nobody expressed aristocratic, Jacobite disdain for the new government more bitingly than Archibald Pitcairne, physician and poet, who was born in Edinburgh on Christmas Day 1652 and who died in 1713, before he could participate in the '15. Here is his view of the General Assembly of the Kirk.

A HOLY CONVOCATION.

Assist me all, ye Muses nyne!
With a beer glass of fourtie nyne[1];
For it is better, ten to one,
Then water of the Hellicon,
To warm the braine, and clear the witt,
And make a satyr dance and skip.
Assist! till I sing what did pass
Att the last meeting of the Ass-
Semblie, begun with frost and snow,
And just dissolved with the thow:
When expectation swelled big,
Both of the Torie and the Whig,
When each, his party to advance,
Did tell quite diff'rent news from France,
Tho' both told nothing but damn'd lies,
Of speaking cats, and prophesies;
Each strove the other to pull down,
And cloak did graple with the gown;

Episcopalls and Presbyters
Were yoak'd together by the ears,
About the form of Government,

17

For never one could both content;
While both did strive to rule the roast-
Whoever wins it's to our cost.
Mean while the cold phlegmatick trimmer,
(Who is a kynd of lukewarm sinner,
And for noe side would lose his dinner,)
Stood by, and gentlie smyl'd to see
Brithren thus live in unitie.
Quoth he, 'This wars amangst divines.
Shamefa' them wins, shamefa' them tines[2].'—

Some stood, some sat, some laid ther heads
Upon ther nighbours shoulder blades;
Some bow'd ther bodies down, but some
Did lean them on ther nighbours bum.
Noe painter could draw the grimmaces
That appeared in ther faces:
Some gasp't, some star'd, some visage wrung,
Some look't as they had smelled dung;
Some winkt, some others I did see
That girn'd and turn'd up white of ee,
Like those who have convulsion fits,
Or are deprived of their wits.
Yet all these postures did agree
Exactly in deformitie.
Extemporarie prayer ended,
Without Amen, for that's condemned
Be all the Presbyterian rable
As a vain superstitious bable,—

[1]a local beer
[2]tine - to lose.

> *Babel: A Satirical Poem on the Proceedings of the General*
> *Assembly in the Year 1692*, the Maitland Club
> (Edinburgh, 1830), pp.5-9.

III. *Ireland and the Revolution: War, Conquest, Jacobite Exile*

To understand the impact of the Glorious Revolution on Ireland,
and the uniquely exilic character of subsequent Irish Jacobitism,
it is essential to grasp the main outlines of the struggles which
had been raging within the Irish ruling class since the civil wars

of the 1640s and 1650s had shattered its fragile early seventeenth-century coherence. Ireland was ruled by a small aristocratic minority. There was nothing odd about that: so was virtually every other European realm. Nor was the fact that the crown of Ireland was attached as an appanage to that of England very abnormal. Multiple monarchies dominated by a core state were a very common way of giving coherence to large territories whilst preserving significant amounts of local autonomy for the peripheral units. What was unusual about Ireland was the existence of three rival groups within the aristocracy.

Late seventeenth-century Ireland had in fact known an unusual degree of stability after 1660, particularly under the two lengthy viceregalties of James Butler, 12th Earl and 1st Duke of Ormonde. He himself belonged, as his family name showed, to that feudal Anglo-Norman nobility which had started to penetrate and conquer Ireland about a century after it had seized Anglo-Saxon England. Ormonde was himself a staunch member and upholder of the Protestant Episcopal Church of Ireland, which was the established church of the kingdom, but the bulk of the old Anglo-Norman families, rather confusingly referred to as "the Old English", had embraced the Counter-Reformation rather than the Reformation, and so were strongly Roman Catholic. There still survived a recognisable group of aristocratic families of Gaelic extraction. After centuries of strife, these had made common cause with the Old English in the mid seventeenth-century civil wars, on grounds of shared religion. Both these groups had suffered heavily from successive waves of confiscations of estates and discrimination against them in state employment. These traumas had started in the Elizabethan era, and after a brief Jacobean peace had reached a crescendo in the Cromwellian conquest and forfeitures. The Restoration era saw the passing in 1662 of an Act of Settlement which with further radical modification in 1665 allowed for some modest concessions to the claims of the dispossessed, but which left them deeply discontented. This was hardly surprising as Roman Catholic recusants who in 1641 had owned about three fifths of all Irish landed estates were by 1665 reduced to roughly one fifth of Irish landed property. Yet with a sovereign who sympathized with his Roman Catholic subjects like Charles II, and more so with a fellow Roman Catholic like James II, the dispossessed had reason not to despair of recovering some or all of their losses.

The unexpected recall of Ormonde early in 1685 by the new monarch, James II, and the eventual nomination of the second Earl of Clarendon to succeed him, marked the beginning of a radical change in Irish affairs. Behind the Anglican Clarendon stood the real strong man of the new regime Richard Talbot, Earl of Tyrconnell. He controlled the army, where Roman Catholic officers and troops replaced Protestants. The Protestant militia of Ireland was disbanded during the scare which marked Monmouth's unsuccessful rising in England against King James. When Tyrconnell became Lord Deputy in 1687, he launched a systematic drive to undermine the Restoration settlement, and to reinstall in power as the Irish ruling class his own group of aristocrats, the so-called Old English. He was inevitably led to challenge the Restoration land settlement, though before the Revolution King James had only agreed, in secret, to plans to restore about half the Cromwellian confiscations.

After the news of the Revolution reached Ireland, Tyrconnell seems briefly not to have been clear whether to fight for James or try to cut a deal with William. His decision to fight for James, with French help, proved in the event catastrophic. A parliament in Dublin in 1689, dominated by the Old English interest, passed legislation which would have had the effect of confiscating almost all Protestant estates, whilst doing remarkably little for Gaelic Ireland, but the decision of battle went against Tyrconnell's Ireland. The Irish treasury was empty. The new-modelled army was weak and of low quality, and French aid proved inadequate. The Ulster Protestants successfully defended Enniskillen and Derry. William landed in Ireland in 1690, occupying Dublin after the Battle of the Boyne. James fled, and the Dutch general Ginkel eventually sealed the Williamite triumph by the conquest of the west, with his victory at the battle of Aughrim and the surrender, on terms, of the Franco-Irish army besieged in Limerick. The treaty of Limerick signed on October 3, 1691 marks the start of exiled Irish Jacobitism. Its terms are important. It was, however, preceded by a debate within the Jacobite camp on the whole question of military emigration, as the first document shows.

i) *Tyrconnell's View*

In August 1691 Tyrconnell, realising that many in the Jacobite army besieged in Limerick were beginning to think that they could carve out a career in the French service, especially if they offered themselves to Louis XIV as a compact formed army and not just as individuals, composed the following denunciation of the idea. It brings out many interesting tensions within the Franco-Irish army. As in Scotland in 1745-46, the French created much dissatisfaction and distrust in their allies. Implicit, but clear in the whole tone of the document, is the clash between the Old English Tyrconnell and Patrick Sarsfield, Earl of Lucan, the dashing cavalryman who was the leading representative of the Gaelic aristocracy, and the main advocate of military emigration. The document is translated from the original French.

Tyrconnell's view: Translation

My dear fellow-countrymen, if ever you were capable of thinking, that is more necessary now than ever, because you are on the verge of ruin.

To wait for help from France is pure self-deception; because I know well enough, and I warned some of my friends long ago, that the French were only trying to prolong matters until the winter, when they mean to carry across to France as many men as they can.

There are those who cry: "Let us go to France where we can remain faithful to our allegiance; where we shall be well paid; and where we can fight for our religion, and so on.

— To the first point I reply that if you can cross to France, which I greatly doubt, your numbers will not exceed ten or fifteen thousand men — It is easy to judge the sort of reception we can expect, by the relationship we have with the French who have been here, and which they will have to maintain for the sake of their reputations. They say that our regular troops are capable of shaping up, after serving under good officers for a while, but that our nobility is crude, lazy, stupid, and ignorant. The strangers who serve France can make up their unit numbers with fresh recruits, but this is out of the question for Irish commanders, who, once they abandon their native land, will never be able to set foot in it again. Believe me, those Frenchmen who are now trying to persuade you, with big promises, to sail to France, will be the first later to denigrate you, in order to obtain the reversion of your regiments.

You would also have to abandon unconditionally your wives, fathers, and mothers, relatives and children to the mercy of our enemies — who, in common prudence must extirpate them, because it is easy to foresee that if the alienated heads of these families were to return, their fellow countrymen and relatives would rally to them. — The ten or fifteen thousand men who may migrate to France as we all know from experience, will be wasted within two years to a third of their original size, even without the hazards of war, and I also have grave doubts whether France would ever let these men return home —

As for the third and final argument for emigration; that it would enable us to fight for our religion, it is surely clear that religion is not what this war is all about, since both Catholics and Protestants are allied to stop or challenge the mounting tyrany of France.

With my last breath I therefore implore you to oppose the enemy with a strong and vigorous faith, believing that though God wishes to punish his people for their sins, he has no desire to destroy them.

Printed from correspondence preserved in the Depot de la Guerre, France, in "Franco-Irish Correspondence December 1688-August 1691", ed. Lilian Tate, *Analecta Hibernica*, No.21 (Dublin, 1959) pp.226-228.

ii) *The Besiegers Realize that War-Weariness and a Desire for Military Emigration Lie behind the Franco-Irish Capitulation on Terms.*

Clearly Tyrconnell's point of view failed to carry the day within his own camp. It was opposed not only by the ambitions of Sarsfield, but also by the acute war-weariness of the French officers, who were as tired of Ireland as Ireland was of them. The Williamite besiegers were quite capable of reading the signs and understanding their apparent luck in securing the surrender of an undefeated force at a time when French reinforcements were expected at almost any moment. Those reinforcements arrived shortly after the surrender. They could have protracted the Irish war, but almost certainly not changed its result. Nobody in or around Limerick wanted that. Here is a Williamite account of the final scenes, drawn from Dr George Clarke's account of the campaigns of the Boyne, Aughrim, and Limerick 1690-91.

After some short stay the army advanced to Galway, which surrendered before any trenches were opened upon articles, and then we marched over Banagher Bridge and so to Limerick, where there was so strong a garrison that we durst not break ground and make approaches to attack it, for they had at least as many foot in the place as we had before it; but it being too soon to go into winter quarters we battered and bombed it, and lay there in expectation of what might happen.—

When they beat the chamade the first thing they desired to know was whether they might be allowed to go and serve where they had a mind, which was consented to, and next day, as I remember, they sent out their demands in writing; but those being very large it was thought better to send them a draft of the terms we would grant them than to retrench and alter theirs. Accordingly articles were drawn up, and the Irish deputed six persons to treat with us upon them. When we met, the first question Sir Toby Butler asked us was what we meant by the title, viz., Articles granted by Lieutenant-General Ginkel, Commander-in-Chief, &c., to all persons in the city of Limerick and in the Irish army that is in the counties of Clare, Kerry, Cork and Mayo, and other garrisons that are in their possession.

I answered that we meant to capitulate with and grant terms to those who were in a condition to oppose us. Sir Toby replied that if we meant to go no further there must be an end of the treaty, and Sarsfield added that he would lay his bones in those old walls rather than not take care of those who stuck by them all along. So the second article was explained to extend to all such as are under their protection in the said counties, which I mention the more particularly because those words, though first agreed to, were omitted by mistake in transcribing that copy of the articles which was signed,—

It may appear very strange that a numerous garrison, not pressed by any want, should give up a town which nobody was in a condition to take from them, at a time when those who lay before it had actually drawn off their cannon and were preparing to march away, and when that garrison did every day expect a squadron of ships to come to their relief, if they had needed any. But when we reflect that the first thing insisted upon at the time they beat the chamade was a liberty to go and serve where they would, and that Sarsfield reckoned upon making himself considerable in France by bringing over such a body of troops, it will be easy to account for their surrender. Besides, the Irish did not find themselves so assisted by France as they expected, and the French officers who were in the town were very weary of the service, so that they first proposed capitulating, as Sarsfield averred openly in the presence of the

French intendant at the time of signing the articles.

From Clarke's "Autobiography" which is printed in the Historical
Manuscripts Commission report on the *Leyborne-Popham MSS.*,
pp.271-281.

iii) *The Military Articles of the Treaty of Limerick*

Though seldom reprinted, in contrast to the Civil Articles,
which have been very often reproduced in print, the Military
Articles of the Treaty of Limerick were certainly closer to the
immediate needs and aspirations of the Irish commanders than
the Civil Articles. Even by the standards of the time Ginkel went
very far in according to his foes not only the honours of war, but
also shipping, and even supplies for horses and men, on credit,
but then as Ginkel was the first to insist, this was a most unusual
termination to a local war.

It was also the genesis of exiled Irish Jacobitism, for the
12,000 Irish soldiers who, along with some 4,000 women, children and old men, left for France, formed a Jacobite diaspora
which maintained its identity for decades.

The Military Articles of Limerick

I. That all persons without any exceptions, of what quality or
condition soever, that are willing to leave the kingdom of Ireland,
shall have free leave to go beyond the seas, to any country (England
and Scotland excepted) where they think fit, with their families,
household-stuff, plate and jewels.

II. That all the general officers, colonels and generally all other
officers of horse, dragoons and foot-guards, troops, dragoons,
soldiers of all kinds, that are in any garrison, place or post now in
the hands of the Irish, or encamped in the counties of Cork, Clare or
Kerry, as also those called rapparees or volunteers, that are willing
to go beyond seas as aforesaid, shall have free liberty to embark
themselves wheresoever the ships are that are appointed to transport
them, and to come in whole bodies, as they are now composed, or in
parties, companies or otherwise, without having any impediment,
directly or indirectly.

III.   That all persons above-mentioned that are willing to leave
Ireland and go into France have leave to declare it at the places and

times hereafter mentioned, viz., the troops in Limerick, on Tuesday next at Limerick; the horse at their camp, on Wednesday; and the other forces that are dispersed in the counties of Clare, Kerry and Cork, the 18th day of this instant, and on no other, before Monsieur Tumeron, the French intendant, and Colonel Withers; and after such declaration so made the troops that will go into France must remain under the command and discipline of their officers that are to conduct them thither; and deserters of each side shall be given up and punished accordingly.

VII.   That to facilitate the transporting of the troops the General will furnish fifty ships, and each ship burden two hundred tons, for which the persons to be transported shall not be obliged to pay, and twenty more, if there shall be occasion, without their paying for them; and if any of the said ships shall be of lesser burden, he will furnish more in number to countervail, and also give two men of war to embark the principal officers and serve for a convoy to the vessels of burden.—

IX.   That the said ships shall be furnished with forage for horses, and all necessary provisions to subsist the officers, troops, dragoons and soldiers, and all other persons that are shipped to be transported into France, which provisions shall be paid for as soon as all is disembarked at Brest or Nantes on the coast of Brittany, or any other port in France they can make.

X. And to secure the return of the said ships (the danger of the seas excepted) and the payment for the said provisions, sufficient hostages shall be given.—

XVII. That all prisoners of war that were in Ireland the twenty-eighth of September shall be set at liberty on both sides; and the General promises to use his endeavours that the prisoners that are in England and Flanders shall be set at liberty also ...

XXVII. That there shall be a cessation of arms at land, and also at sea with respect to the ships, whether English, Dutch or French, designed for the transportation of the said troops, until they be returned to their respective harbours; and that on both sides they shall be furnished sufficiently with passports, both the ships and men; and if any sea commander or captain of a ship, or any officer, troop, dragoon, soldier or other person, shall act contrary to this cessation, the persons so acting shall be punished on either side, and satisfaction shall be made for the wrong done; and officers shall be sent to the mouth of the river of Limerick to give notice to the commanders of the English and French fleets of the present conjuncture, that they may observe the cessation of arms accordingly ...

iv) *The Civil Articles of the Treaty of Limerick*

The second clause (the phrase "and all such as are under their protection in the said counties"), which had the effect of vastly widening the number of those who could claim the very real benefits of the surrender terms, was omitted in the first fair copy, and therefore in early printed versions, but restored by William III, on the insistence of the Williamite negotiators at Limerick. William was genuinely anxious to pursue a policy of moderation towards his new Roman Catholic subjects in Ireland, who formed a very large majority of the population of that kingdom, and the pledge in the first clause to try to ensure that Roman Catholics should not be disturbed in the exercise of their religion was not insincere. A Jacobite aristocracy William clearly could not tolerate, but the gravest discrimination against Roman Catholics in Ireland came under Queen Anne.

The Civil Articles

In consideration of the surrender of the city of Limerick and other agreements made between ... Lieutenant-General Ginkel, the governor of the city of Limerick and the general of the Irish army, bearing date with these presents, for the surrender of the said city and submission of the said army, it is agreed that:

I. The Roman Catholics of this kingdom shall enjoy such privileges in their exercise of their religion as are consistent with the laws of Ireland, or as they did enjoy in the reign of King Charles the Second; and their Majesties, as soon as their affairs will permit them to summon a Parliament in this kingdom, will endeavour to procure the said Roman Catholics such farther security in that particular as may preserve them from any disturbance upon the account of their said religion.—

VII. Every nobleman and gentleman comprised in the said second and third articles shall have liberty to ride with a sword and case of pistols if they think fit, and keep a gun in their houses for the defence of the same or for fowling —

IX.   The oath to be administered to such Roman Catholics as submit to their Majesties' government shall be the oath abovesaid and no other —

XII.   Lastly, the Lords Justices and General do undertake that their Majesties will ratify these articles within the space of eight months or sooner, and use their utmost endeavours that the same shall be ratified and confirmed in Parliament —

v) *Confirmation of the Missing Clause*
In order to leave no doubt about the acceptance of the missing clause, William and Mary, in accepting the Limerick Articles, added a rider. Because the settlement was regarded as over-generous by Williamite extremists, (it did ship an army to Louis XIV, as well as allow any Irish officer who had fought against William III at Limerick guarantees for peaceful possession of his estates if he remained in Ireland), further legislation of the Irish parliament (9 William III, Cap.II) fully confirmed the Articles. The elimination of a high percentage of the surviving minority of Irish Roman Catholic landlords was not in fact the direct result of the Treaty of Limerick.

Present,
Scravemore
H. Maccay
T. Talmash

And whereas the said City of Lymerick hath been since, in pursuance of the said Articles, surrendered unto Us, Now know ye, that We having considered of the said Articles, are Graciously pleased hereby to declare, that We do for Us, Our Heirs and Successors, as far as in Us lies, Ratifie and Confirm the same, and every Clause, Matter and Thing therein contained. And as to such Parts thereof, for which an Act of Parliament shall be found to be necessary, We shall Recommend the same to be made good by Parliament, and shall give Our Royal Assent to any Bill or Bills that shall be Passed by Our Two Houses of Parliament to that purpose. And whereas it appears unto Us, that it was agreed between the Parties to the said Articles, that after the words, Limerick, Clare, Kerry, Cork, Mayo, or any of them in the second of the said Articles, the words following: Viz., *And all such as are under their Protection in the said Counties*, should be inserted, and be part of the said Articles. Which words having been casually omitted by the Writer, the omission was not discovered till after the said Articles were Signed, but was taken notice of before the second Town was surrendered: And that our said Justices, and General, or One of them, did promise that the said Clause should be made good, it being within the Intention of the Capitulation, and inserted in the Foul Draught thereof. Our further Will and Pleasure is, and We do hereby Ratifie and Confirm the said omitted Words, Viz. *And all such as are under their Protection in the said Counties* Hereby for Us, Our Heirs and Successors, Ordaining and Declaring, that all and every Person and Persons therein concerned, shall and may have, receive, and enjoy the Benefit thereof, in such and the same manner, as if the said Words had been inserted in their proper place, in the said second Article; any Omission, Defect, or Mistake in the said second Article, in any wise notwithstanding.

From the *Harleian Miscellany*,
(London, ed. 1808-1811), Vol.X, pp.141-149.

vi) *The Penal Laws: Two Examples*
The systematic exclusion of Roman Catholics from positions of political weight in Ireland necessarily involved their exclusion not only from positions of political authority, but also from the landlord class, which in effect was political authority in the countryside. Irish parliaments, dominated by Protestant landowners who had been thoroughly frightened by the threat to their property and power under Tyrconnell, systematically erected a legislative structure designed to squeeze out of Ireland both Roman Catholic landlords, and indeed their form of faith. The latter objective proved impractical. The full battery of persecution was usually only applied spasmodically during occasional crises, and by the middle of the eighteenth century few educated Irish Protestants wanted or saw the need for a campaign to extirpate the religion of the majority. These two documents remind us that the campaign to pressure the remaining minority of Roman Catholic landowners into conformity with the Protestant majority of their class was formidable, broadly effective, and the key to the absence of Jacobite rebellions in eighteenth-century Ireland. They had no potential leadership.

a) *An Act Excluding Papists from Public Trust in Ireland, 1691*

An Act for the Abrogating the Oath of Supremacy in Ireland and Appointing other Oaths

IV.   And forasmuch as great disquiet and many dangerous attempts have been made to deprive their Majesties and their royal predecessors of the said realm of Ireland by the liberty which the popish recusants there have had and taken to sit and vote in Parliament, be it enacted ... that from and after the last day of January next no person that now is or shall be hereafter a peer of that realm or member of the House of Peers there shall vote or make his proxy in the said House of Peers, or sit there during any debate in the said House, nor any person that after the said last day of January shall be a member of the House of Commons shall be capable to vote in the said House, or sit there during any debate in the same after their Speaker is chosen, until he first take the oaths herein and hereafter mentioned and expressed, and make, subscribe and audibly repeat this declaration following:

I, A.B., do solemnly and sincerely in the presence of God profess, testify and declare that I do believe that in the sacrament of the Lord's Supper there is not any transubstantiation of the elements of bread and wine into the body and blood of Christ at or after the consecration thereof by any person whatsoever, and that the invocation or adoration of the Virgin Mary or any other saint and the sacrifice of the mass as they are now used in the Church of Rome are superstitious and idolatrous.—

IX.   Provided always, that this Act or anything herein contained shall not extend to hinder or disable any person or persons who on the third of October one thousand six hundred ninety-one were inhabiting or residing in Limerick or any other garrison then in the possession of the Irish, or any officers or soldiers then in arms by virtue of any commission of the late King James or those authorized by him to grant the same in the several counties of Limerick, Clare, Kerry, Cork and Mayo or any of them, or any commissioned officers then in their Majesties' quarters that did belong to the Irish regiments then in being, or were then treated with, or who were not prisoners of war and who had not then taken protection, and have since returned and submitted to their Majesties' obedience, from using, exercising and practising his or their profession or calling of barrister-at-law, clerk in chancery or attorney or practiser of law or physic, but they may freely use, exercise and practise the same as they did in the reign of the late King Charles the Second, anything herein contained to the contrary notwithstanding ...

From the Irish *Statutes of the Realm*, Vol.VI, pp.254-257.

b) *An Act of the Irish Parliament To Prevent The Growth of Popery, 1704*

It is perhaps necessary to warn the reader of these extracts against confusing ownership of land with access to use of land. Few big landlords actively farmed more than a small fraction of their estates. There was an active land market of some complexity, full of middlemen, tenants and subtenants, and outside Ulster these were overwhelmingly Roman Catholic. Even the restriction on leases to Roman Cathlics in clause VI must be seen in its economic context: thirty-one years was a very long term for an agricultural lease.

An Act to Prevent the Further Growth of Popery

Whereas divers emissaries of the Church of Rome, popish priests and other persons of that persuasion, taking advantage of the weakness and ignorance of some of her Majesty's subjects, or the extreme sickness and decay of their reason and senses, in the absence of friends and spiritual guides, do daily endeavour to persuade and pervert them from the Protestant religion, to the great dishonour of Almighty God, the weakening of the true religion, by his blessing so happily established in this realm, to the disquieting the peace and settlement, and discomfort of many particular families thereof; and in further manifestation of their hatred and aversion to the said true religion many of the said persons so professing the popish religion to this kingdom have refused to make provision for their own children, for no other reason but their being of the Protestant religion; and also have, by cunning devices and contrivances, found out ways to avoid and elude the intents of an Act of Parliament made in the ninth year of the reign of the late King William the Third for preventing Protestants intermarrying with papists, and of several other laws made for the security of the Protestant religion; and whereas many persons so professing the popish religion have it in their power to raise divison among Protestants by voting in elections for members of Parliament, and also have it in their power to use other ways and means tending to the destruction of the Protestant interest in this kingdom, for remedy of which great mischiefs, and to prevent the like evil practices for the future, be it enacted —

III.   And to the end that no child or children of popish parent or parents, who have professed or embraced, or who shall profess or embrace, the Protestant religion, or are or shall be desirous or willing to be instructed and educated therein, may in the lifetime of such popish parent or parents, for fear of being cast off or disinherited by them, or for want of fitting maintenance or future provision, be compelled and necessitated to embrace the popish religion, or be deterred or withheld from owning and professing the Protestant religion, be it further enacted ... that from and after the said twenty-fourth day of March one thousand seven hundred and three, upon complaint in the High Court of Chancery by bill founded on this Act against such popish parent, it shall and may be lawful for the said court to make such order for the maintenance of every such Protestant child, not maintained by such popish parent,—

IV.   And that care may be taken for the education of children in the communion of the Church of Ireland as by law established, be it enacted ... that no person of the popish religion shall or may be guardian unto, or have the tuition or custody of, any orphan child or children under the age of twenty-one years; but that the same, where the person having or entitled to the guardianship of such orphan child or children is or shall be a papist, shall be disposed of by the High Court of Chancery to some near relation of such orphan child or children, being a Protestant and conforming himself to the Church of Ireland as by law established, to whom the estate cannot descend, in case there shall be any such Protestant relation fit to have the education of such child; otherwise to some other Protestant conforming himself as aforesaid —

VI.   And be it further enacted — that every papist or person professing the popish religion shall from and after the said twenty-fourth day of March be disabled, and is hereby made incapable, to buy and purchase, either in his or their own name, or in the name of any other person or persons to his or her use, or in trust for him or her, any manors, lands, tenements or hereditaments, or any rents or profits out of the same, or any leases or terms thereof other than any terms of years not exceeding thirty-one years, whereon a rent not less than two thirds of the improved yearly value, at the time of the making such lease of the tenements leased, shall be reserved and made payable during such term ...

Printed in the *Irish Statutes at Large*, Vol.IV, pp.12-31.

IV: Revolution in the American Provinces of the English Nation

The group of colonies in North America stretching from New England to the vague frontiers of Spanish power, which lay somewhere to the north of present-day Florida, had grown substantially in number since the Restoration of 1660. With the exception of New Hampshire, the additional colonies — New York, New Jersey, Pennsylvania and the Carolinas — were all proprietary grants, and while few proprietors asserted the sort of sweeping authority which Charles I had granted to the Lords Baltimore in Maryland, they all wielded extensive power. On the other hand, the white inhabitants of these settlements (there were increasing numbers of black slaves, especially in the Chesapeake region) were emphatic that they were Englishmen, as well as Americans, and that they inhabited provinces of the English nation. Late Stuart absolutist government had closed in on these provinces after troops had to be sent to Virginia in 1676 to cope with the problems created by Bacon's Rebellion. By 1688 the New England Colonies, with their stubborn Congregationalist oligarchies, had been deprived of the virtual independence they had long enjoyed, and had been brought within a great new Dominion of New England. Its foundation was laid on an assault on colonial charters by crown lawyers, who used *quo warranto* proceedings to recall them. Governor Sir Edmund Andros ruled the Dominion for James II, with emphasis upon profit and dependency.

The rule of Andros was deeply unpopular with the bulk of the New England population, so the Glorious Revolution in Old England came as an unexpected but welcome surprise to most American settlers, but especially to the New Englanders. The authority which Andros wielded was entirely dependent on his ability to call on military and naval support from James II. On April 18 Boston exploded as armed colonists seized control of the town and seized and imprisoned Andros. Within four months, major rebellions occurred in Massachusetts, New York and Maryland. The New England colonies resumed their independence, and though relations with the Williamite government in London were far from easy, American Englishmen were committed to a radical Whig interpretation of the Glorious Revolution. There were individual Jacobites in late seventeenth and early eighteenth-century America, but there was no social or ideological basis for a Jacobite movement there.

i) *Massachusetts and the Rights of Englishmen*
There was clearly a great incentive for the colonists to try to

make metropolitan opinion aware of what had happened in America, and to try to do so in such a way as to propagate colonial interpretations of the significance of these events. Nathaniel Byfield's *An Account of the Late Revolution in New England Together with the Declaration of the Gentlemen, Merchants, and Inhabitants of Boston and the Country adjacent* (London, 1689) is a good example of the genre.

The Declaration of the Gentlemen, Merchants, and Inhabitants of BOSTON, and the Country Adjacent. April 18. 1689

II. To get us within the reach of the desolation desired for us, it was no improper thing that we should first have our Charter Vacated, and the hedge which kept us from the wild Beasts of the field, effectually broken down. The accomplishment of this was hastened by the unwearied sollicitations, and slanderous accusations of a man, for his Malice and Falshood, well known unto us all. Our Charter was with a most injurious pretence (and scarce that) of Law, condemned before it was possible for us to appear at Westminster in the legal defence of it; and without a fair leave to answer for our selves, concerning the Crimes falsly laid to our charge, we were put under a President and Council, without any liberty for an Assembly, which the other American Plantations have, by a Commission from His Majesty.—

IV.   In a little more than half a Year we saw this Commission superseded by another, yet more Absolute and Arbitrary, with which Sir Edmund Andross arrived as our Governour: who besides his Power, with the Advice and Consent of his Council, to make Laws and raise Taxes as he pleased; had also Authority by himself to Muster and Imploy all Persons residing in the Territory as occasion shall serve; and to transfer such Forces to any English Plantation in America, as occasion shall require. And several Companies of Souldiers were now brought from Europe, to support what was to be imposed upon us, not without repeated Menaces that some hundreds more were intented for us —

VI.   It was now plainly affirmed, both by some in open Council, and by the same in private converse, that the people in New England were all Slaves, and the only difference between them and Slaves is their not being bought and sold; and it was a maxim delivered in open Court unto us by one of the Council, that we must not think the Priviledges of English men would follow us to the end of the World:

Accordingly we have been treated with multiplied contradictions to Magna Charta, the rights of which we laid claim unto.—

An Account of the Late Revolution in New England, pp.7-13.

ii) *Maryland and the Protestant Revolution*

Maryland, a proprietorial colony ruled by Lord Baltimore through a local council which was also the upper house of the General Assembly, or local legislature, had been afflicted by acute tensions which had already produced insurrections in 1659, 1676, and 1681. The Calvert family, of which Lord Baltimore was the head, was Roman Catholic, and the colony was designed as a refuge for their co-religionists. Though very strongly represented amongst office-bearers, and on the council, Roman Catholics were a small minority in Maryland in 1689. The Calverts were strongly identified with James II and the rebellion by members of the newly formed Protestant Association in the summer of 1689, not only swept away the Calvert regime, but also prepared the way for the conversion of Maryland into a royal province in 1691, and for the formal establishment of the Church of England. The declaration issued by the Protestant Association in July 1689 was the prelude to these changes.

The Declaration of the Protestant Association, July 25, 1689

— His Lordships right and title to the Government is by virtue of a Charter to his father Cecilius from King Charles the first ... how his present Lordship has managed the power and authority given and granted in the same wee could mourn and lament onely in silence, would our duty to God, our allegiance to his Vicegerent, and the care and welfare of ourselves and posterity permit us.—

How the jus regale is improved here, and made the prorogative of his Lordshipp, is so sensibly felt by us all in that absolute authority exercised over us, and by the greatest part of the Inhabitants in the service of their persons, forfeiture and loss of their goods, chatteles, freeholdes and inheritances.—

... These and many more even infinit pressures and Calamitys, wee have hitherto layne with patience under and submitted to, hoping that the same hand of providence that hath sustained us under them would at length in due time release us. And now at length for as much as it hath pleased Almighty God, by meanes of the great prudence and conduct of the best of Princes, our most gracious King William, to putt a check to that great inudation of Slavery and Popery, that had like to overwhelm their Majestys Protestant Subjects in all their Territorys and Dominions ... Wee hoped and expected in our particular Stations and qualifications, a proportionable shew in soe great a blessing.

But our greatest grief and consternation, upon the first news of the great overture and happy change in England, wee found ourselves surrounded with strong and violent endeavours from our Governors here (being the Lord Baltemores Deputys and Representatives) to defeat us of the same.

Wee still find all the meanes used by these very persons and their Agents, Jesuits, Priests, and lay papists that are of malice can suggest to devise the obedience and loyalty of the inhabitants from their most sacred Majestys, to that height of impudence that solemn masses and prayers are used ... in their Chapells and Oratorys for the prosperous success of the popish forces in Ireland, and the French designs against England, whereby they would involve us, in the same crime of disloyalty with themselves and render us obnoxious to the insupportable displeasure of their Majesties —

Wee have considered that all the other branches of their Majesty's Dominions in this part of the world ... have done their duty in proclaiming and asserting their undoubted right in these and all other their Majesties Territoryes and Countys —

These are the reasons, motives and considerations which wee doe declare have induced us to take up Arms to preserve, vindicate, and assert the sovereign Dominion and right of King William and Queen Mary to this Province; to defend the Protestant Religion among us, and to protect and [s]helter the Inhabitants from all manner of violence, oppression and destruction, that is plotted and designed against them —

For the more effectual Accomplishment of which, wee will take due care that a full and free Assembly be called and conven'd with all possible expedition by whom we may likewise have our condition, circumstances, and our most dutyfull addresses represented and tendered to their Majesties —

Printed as document 57, "The Insurrection Accomplished" in Michael G. Hall, Lawrence H. Leder, and Michael G. Kamman (eds), *The Glorious Revolution in America; Documents on the Colonial Crisis of 1689* (University of North Carolina Press, Chapel Hill, for the Institute of Early American History and Culture at Williamsburg, Virginia, 1964), pp.171-175.

CHAPTER 2:

THE FIRST JACOBITE REBELLION:

Dundee's Rising in Scotland

The Irish war which came to an end with the Treaty of Limerick hardly qualifies as a rebellion. James II, the legitimate ruler of the Kingdom of Ireland, was recognized as sovereign by the regime of Lord Deputy Tyrconnell, and indeed had become the first King of England in three centuries to actually visit his Kingdom of Ireland when he landed at Kinsale in March 1692. It is true that after a rapturous reception, based on Roman Catholic expectations of a total restoration of their faith and former ruling class, his relations with his Irish supporters steadily soured. In Irish tradition he is James of the dung, and he sailed from Kinsale to France after the Battle of the Boyne as disillusioned with his Irish army as they with him. It may be that at various points Tyrconnell had aimed at an independent Ireland, and by the end of the campaigns Sarsfield was at least as concerned about his own future as that of James II. Nevertheless, the army of Roman Catholic Ireland fought in the name of the established sovereignty of James II, King of Ireland. They became rebels only in retrospect, and only because they lost.

The first Jacobite rebellion occurred in Scotland. Its civil and military leaders, Colin Lord Balcarres and John Graham of Claverhouse, Viscount Dundee, had attended the Convention of the Estates of the Realm summoned to Edinburgh by the Prince of Orange. It assembled on March 14, 1689. By March 18 Dundee had retired to his castle of Dudhope outside the town of Dundee, protesting that his life was in danger. In fact his motivation was primarily political. He and Balcarres had been commissioned by King James to manage his troops and civil affairs in Scotland. Dundee and Balcarres were in effect manoeuvring to take over Scottish government, in the name of James VII, but in practice as part of a Protestant Episcopal conservative reaction, very like the Anglican reaction which had gone so far in England before the landing of William of Orange.

The Earl of Melfort, brother of Lord Perth, Chancellor of Scotland, had become principal adviser to King James in Ireland. The Irish disliked Melfort as much as the Scots had. There were policy disputes which helped explain these quarrels between Melfort and his Irish allies. For Melfort, the priority after a Jacobite rising occurred in Scotland was to throw a significant force from Ireland into Scotland, to link up with that rising. His Irish colleagues, many of whom were not particularly worried about their sovereign's other two thrones provided they could create an independent Ireland under French protection, argued that this would create a dangerous dispersion of effort undermining success on every front. Significantly, in the middle of these Irish disputes, Dundee was writing to King James warning him that there was no place for Melfort in the future politics of Scotland.

Ironically, the letter which King James had sent to the Scottish Convention, penned by Melfort, was so dictatorial and tactless as to destroy hope of political support. Balcarres was seized and imprisoned and by mid April Dundee had signalled his appeal to arms by raising the royal standard on Dundee Law, a hill outside the burgh of Dundee. The Estates had proclaimed William and Mary joint sovereigns of Scotland in Edinburgh on April 11, and the burgh of Dundee was staunchly Williamite. The stakes were high, and we have accounts of the subsequent civil war from both sides.

I. The Jacobite View of the Rising

James Philip of Almerieclose, the author of the remarkable Latin poem "The Grameid", which describes the 1689 campaign, came from a family of staunchly royalist and Episcopal persuasion. His father was a bailie (or magistrate) of the small seaside town of Arbroath, near which the family built up a small estate, Almerieclose. He joined Dundee's rising at Dudhope, and acted as his standard-bearer. His poem provides an insight into the mind of an early Jacobite, as well as details of the support which rallied to Dundee. It starts with echoes of Virgil's "Aeneid" and Lucan's "Pharsalia" and includes a list of the Jacobite chiefs modelled on Homeric usage. Inevitably, his classical rhetoric leads to partisan exaggeration and it is disappointing that he never reached the battle at Killiecrankie in his verse.

GRAMEIDOS

LIBER PRIMUS.

Bella Caledonios civiliaque arma per agros
Instructasque acies, variisque horrentia signis
Agmina, et horriferae canimus certamina pugnae,
Magnanimumque Ducem, pulso pro Rege cientem
Arma, acresque viros, ipsumque in saeva ruentem
Vulnera, terribilemque in belli pulvere Gramum
Ingentemque heroem animis armisque potentem,
Pangimus et saeclis Mavortia facta futuris. —

Translation:
We sing the Scottish wars, and civil strife, the lines of battle, and
ranks bristling with many standards, the encounters of a horrid
contest. And we sing the noble Leader, calling brave men to arms
for an exiled King, and himself rushing to meet cruel wounds. We
sing the Graham, the great Hero, terrible in the dust of battle, mighty
in spirit and in arms. We tell of war-like deeds for times to come.—

—Therefore, from the various regions of the Scottish coast there
gathered to the war for fair liberty a band of noble leaders. And first
brave Stewart of Appin prepares his arms, and, with the whole body
of his clansmen, he leaves the shores bordering Leven, rich in fish,
carrying blue banners, charged with yellow figures. Him two
hundred men follow to dread war, all of them tall, terrible in form
and in arms —

Stewart himself, in their midst, is of great stature, and though so
young, that the yellow down does not yet cover his cheeks, he went
forth, the leader with his uncle of his father's clan, and carrying with
him its whole strength. Grandly he advances into the camp with his
splendid force. Now, also, the illustrious son of warlike MacNeill
comes from the winding shore of Barra's isle, around whom, as their
chief, a great company of the youth of his name presses on the right
hand and on the left. Carrying his immense battle-axe he advances
on foot, panting as he goes, leading his tall clansmen, himself the
tallest, and his shoulders covered with a Tyrian mantle. He displays
as many colours woven into his plaid as the rainbow in the clouds
shows in the sunlight. —

Here also from the distant shores of Raasay hastens, in striking
arms, the bold son of Malcolm, leading in long line a noble band of

clansmen, gleaming in brass, and bearing on their shoulders their heavy weapons. —

First, from his northern shores, the brave Glengarry leads three hundred illustrious youths in the first flower of vigorous manhood, each of whom a tartan garb covers[1], woven with Phrygian skill in triple stripe, and, as a garment, clothes their broad chests and flanks. A helmet defends the temples of the men. A coloured plaid veils their shoulders, and otherwise they are naked. The chief himself, mounted on a foaming steed, and towering in glittering arms, advances into the plain, claymore in hand, his cloak shining with gold, and a broad baldric with buckled clasp crossing his left breast. Following him closely comes his brother Allan, the brave, with a hundred men all clothed in garments inter-woven with the red stripe, their brawny calves bound with the red buskin. Afar they bristle with spears, and they stand firm with sword belted round their loins, with shields strengthened with brazen knobs protecting their bodies. Next came Glencoe terrible in unwonted arms, covered as to his breast with raw hide, and towering far above his whole line by head and shoulders. A hundred men, all of gigantic mould, all mighty in strength, accompany him as he goes to the war. He himself, turning his shield in his hand, flourishing terribly his sword, fierce in aspect, rolling his wild eyes, the horns of his twisted beard curled backwards, seems to breathe forth wrath wherever he moves. —

Besides these, from the high rocks of Argyll, there hastens the flower of young men, Dunderaw, the bold son of the faithful Macnachtan. As he is conspicuous in shining armour, so he is noble in spirit, and worthy of his great origin. Nor is he inferior to his father, whom the glory of reducing the Campbell to the laws, raised high on the wings of fame.—

[1] Some of the earliest references to clan tartans occur in this poem.

James Philip of Almerieclose, *The Grameid An Heroic Poem Descriptive of the Campaign of Viscount Dundee in 1689*, ed. Alexander D. Murdoch, Scottish History Society, Vol.III (Edinburgh, 1888), pp.1-157.

II. The Williamite Point of View

We are fortunate in possessing the military memoirs of the Williamite commander who, despite his defeat at Killiecrankie, fought the campaign through to a totally successful conclusion when his cavalry overran and routed the last Jacobite army on the alluvial flats beside the River Spey known as the Haughs of Cromdale on May Day 1690. General Hugh Mackay of Scourie ('the Dutch General' of the "Grameid") was a Highlander from a cadet branch of the chiefly house whose head was Lord Reay. Mackay was born about 1640. His first commission, as an ensign, was in Dumbarton's Regiment which Charles II sent to assist Louis XIV in his invasion of the Dutch republic in 1672. Marrying a Dutch lady, he resigned his commission from Charles II to join the Scots Brigade in the Dutch service. Like most of the officers of that Brigade, he refused the summons of James VII to leave the Prince of Orange in 1688. Instead, Mackay led the Scots Brigade home in the invasion of the Prince of Orange. A pious Calvinist, Mackay was to be killed at the head of his troops at the Battle of Steinkirk in 1692, and his eldest daughter was to marry George, third Lord Reay, head of Clan Mackay.

The Convention taking into consideration the untoward humours of many of the nobility and gentry, the combination of the Highland clans who apprehended the Earle of Argyles appearing greatness, and the genereal disaffection of the northern provinces, as well as of the borders, and of several of the chiefest corporations of the kingdom, not excepting Edinburgh, whereof the greater part of the inhabitants appeared not well pleased with the late happy, and for the general interest of the Protestant religion, as well as the liberty of Europe, so necessary a revolution, resolved to levy upon Scots pay 6000 foot in ten regiments, 12 troops of horse, making 600, and a regiment of 300 dragoons; and, accordingly, distributed commissions to such noblemen and gentlemen as did undertake to levy them, with levy-money, giving pouer to the colonels, as well as to the captains of horse, to make all their officers, whereby it fell out that those troops never came to any perfection, tho during the first six or seven months very punctually paid, because the chief officers, being all noblemen of no service, chose the officers of their regiments and troops, according as they had a kindness for their persons, or as they judged them popular, to get a number of men together, to the disorder of those troops, helping not a little, that the General found himself presently engaged in the war, so that he could neither see them, nor give order for their composition or discipline.

—But the General judging the consequence of letting Dundee, who wanted not his arguments, to persuade men to his measures, play his personage among the nobility and gentry of the north, and knowing that all the Duke of Gordons interest, which is considerable in command of men, would joyn with him as one man, having dispatched the Master of Forbes eldest son to the Lord of that name, who also hath a pretty command of men, and is no friend to Gordon, to oppose the first endeavours of Dundee, and labour to disabate the inhabitants of the northern provinces, and overturn Dundees persuasions, as well as his endeavours to form a party, resolved, upon the first advertisement from the said Master (to whom he had given written instructions how to believe in those matters), to march northward himself with what small number of forces he would spare from the siege of the Castle of Edinburgh, with the security of the government, and that of Stirling;—

The General engaged the Earle of Mar also, to cause observe Dundee with 3 or 400 Highlanders about the braes or height of the province of Marr, where he was very likely to pass; for about this time Mar began to change in favour of their Majesties interest and service; and likewaies he ordered the Laird of Grant, a person of a considerable estate and Highland interest, and following, to make all diligence to the north, and not only to hinder the passage of his own country, called Strathspey, from the Lord Dundee, but also to cause guard all the foords of Spey, which he might easily have done, had he used diligence, and followed his directions; but instead of that, Grant stayed some days after the General at Edinburgh, while he believed him before him to the north: which wrong step of his was certainly without any design of prejudice to the service, tho' highly punishable, had he been a man of service.—

It is necessary to remember, that all this time the General could not regulate himself by the Kings instructions, but rather by order of the Convention, which, immediately upon his landing, conferred upon him the General command of all the forces of the kingdom, raised and to be raised, which he made no difficulty to accept of, tho he had no particular instruction for it from the King, being sure his Majestie would be well satisfied since the Convention had not continued him in the administration of the government as that of England had done, that he, to whom his Majestie intrusted the service of that kingdom for him, should be also intrusted by them during their sovereignity, with the chief command of the forces whereof they had ordered the levie.—

The first day he set forward from St. Johnston he lodgede over against Dunkeld, where by 12 of the clock at night he received a letter from the Lord Murray signifying Dundee's entry into Athole, and his own retreat from the castle of Blair, (which till then he made the fashion to keep blockt) and his passing a strait and difficult pass two miles below the said house, leaving it betwixt him and the ennemy, the farther side whereof he affirmed to have left guarded, for our free passage to the Blair where he supposed Dundee to be already; altho Lieutenant-Colonel Lawder, whom the General commanded presently upon Murray's advertisement for the better securing of the pass, denied to have met with any of his men there. Next morning by the break of day the General marched, having dispatched orders to Perth to haste up the other six troops and come to the entry of the pass, which was eleven miles from his former nights camp, about 10 of the clock, where he let his men rest two hours to take some refreshment;

—Being come up to the advanced party he saw some small partys of the ennemy, the matter of a short mile, marching slowly along the foot of a hill which lay towards Blair,—he galloped back in all haste to the forces, and having made every battalion form by a Quart de Conversion to the right upon the ground they stood, made them march each before his face up the hill, by which means he prevented that inconveniency, and got a ground fair enough to receive the ennemy, but not to attack them, there being, within a short musket shot to it, another eminence before our front, as we stood when we were up the lowest hill, near the river, whereof Dundee had already gott possession before we could be well up, and had his back to a very high hill, which is the ordinary maxim of Highlanders, who never fight against regular forces upon any thing of equal terms, without a sure retreat at their back, particularly if their ennemies be provided of horse; and to be sure of their escape, in case of a repulse, they attack bare footed, without any cloathing but their shirts, and a little Highland dowblet, whereby they are certain to outrun any foot, and will not readily engage where horse can follow the chase any distance. Their way of fighting is to divide themselves by clans, the chief or principal man being at their heads, with some distance to distinguish betwixt them. They come on slowly till they be within distance of firing, which, because they keep no rank or file, doth ordinarly little harm. When their fire is over, they throw away their firelocks, and every one drawing a long broad sword, with his targe (such as have them) on his left hand, they fall a running toward the ennemy, who, if he stand firm, they never fail of running with much more speed back again to the hills, which they usually take at their back, except they happen to be surprized by horse or dragoons marching through a plain, or camping negligently; as the General four days thereafter surprized ten of them at Perth, and Sir Thomas Livingston the ensuing year in Strathspey, as we shall have occasion to touch hereafter.

All our officers and souldiers were strangers to the Highlanders way of fighting and embattailling, which mainly occasioned the consternation many of them were in; which, to remedy for the ensuing year, having taken notice on this occasion that the Highlanders are of such a quick motion, that if a battalion keep up his fire till they be near to make sure of them, they are upon it before our men can come to their second defence, which is the bayonet in the mufle of the musket. I say, the General having observed this method of the ennemy, he invented the way to fasten the bayoned so to the musle without, by two rings, that the soldiers may safely keep their fire till they pour it into their breasts, and then have no other motion to make but to push as with a pike.—

The General — resolved then to stand it out, tho' with great impatience, to see the ennemy come to a resolution, either of attacking or retiring, whereof they had more choice than he; and to provoke them, he ordered the firing of three little leather field-pieces, which he caused carry on horse-back with their carriages, which proved of little use, because the carriages being made too high to be more conveniently carried, broke with the third firing.—

—about half an hour before sunset, they began to move down the hill.—

The General observing the horse come to a stand, and firing in confusion, and the foot beginning to fall away from him, thinking happily that the horse would—follow his example, and in all cases to disengage himself out of the croud of Highlanders which came doun just upon the place where he was calling to the officers of the horse to follow him, spurr'd his horse through the ennemy.—Having passed through the croud of the attacking Highlanders, he turned about to see how matters stood, and found that all his left had given way, and got down the hill which was behind our line, ranged a little above the brow thereof, so that in the twinkling of an eye in a manner, our men, as well as the ennemy, were out of fight, being got doun pall mall to the river where our baggage stood.—

Major General Hugh Mackay, *Memoirs of the War Carried on in Scotland and Ireland 1689-1691*, Bannatyne Club, Vol.45 (Edinburgh, 1833) pp.7-59.

III. The Final Collapse of the Rising

Dundee's death at the moment of his striking victory at Kil-liecrankie did not mark the end of his rising, but reinforcement from Ireland had always been both a hope and a necessity for Dundee's relatively meagre forces. Apart from a ragged regiment under Colonel Alexander Cannon, which did reach the Scots Jacobites from Ireland in July 1689, that reinforcement never came. After Killiecrankie had been fought on July 27, Cannon took over the command, for which he was not well suited, and in the latter part of August tried to break out of the Highlands along the Tay Valley, through the natural gap in the Highland Line controlled by the small town of Dunkeld. There was a Williamite garrison consisting of the Cameronians, strongly Whig Presbyterians from the traditionally radical western parts of Lowland Scotland. In vicious street fighting around the cathedral the Cameronians so mauled the Highlanders that they retreated to Lochaber to lick their wounds. The Cameronian commander, the young soldier-poet Colonel William Cleland, like Dundee, died in the moment of victory.

Early in 1690 Major-General Thomas Buchan was sent by James to try to put fresh life into the defeated Jacobite army. He arrived in time to preside over the final débâcle on May Day 1690 on the Haughs of Cromdale. This did not stop dispersed groups of Jacobites wandering round the Highlands under arms. The following documents explain why such groups soon lost heart. The documents are a series of newsletters, obviously written from the point of view of a supporter of the government of the Estates.

Saturday Aug.16 to Tuesday Aug.19, 1690. No.134.

Edinburgh, August 12.

The Highlanders, that hitherto continued lurking in the hills during the time that Major-General Mackay was in the Field with the army, are now coming abroad again, & threaten to plunder & rob upon the skirts of Aberdeenshire; whereupon Sir Thomas Levingston is ordered to march against them, with three Regiments of Foot, & ten troops of horse & Dragoons.

Our Letters from Innerlochy tell us, That a party of that garrison having been abroad to discover the Rebels' places of abode & retreat, had engaged with a party of them, defeated them killed some, & taken others prisoners.

Tuesday Aug.19-Saturday Aug.23, 1690.

Edinburgh, Aug.16, 1690.—

About Twelve o'clock yesterday, Major Mackay & Sir Thomas Levingston's regiments of Dragoons were ordered to march immediately northward with all possible expedition; and the Major-General himself is to march to-morrow with a Battalion of Ramsay's & Lawther's Regiments to join them & the other Forces that are in pursuit of the Rebels.

Letters are just now come from Aberdeen, bearing date of the 12th, that give an account of the march of the Highland Rebels to Inneraries within ten miles of Aberdeen; & that the Master of Forbes and Lieutenant-Colonel Jackson, with six troops of horse & Dragoons were within & about the town; that they had put all the fencible men in arms, & raised a breastwork without the town & planted 20 pieces of cannon round the work at that part of the town where it was weakest; & doubted not but they should be able to defend it until the foot came up commanded by Colonel Cunningham & the other six Regiments that were hourly expected; which the post that brought those letters says he met marching in all diligence from Munross towards Aberdeen where he believed they would arrive this night. The same letters add, That the Highlanders in their march towards Aberdeen did not plunder & rob as they used to do; but took horses & provisions only wherever they found them. They are commanded by Cannon & Buchan; & some say that the Earl of Dunfermling is amongst them.—

Saturday Sept.6 to Saturday September 13, 1690.

Edinburgh, Sept.4.

By the last letters from the north, we have an account that the Earl of Dumferling, Cannon & Buchan at the head of some horse, have rambled through Murray, have crost the River of Spey, near the Bogue of Geeth, & gone as far as the River of Ness, which they passed above the town of Inverness, without venturing to come near the town. They have committed several robberies & plunderings all along as they march'd, taking away all the horses they could find. Those Gentlemen's houses & lands suffered most whom they knew to be best affected to the Government: & such as they believed to be well inclined to their party, they treated with more civility. They endeavoured to take or surprise Mr. Forbes' of Cullodens house, about 2 miles from Inverness; but they were disappointed the house being well manned. M. G. Mackay is in pursuit of them, & is now come to Inverness, the Rebels flying before him all along as he marches. When they past the Ness, they endeavoured to get the Frasers in the Aird, who are the chief inhabitants of those parts, to join them; but they could find none to come into them, they chusing rather to suffer all the depredations & plunderings then committed upon their lands, than to join with them in their rebellious practises against their Majesties government. From Inverness, the M. G. sent a summons to the Earl of Seaforth to lay down his arms, to come in & submit to the Government; but his answer was, That he kept his party in arms to defend himself against both parties. —-

Saturday Sept.13 to Tuesday Sept.16, 1690.

Edinburgh, Sept.9, 1690.

By the last letters from the North we have an account that M. Gen. Mackay was at Inverness on the 3ᵈ instant being returned from Ross, whither he was gone with a thousand horse & 1600 foot, & quartered two nights in Strapeffer upon the Earls of Seaforth's lands: which obliged the Earl to lay down his arms, come in & submit himself, offering good security for himself & his friends, to behave themselves peaceably & dutifully under their Majesties' Government; Whereupon the Maj. Gen. having secured all the country, returned back to Inverness; the Earl of Seaforth, & some of the chiefs of that clan, coming along with him. From thence he marches towards Aberdeen. The Steward of Appin, a Gentleman of considerable interest in those parts, is likewise come in, submitted & given security to the Government for himself & all his followers.—

Saturday Sept.27 to Saturday October 4, 1690.

Edinburgh, Sept.23, 1690.

Last week were seized in this Town two men for spies to give Intelligence to the Rebels; one of them belonged to L. C. Greimes, the other to the Laird Ladwharn, who had both joyn'd the Rebels. Upon their examination the first confess'd That he was servant to L. C. Greimes, but that he had freely deserted his service, with a resolution never to return to it again: That notwithstanding all the plunder & pillage, that the Rebels have lately got when they ravaged up & down the country, yet they were in great straits for want of forrage & provisions, which forced many to desert them: That all their forces consisted of about 400 horse & 200 foot when he left them, which was before they came down to the neighbourhood of Stirling, & that they were mouldring away & growing less every day. The other Prisoner being called & examined confirmed the same; & then they were both remitted to prison.—

Saturday Oct.4 to Tuesday October 7, 1690.

[Edinburgh] Sept.30.

We have heard no more of the Rebels, but from all parts are informed that they are dispersed.

Printed in "The End of the Active Resistance to William of Orange in Scotland" in *Highland Papers Volume IV*, ed. J. R. N. Macphail, Scottish History Society, 3rd Series, Volume XXII (Edinburgh, 1934), pp.107-120.

CHAPTER 3:

THE GROWTH OF DISCONTENT AND JACOBITE SYMPATHIES IN ENGLAND AND SCOTLAND 1690-1695

I. The Unpopular and Plot-Ridden Nature of William's Rule in England by 1690

The high-handed nature of William's government, and the rapidly-mounting costs to England of his great war with France, in increased taxes and repeated interruption of foreign trade by French naval and privateering activity, went far to undermine his popularity. Ironically, high on the list of those whose consciences were not in the least perturbed by the thought of serving William in his new capacity as King of England were several of the supple rascals who, even at the price of nominal conversion to Roman Catholicism, had served the authoritarian regime of James II to the bitter end. Too many of them remained in, or re-entered office for even the most middle-of-the-road Londoner to fail to notice the absence of what one of the following letters (that of May 31, 1691) calls "a Reformation as to places of trust". The fact that during the period covered by these letters Robert Spencer, Earl of Sunderland, one of the most feared and distrusted of the close confidants of King James, kissed King William's hands as he entered service under him, is significant. All these letters are by Richard Lapthorne, a moderately prosperous London businessman, to a correspondent in the country.

November 16th 1689

—On Monday last the Lord Preston late secretary of State to King James came to sit in the house of Lords as a peere, but the Lords inquiring into the patent found it bore date in January after ye Abdication and sealed at St. Germans for which hee was refused and also comitted to the Tower.—

January 3rd 1690

The King is hastening to ye Hague and its sayd the parliament is to continew sitting in absentia Regis and the Queene to preside and for that end her parliament Robes are a preparing. On Wednesday last the lord Preston Captaine Aston and Captaine Elliot were seized in a smack a litle below Gravesend going for France and there was taken with them a pacquett of Letters with a peece of Lead affixed that when thrown overboard they might presently sink.—

January 17th 1690(I)

This day was tryed the Lord Preston at the old Bayly and convicted of High Treason. hee had all faire play Imaginable and 9 Counsell assigned him. the Tryall held 8 or 9 houres though the Evidence very plaine. The owner of the smack and the master proved the contract exactly and Captaine Billop the master of the Kings yatch that seized them the maner of it and taking the letters and instructions which were read in Court: their offer to bribe him to throw the papers overboard or to joyne with them. the papers gave an account of the posture wee stood in here: in what condition our Fortifications: how they should fight us: with the Draught of a Declaration for King James such as Colemans and a key to explaine what was misterious in the letters and papers and Munday morning wilbe tryed Ashton and Ellyot.—

The King went away yisterday morning for the Hague.

January 20th 1690

Capt. Ashton was tryed yisterday at the old Bayly upon the same plott and the Lord Preston and hee received their sentence of death as for high treason. the sessions ended last night and Captain Ellyot put off till next Sessions unless tryed in Westminster Hall.

January 31st 1690

On Wednesday last Captain Ashton was caryed in a Coach to Tiburne and there only hanged and after his body was caryed back in a Herse to bee interred by his freinds. The discourse about the Lord Preston is various. Some say hee is penning a further discovery, others say otherwise and I heard one say this evening that a warrant was signed for his execution but Quere de hoc.—

May 16th 1691

—This week was sentenced at the Kings bench bar a parson of
Buckinghamshire, being convicted at the Assizes in the Cuntry for
drinking King James health and confusion to King William and
Queen Mary hee had taken notwithstanding the oaths of Aleagiance
and Supremacy, to pay 100 marks and caryed before all the Courts
in Westminster Hall with a Labell in his hat of his ofence and the
like to bee don at 3 Assizes in the Cuntry. hee sayd by way of
excuse hee was drunk — a sweet Apology for a Divine — The
busines[1] also between the Bp. of Exon and Dr Bury touching Exeter
Colledge was tryed and a speciall veredict found. Its sayd Dr.
Beveridge elect for Bath and Wells refused to take it and so is put
out of being the Kings chaplyn and forbid come to Court.

May 31st 1691

The lord Prestons pardon is now generally affirmed to bee sealed
and also Crones and both since released out of prison and that the
lord Prestin as tis sayd hath highly meritted his by making a great
detection of persons as well as things which I will beleive when I
see a Reformation as to places of trust. Col. Norton and Col. Tytus
lye dangerously sick. Some lords and other gents in a Night fray
lately killed a Bedle in Coven garden. The lord Archbp elect of
Canterbury is to bee consecrated tomorow and Dr. Sherlock
preaches the Sermon.

Printed in *The Portledge Papers*, ed. Russell J. Kerr and Ida Coffin
Duncan (London, 1928).

II. The Failure of Forfeiture in Scotland

The Jacobite rising in Scotland came to an end in 1692. Generals
Buchan and Cannon left from the port of Leith outside Edinburgh, along with a party of followers, to make their way to
France. There was no further resemblance between the fates of
the Scottish and Irish aristocracies. Whereas virtually an entire
Jacobite aristocracy (or to be more precise two: Gaelic and Old
English) left Ireland forever, there were no effective forfeitures
on any scale in Scotland, apart from the estates of the late Viscount Dundee, which in fact proved difficult to transfer into

politically trustworthy hands. In the Highlands it would not have been feasible to forfeit the Jacobite chiefs, most of whom were in fact formally received into King William's peace by 1692. These two documents from the records of the Scots Privy Council show the process of evacuating Cannon and Buchan, and the fact that some government supporters did feel that the only long-term security for the new regime lay in forfeiture and regrant. Both the style of the second document, and the proposal in it elsewhere for £150 per annum to the governor of Inverlochy, strongly suggest the possibility that the author was Colonel John Hill, who commanded there.

1692. Mar.23.

The Lords of th^r Maties Privy Councill doe hereby recomend to the Lord High Chancellour, to signe a pass in there name, for the ship, coalls, and baggage therein, skipper and ships crew, which are to transport Major Generall Buchan and Major Generall Cannane, and these allowed to goe alongst with them, for their passadge from Leith to the port of Haverdegrace in ffrance, conforme to there particular passes, and appoints the Councill Seal to be thereto appended. Sic Subscribitur, Douglas, Lothian, Leven, Stair, Jo. Lauder, Pat. Murray, W. Anstruther.

Memoriall to the King.

A.D. 1692, before 26 Apr.

Thers nothing can contribut mor to the reputation and security of ther May^{tys} goverment, then the rewarding and advancing such as ar true, and ar knouen to go upon the sam interest w^t the government, and the making proper examples of justice. Som of the most irreclammable familys that stand upon a foot oposit to the nation, as weill as ther Majestys, the D. of Gordons family is the head of the papists in Scotland, and hath alwys bein considered so. The E. of Seaforth hath turned papist, and both thes ar great famillys, the leaders of clans, vassalls, and followers. If the law be allowed to have its cours against them, the process of treason, now depending, will doub[t]less reach to forfaultour; and if ther wer competent allowances given to them and ther ladys, ther male childring takin and educat protestant, if the King did bestow ther estats upon them, it wer no hardship to disobleg the clans, bot an incredible advantage to that nation to hav thes familly[s] protestant;—

51

—therfor its proposed that the E. of Dumferlens estat in Murray shir, which is about six or seven hundreth pounds ster. be givin to the Lord Rae, the M'Kays bein all weill inclin'd to the goverment, besids the merit of Liftenant Gen. M'Kay, and they have, w^t reward, appeard severall tims in armes, in conjunction w^t ther Ma^{tys} forces, when they wer in greatest difficultys, and they particularly obliged my Lord Seaforth to render himself. Colonell Aeneas M'Kay, who is uncle and tutor to my Lord Rae, and who formerily brought out the M'Kays, offers to bring a full battalion of foot, weill armed, any time of ther May^{tys} reing, on ther oun charges, to any place of that kingdom they shall be required. Its proposed that the E. of Dinfermlins estat in Aberdeen shir, which may be about the sam value, sex or seven hundreth lbs ster. may be given to my Lord Forbess, who will bring tuo hundreth horse to ther May^{tys} service any tim they shall be required. Thes tuo clans ar both weill affected to ther Majesty service, and ther chieftans ar so low in ther fortuns, tho ther followings and freinds be considerable, that its proper for the goverment to support them.

Privy Council Records, printed in *Papers Illustrative Of The Political Condition Of The Highlands Of Scotland From 1689 To 1696*, Maitland Club, Vol.64 (Glasgow, 1845), pp.78-81.

III. The Massacre of Glencoe

i) *The Facts*

In the very early hours of February 13, 1692, soldiers from Argyll's Regiment under the command of Captain Robert Campbell of Glenlyon began a massacre which has ever since lived in infamy. This was a murderous attack upon the small clan of MacDonalds or MacIains of Glencoe, with whom they had been peaceably quartered for the past week, enjoying the hospitality they were now so shamefully abusing. As Highland massacres went, it was not a big one, claiming probably only 36 lives all told, but including that of the old chief so vividly described in the "Grameid". The operation was in fact botched. Other troops sent to block escape routes failed to arrive in time. By March 1692, when Argyll's Regiment, including Campbell of Glenlyon's men, were quartered in Leith, the port of Edinburgh, the Scottish capital was full of stories of the episode. The news of the massacre had reached London by February 27, but it was government policy to hush the matter up. Jacobite publicists saw it at once as a gift, and when on April 12, 1692, copies of the *Paris Gazette* reached London, the massacre became common knowledge. King William nevertheless stonily refused any official enquiry. The naval victory of La Hogue strengthened his hand. By 1693 pressure for an official enquiry by the Scots Parliament was mounting, and finally in 1695 William's political position was so weak in Scotland that he had to concede a parliamentary Commission of Enquiry whose moderate, just, and wise report is as damning as it is restrained. Note the way that the victims were drawn into the proceedings.

Protection for Glenco and others, 1695, be the Commission

1695, Jun.15.

At Edinburgh, the Fyfteinth of June, MD.C. and Nyntie fyve yearis, The Lords Commissioners appointed by his Majestie for inquyring into the mater of Glenco, considering that, by that order, the persons afternamed came to this place to mak ther appearance before them, viz., Johnne Macdonald of Glenco, Alex^r Macdonald his brother, Alexander Macdonald of Auchatriaten, Alex^r MacDonald of Dalnes, Ronald Macdonald in Lockintuin, Ronald Macdonald in Innerrigen, Duncan Mackeanrig in Innerrigen, Donald Macstarken in Larach, Alex^r Macdonald in Braickled, and Angus Macdonald in Strone. They doe heirby give personal protection to all the above named persons ag^t all captions, arrestis, or other diligence of that sort, from the date heirof inclusive, to the tenth of Julij next to come. Wherof all concerned are to take notice, and to observe the same, as they will be answearable.

ANNANDALE, P.
J. MURRAY.
JA. STEUART.
AD. COKBURNE.
WILL. HAMILTON.
JA. OGILVIE.
A. DRUMMOND.

Report of the Commission given by his Majesty, under the Great Seal, 29th April, 1695, for inquiring into the Slaughter of the Men of Glenco, 13th February, 1692

At Halyrudhouse, 20th June, 1695.

—The things to be remark'd preceding the said slaughter were, that it's certain that the Lairds of Glenco and Auchintriaten, and

53

their followers, were in the insurrection and rebellion made by some of the Highland clans, under the command, first of the Viscount of Dundee, and then of Major Gen. Buchan, in the years 1689 and 1690. This is acknowledg'd by all. But, when the Earl of Braidalbine called the heads of the clans, and met with them in Auchallader, in July 1691, in order to a cessation, the deceas'd Alexander Macdonald of Glenco was there, with Glengary, Sir John Maclene, and others, and agreed to the cessation;—And here the Commissioners cannot but take notice of what hath occur'd to them in two letters from Secretary Stair, to Lieutenant-Colonel Hamilton, one of the 1st, and another of the 3^{d} of December, 1691, wherein he expresses his resentment, from the marring of the bargain that should have been betwixt the Earl of Braidalbin and the Highlanders, to a very great hight; charging some for their despite against him, as if it had been the only hinderance of that settlement: Whence he goes on, in his of the 3^{d} of Decemb., to say, that, since the government cannot oblige them, it is oblig'd to ruine some of them, to weaken and frighten the rest, and that the Macdonalds will fall in this net: — And, in effect, seems, even at that time, which was almost a month before the expiring of the King's indemnity, to project, with Lieutenant-Colonel Hamilton, that some of them should be rooted out and destroyed.—and the Colonel produces Ardkinlas's answer to that letter, dated the 9th of January, 1692, bearing that he had indeavoured to receive the great lost sheep Glenco, and that Glenco had undertaken to bring in all his friends and followers as the Privy Council should order; and Ardkinlas farther writes, that he was sending to Edinburgh, that Glenco, tho' he had mistaken in coming to Colonel Hill to take the oath of allegiance, might yet be welcome, and that, thereafter, the Col. should take care that Glenco's friends and followers may not suffer till the King and Council's pleasure be known; as the said letter, mark'd on the back, with the letter B, bears;—

After that Glenco had taken the oath of allegiance, as is said, he went home to his own house, and, as his own two sons above nam'd depone, he not only liv'd there for some days quietly and securely, but call'd his people together, and told them he had taken the oath of allegiance, and made his peace, and therefore desir'd and engag'd them to live peaceably under King William's government; as the depositions of the said two sons, who were present, mark'd with the letter E, bear.

—Glenlyon, a captain of the Earl of Argyle's regiment, with Lieutenant Lindsay, and Ensign Lindsay, and six score soldiers, return'd to Glenco about the 1ˢᵗ of February, 1692, where, at their entry, the elder brother, John, met them, with about 20 men, and demanded the reason of their coming; and Lieutenant Lindsay shewed him his orders for quartering there, under Colonel Hill's hand, and gave assurance that they were only come to quarter; whereupon they were billeted in the country, and had free quarters, and kind entertainment, living familiarly with the people until the 13ᵗʰ day of Feb.; and Alexander farther depones, that Glenlyon, being his wife's uncle, came almost every day, and took his morning drink at his house, and that the very night before the slaughter, Glenlyon did play at cards, in his own quarters, with both the brothers; and John depones, that old Glenco, his father, had invited Glenlyon, Lieutenant Lindsay, and Ensign Lindsay, to dine with him upon the very day the slaughter happened. But, on the 13ᵗʰ day of February, being Saturday, about four, or five, in the morning, Lieutenant Lindsay, with a party of the foresaid soldiers, came to old Glenco's house, where, having call'd, in a friendly manner, and got in, they shot his father dead, with several shots, as he was rising out of his bed; and, the mother having got up, and put on her clothes, the soldiers stripp'd her naked, and drew the rings off her fingers with their teeth;—

The testimonies above set down being more than sufficient to prove a deed so notoriously known, it is only to be remarked, that more witnesses of the actors themselves might have been found, if Glenlyon and his soldiers were not at present in Flanders, with Argile's regiment;—

But Secretary Stair, who sent down these instructions, as his letters produc'd written with his hand to Sir Tho., of the same date with them, testifie, by a previous letter, of the date of the 7th of the said month of January, written and subscribed by him, to Sir Tho., says, "You know in general that these troops posted at Inverness and Inverlochie, will be ordered to take in the house of Innergarie, and to destroy entirely the country of Lochaber, Locheal's lands, Kippoch's, Glengarie's, and Glenco;" and then adds, "I assure you your power shall be full enough, and I hope the soldiers will not trouble the government with prisoners;"—But, in his letter of the 16ᵗʰ of January, of the same date with the additional instructions, tho' he writes in the 1ˢᵗ part of the letter, "the King does not at all incline to receive any after the diet but on mercy;" yet he thereafter adds, "but, for a just example of vengeance, I intreat the theiving tribe of Glenco may be rooted out to purpose." And, to confirm this, by his letter of the same date, sent with the other principal duplicate, and additional instructions, to Colonel Hill, after having written that such as render on mercy might be saved, he adds, "I shall intreat you that, for a just vengeance, and publick example, the tribe of Glenco may be rooted out to purpose.—

And, upon the whole matter, it is the opinion of the Commission, First, that it was a great wrong that Glenco's case, and diligence as to his taking the oath of allegiance, with Ardkinlas's certificate of his taking the oath of allegiance on the 6th of January, 1692, and Col. Hill's letter to Ardkinlas, and Ardkinlas's letter to Colin Campbel, Sheriff-Clerk, for clearing Glenco's diligence and innocence, were not presented to the Lords of his Majesty's Privy Council, when they were sent into Edinburgh, in the said month of January, and that those who advis'd the not presenting thereof were in the wrong, and seem to have had a malicious design against Glenco; and that it was a farther wrong, that the certificate as to Glenco's taking the oath of allegiance was delete and obliterate after it came to Edinburgh, and that, being so obliterate, it should neither have been presented to, [n]or taken in by, the Clerk of the Council, without an express warrant from the Council. Secondly, that it appears to have been known at London, and particularly to the Master of Stair, in the month of January, 1692, that Glenco had taken the oath of allegiance, tho' after the day prefix'd; for he saith, in his letter of the 30th of January, to Sir Tho. Livingston, as is above remark'd, "I am glad that Glenco came not in within the time prescribed." Thirdly, that there was nothing in the King's instructions to warrant the committing of the foresaid slaughter, even as to the thing it self, and far less as to the manner of it, seeing all his instructions do plainly import, that the most obstinate of the rebels might be received into mercy upon taking the oath of allegiance, tho' the day was long before elaps'd,—

—And this their humble opinion the Commissioners, with all submission, return, and lay before his Majesty, in discharge of the foresaid Commission.

(Sic Subscribitur) TWEDDALE.
ANANDALE.
MURRAY.
JA. STEWART.
ADAME COCKBURN.
W. HAMILTON.
JA. OGILVIE.
A. DRUMMOND.

Address by the Parliament to the King, touching the Murder of the Glencoe Men

[1695, Jul.10.]

—We found, in the first place, that the Master of Stairs letters had exceeded your Majesties instructions towards the killing and destruction of the Glenco men.—

We proceeded to examine Collonell Hills part of the business, and were unanimous that he was clear and free of the slaughter of the Glencoe men; for, tho your Majesties instructions, and the Master of Stairs letters, were sent straight from London to him, alse well as to Sir Thomas Livingstoun, yet he, knowing the peculiar circumstances of the Glencoe men, shunned to execut them, and gave no orders in the matter till such time as, knowing that his Lieutennent Collonell had receaved orders to take with him four hundred men of his garison and regiment for the expedition against Glencoe, he, to save his honour and authority, gave a general order to Hamilton his Lieuetennent Collonell, to take the four hundred men, and to put to due execution the orders which others had given him.

Lieuetennent Collonell Hamiltons part came next to be considered, and he being required to be present, and called, and not appearing, wee ordered him to be denounced, and to be seised on wherever he could be found.—

In the last place, the depositions of the witnesses being clear as to the share which Captain Campbell of Glenlyon, Captain Drummond, Liuetennent Lindsay, Ensign Lundy, and Serjand Barber, had in the execution of the Glencoe men, upon whom they were quartered, wee agreed that it appeared that the saids persons were the actors in the slaughter of the Glencoe men under trust, and that we should address your Majesty to send them home to be prosecuted for the same, according to law.—

And likewayes, considering that the actors have barbarously killed men under trust, wee humbly desire your Majesty would be pleased to send the actors home, and give orders to your Advocat to prosecut them according to law, there remaining nothing else to be done for the full vindication of your Government of so foull and scandalous an aspersion as it has lyen under upon this occasion.

We shall only add, that the remains of the Glencoe men who escaped the slaughter, being reduced to great poverty by the depredation and vastation that was then committed upon them, and, having ever since lived peaceably under your Majesties protection, have now applyed to us, that wee might interceed with your Majesty, that some reparation may be made them for their losses. Wee do humbly lay their case before your Majesty as worthy of your royal charity and compassion, that such orders may be given for supplying them in their necessities as your Majesty shall think fitt.

And this, the most humble address of the Estates of Parliament, is, by order, and their warrand, and in their name, subscribed by,

MAY IT PLEASE YOUR MAJESTY,
Your Majesties most humble, most obedient, and most faithful
Subject and Servant,
Sic subscrisbitur, ANNANDALE—

Printed in *Papers Illustrative Of The Political Condition Of the Highlands of Scotland*, pp.99-149.

ii) *The Issue*

The Massacre of Glencoe provided Jacobite propaganda with an ideal, because absolutely true, atrocity story with which to lambast the Williamite regime. It has been seen more recently as a sinister piece of evidence of an official plan for total genocide directed against the Scottish Gaels. This really does not appear to be a sensible view, not least because such a plan clearly never existed. More seductive has been a recurring emphasis on the massacre as part of a 'clan feud' between Campbells and MacDonalds. Now clearly the Argyll Campbells were the most prominent of the minority of clanned groups which were pro-Revolution. Equally, few of the many MacDonald clans were other than Jacobite in sympathy. However, no clan had eternal enemies, or eternal friends. Everything depended on circumstances, and all of them were used to living with governments of which they were unenthusiastic admirers.

The friendly reception given to Glenlyon's soldiers by the MacDonalds of Glencoe was significant. The Glencoe people thought that the military were on their way to launch a punitive strike against the MacDonells of Glengarry. This thought appears to have caused little distress. Most likely, people considered Alasdair MacDonell of Glengarry to be an irresponsible windbag who had pulled the coming disaster on his own head by refusing to come to terms with the new regime. The real issue raised by the massacre of Glencoe to contemporaries, regardless of kinship, party, or even religious affinity, was the behaviour of the British executive which first ordered the massacre, then stubbornly defended those guilty of it. For a long time William refused to have an enquiry. When he was forced to concede one and it made the Master of Stair's temporary resignation from office inevitable, William underlined his contempt for the whole business by safeguarding Stair from prosecution and awarding him revenues. The following documents show William's support of Stair despite the damning evidence against him, and the arguments of Andrew Fletcher of Saltoun in 1698, the year after a great cycle of war with France had ended, that by refusing to punish the worst agents of the tyranny of James VII, and indeed by often retaining them in office, William III had necessarily raised the question of whether the Revolution had really changed the nature of executive government. Nor was the popularity of that government enhanced by the famine Jacobites called "King William's Seven Ill Years."

a) *Scroll of Discharge to John Viscount Stair (1695)*

His Majesty considering that John Viscount of Stair, hath been employed in his Majesty's service for many years, and in several capacities, first as his Majesty's Advocate, and thereafter as Secretary of State, in which eminent employments persons are in danger, either by exceeding or coming short of their duty, to fall under the severities of law, and become obnoxious to prosecutions or trouble therefor; and his Majesty being well satisfied that the said John Viscount of Stair, hath rendered him many faithful services, and being well assured of his affection and good intentions, and being graciously pleased to pardon, cover, and secure him now after the demission of his office, and that he is divested of public employment, from all questions, prosecutions, and trouble whatsoever;—and particularly any excess, crime or fault done or committed by the said John Viscount of Stair, in that matter of Glenco, and doth exoner, discharge, pardon, indemnify, and remit the said John Viscount of Stair, &c.

b) *Scroll of Grant to John Viscount of Stair (1695)*

Whereas by the Act of Parliament abolishing Episcopacy, the rents, revenues, feu and teind duties, and others whatsoever, formerly pertaining to the bishops, are now in his Majesty's hands, and at his disposal; and his Majesty being graciously pleased to give a mark of his favour to John Viscount of Stair, and to prevent his trouble that may arise from the collecting of the tithes and feu duties of the parish of Glenluce, in which he is the principal heritor;— Therefore his Majesty gives, grants, and in take and assedation, lets all whole the foresaid teind duties and others whatsoever, due and payable out of the parish and regality of Glenluce, to the bishops of Galloway formerly, for the space years next to come, the entry or commencement of this take being from the date of Whitsunday last past, in the year of God 1695 years, and so forth, to continue during the whole space and years foresaid, to, and in favour of John Viscount of Stair, and his heirs for the time foresaid, for the payment of twenty shillings Scots money yearly,—

From the Stair family archives. Printed in *Papers Illustrative Of The Political Condition Of The Highlands Of Scotland*, pp.143-44

c) Extract from Andrew Fletcher of Saltoun's *Two Discourses Concerning the Affairs of Scotland Written in the Year 1698* (Edinburgh, 1698)

—When it is confessed and acknowledged that there have been bold attempts and treacherous practices to destroy the religion, overturn the constitution of government, and suppress the liberty of a nation, and yet no example made of the advisers, and those who have been eminently subservient to such designs; such a people has as much laid the foundation of their own ruin, as if they had declared that those who shall hereafter engage themselves in the like attempts, need fear no punishment. Upon a revolution followed by a war, circumstances of affairs may be such that till the war be at an end, it is not fit to punish great offenders. But there was no reason, nor any well-grounded political consideration, why immediately upon the late revolution, the most notorious of those offenders should not have been punished; by which means we should have been delivered from our worst men, who have since been very bad instruments in affairs, and have terrified the rest by their example: we might then have quieted the minds of the people by an indemnity; brought the nation to a settlement, and prevented the war which ensued in this country. Yet (because in matters of prudence men are of different sentiments) though it should be granted, that during the war it was not fit to make any examples, what pretence can there be now of exempting from punishment those who have been notoriously criminal, both under the late reigns, and under this?

which when it is done, what conjuncture of time can be so proper for applying the healing remedy of an act of indemnity and oblivion to the rest, as the present, by reason of the peace?—

—Is it not enough, that the punishment of those who endeavoured to enslave us under the late reigns has been delayed till now? Because they have renewed the same practices under this, must it still be delayed, to the end that (as they have already done in the affair of Glencoe) they may continue to give his majesty the same bad counsel with which the late kings were poisoned? Now, to pardon them we have this encouragement, that having passed over former crimes, we embolden them to commit new, and to give fresh wounds to that country which has already so often bled under their hands.—

My opinion therefore is that an act of indemnity (excepting only assassins and other notorious criminals, whom we cannot at present reach) is more suitable to our present condition than an act of banishment: and that to procure the nation so great a blessing, the parliament should proceed, without delay, to the punishing of the greatest criminals, both of this and the last reigns without which an oblivion will be one of the greatest injuries that can be done to us.

The Second Discourse Concerning the Affairs of Scotland; Written in the Year 1698

The affairs of which I have spoken in the preceding discourse are such as the present conjuncture makes a proper subject for the approaching session of parliament: but there are many other things which require no less their care, if the urgent and pressing distresses of the nation be considered. I shall therefore will all due respect to the parliament offer my opinion concerning two, which I presume to be of that nature.

The first thing which I humbly and earnestly propose to that honourable court is, that they would take into their consideration the condition of so many thousands of our people who are at this day dying for want of bread. And to persuade them seriously to apply themselves to so indispensable a duty, they have all the inducements which those most powerful emotions of the soul, terror and compassion, can produce. Because from unwholesome food diseases are so multiplied among the poor people, that if some course be not taken, this famine may very probably be followed by a plague; and then what man is there even of those who sit in parliament that can be sure he shall escape? And what man is there in this nation, if he have any compassion, who must not grudge himself every nice bit and every delicate morsel he puts in his mouth, when he considers that so many are already dead, and so many at that minute struggling with death,—

Reprinted in *Fletcher of Saltoun: Selected Writings* ed David Daiches (Edinburgh, 1979) pp.41-45.

CHAPTER 4:

PLOTS DUBIOUS, PLOTS REAL, AND PEACE
1692-1697

I: The Shadow of Invasion, 1692

The abdication of King James — if 'abdication' it was — had coincided with the opening of general European war. French aggression in the Rhineland in 1688 which broke European peace had not only given William of Orange his window of opportunity, with French armies so engaged, to invade England. It also elicited a warlike reaction from Holland, Austria and the German electorates and principalities, uniting Catholic and Protestant powers against France.

Not until 1692, with the Irish war lost and the conflict on the continent dragging on, did King Louis seek to strike at England. His purpose was to restore to the British crowns their natural sovereign, the exiled James; the sanctity of legitimate monarchy was ever in his mind. During the spring months of 1692, in the Cotentin peninsula which thrusts northwards towards England from the rest of Normandy there were concentrated ten Irish regiments which France had re-formed, re-equipped and was maintaining from the 15,000 'wild geese' who had come over as a consequence of the Treaty of Limerick; also a matching number of French regulars. James was with this mighty force to accompany it in the invasion of England. But the Irish regiments were still James' troops; they were not yet formally in the French Service.

This was to be the first of a succession of invasion projects which were to recur at intervals for the next hundred years or more. The first five of these, in 1692, 1696, 1708, 1744 and 1745 (like the one from Spain of 1719) would be associated with the Jacobite Cause. But their main purpose would ever be fulfillment of the Gallic dream of getting the better of Britain in the struggle for world supremacy.

To Louis, in 1692, it would seem that a cross-Channel invasion of England must succeed. The success of William's invasion four years past had no doubt been due to the luck of the
winds which prevented the superior English fleet intercepting
his own force. But in 1690 the French navy, led by Louis' bril-
liant bastard son the Comte de Tourville, had roundly beaten the
combined Anglo-Dutch fleet off Beachy Head. By 1692, moreover, contacts between English notables and the exiled court at
the Palace of St Germain near Paris had become frequent, as
William's popularity in England waned; and James had persuaded himself, and Louis as well, that the English navy he had
so lovingly built up in the years before 1688 would not stand in
the way of an invasion he, personally, was leading. The French
intention was that the Brest fleet, under Tourville, should come
up the Channel, defeat the English navy and transport the invasion force to Torbay before it could be joined by the Dutch fleet.
In England there was now widespread fear of invasion.

(i) *King James' Declaration*

James, confident of success, had printed and circulated widely
a declaration to his subjects, remarkable for its arrogant, uncompromising tone, even though it promised religious toleration.

(a)

Declaration

Whereas the most Christian King, in pursuance of the many
obliging promises he has made Us, of giving Us his Effectual
Assistance for the recovering of our Kingdoms, as soon as the
condition of his Affairs would permit, has put us in a way of
endeavouring it at this time; and in order to it, has lent Us so many
of his Troops, as may be abundantly sufficient to unty the hands of
our Subjects, and make it safe for them to return to their Duty, and
repair to Our Standard; and has notwithstanding for the present,
according to Our desire, (unless there should appear further
necessity for it) purposely declind sending over Forces so
Numerous, as might raise any jealousie in the minds of Our good
Subjects, of his intending to take the Work wholly out of their
hands, or deprive any true Englishman of the part he may hope to
have in so Glorious an Action, as is that of Restoring his Lawful
King, and his Ancient Government; (all which Foreign Troops, as
soon as we shall be fully setled in the quiet and peaceable

Possession of our Kingdom, We do hereby promise to send back, and in the mean time to keep them in such exact Order and Discipline, that none of Our Subjects shall receive the least Injury in their Persons or Possessions, by any Soldier or Officer whatsoever.) Tho an Affair of this nature speaks for it self, nor do We think Our selves at all bliged to say anything more upon this occasion, than, That We come to Assert our Just Rights, and to deliver our People from the oppression they lye under...

> Quoted in *Second Letter to a Friend concerning a French Invasion in which the Declaration Lately Dispersed under the Title of His Majesty's most Gracious Declaration to all His Loving Subjects Commanding their Assistance against the Prince of Orange and His Adherents is entirely and exactly published with some short observations on it;* published in 1692 by Randal Taylor, near Amen-corner (written by William Sherlock).

(ii) *An Anglican Rejoinder*

William Sherlock, the latter-day Anglican convert to support for King William wrote another pamphlet the directness of which compares well with his tortured *apologia* of 1689.

> He wanted nothing but Power to make himself Absolute, and to make us all Papists, or Martyrs, or Refugees; and that he will now have: For if a French Power can Conquer us, it will make him as absolute as the French King will let him be; or to speak properly, it will make him, though not an Absolute Prince, yet an Absolute Viceroy, and Minister of France: He will Administer an Absolute Power and Government, under the influence and direction of French Councels: and then we know what will become of the Liberties and Religion of England... And whatever some fancy, they will find it a very easy and natural thing, for the late King, if he return by Force and Power, to make himself Absolute by Law: Princes always gain new Powers by the ineffectual opposition of Subjects: If they lose their Crowns and recover them again, they receive them with an addition of some brighter Jewels, and turn disputed Prerogatives into Legal and undoubted Rights—

> All this is upon a supposition of the late King's return, which I declare to you I am not afraid of, though it is fit to mind those men who are so fond of it, what they may reasonably expect, if he should return; which possibly may abate their zeal in this cause, and that may prevent the mischiefs of an attempt; for without a hopeful Conspiracy in England, the French King is too wary to make such an Attempt.

But if they have any love to their Countrey, any pity left in them for the lives and fortunes of English Protestants, I beseech them to consider what the Calamities and Desolations of Civil War will be; for that it must end in, if there be an Invasion from abroad strengthned with a powerful Conspiracy at home: King William, as I said before, will not Desert or Abdicate;—

It must then come to Blows, if an attempt be made; and the fortune of one Battel may not decide it; and those who are too young to remember the desolations which the late Civil Wars in England made, let them look into Ireland, and see to what a heap of rubbish a flourishing and fruitful Countrey is reduced by being the scene of a Three Years War.

It is made a popular pretence to raise discontents, and to make people disaffected to the present Government, that the Taxes for maintaining this War are grown so intolerable, and there is no prospect of an end of them: Now I must confess, that the Taxes fall very heavy upon some, and am sorry that the present posture of our Affairs does require it, and that there can be no easier ways found to supply the plain and pressing necessities of the State: But we ought to consider, that still all this is infinitely easier than Popery and French Slavery, if we regard only our Estates.

Letter to a Friend Concerning a French Invasion To Restore the Late King James to his Throne and What may be Expected from Him Should He be Successful in It.
(London: 1692; published by Randal Taylor, near Amen-Corner).

(iii) *Failure of the Invasion Attempt*

Louis' confidence in the invasion project was misplaced though it might well have succeeded had the luck of the winds been with Tourville. Persistent easterlies slowed Tourville's coming up the Channel, as they enabled the Dutch and English fleets to join forces and intercept him. In a hard fought action off Cap Barfleur Tourville was battered by superior numbers. Some of his ships seeking safety by beaching themselves on the Cotentin shore were burned by boats' parties of intrepid English sailors under the eyes of James and his would-be invasion force. The invasion plan was dropped.

The Memoirs of the Duc de Saint-Simon record the view taken at Versailles of the disaster to their King's navy. These justly famous memoirs give the 'insider's-view' of the French court for the remainder of Louis' reign and beyond; they consist of contemporary record, polished up in subsequent years.

Translation

The King [now] suffered a cruel disappointment. He had at sea a fleet commanded by the famous Tourville as admiral. The English had another which with the addition of the Dutch was twice his strength. He was coming up the Channel and the King of England was on the Normandy coast ready to cross to England after victory at sea had been won. He relied so completely on his secret dealings with most of the English senior officers that he persuaded the King to order Tourville to do battle, the outcome of which he believed could not be in doubt with more than half the English ships, as he hoped, defecting when action was joined. Tourville, so renowned for valour and ability, sent two emissaries to the King to warn of the great danger of relying on the King of England's information which had so often proved false; and to warn too of the lack of harbours or any haven for escape should victory go to the English who would burn his fleet and destroy the rest of the King's navy.

These representations were of no avail. Tourville was ordered to fight whatever the circumstances irrespective of whether he was stronger or weaker than the enemy. He obeyed, did wonders as did his senior and junior officers alike, but not a single enemy ship showed weakness or came over. Sheer weight of numbers overwhelmed Tourville and though he saved more of his ships than anyone could have thought possible, nearly all of them were lost or burned after the battle at La Hougue. From the shore the King of England watched the fight. The accusation was made against him that he showed partiality for his own countrymen though not one of them had lived up to the promises on the strength of which he had insisted that battle be joined.

Mémoires de Saint-Simon, ed. A. de Boislisle
(Paris, 1879), Tome I, pp. 51-2.

II. A Triumph of Providence
— The Assassination Plot of 1696

The death of Mary II on December 28, 1694, was unexpected. She was only thirty-two, and she left her disconsolate spouse William III lonely, isolated, and unpopular. The elections of 1695 returned a predominantly Whig English Parliament, with which he proved to be not on the best terms. Price rises and

inflation, both greatly stimulated by war expenditures, were causing great distress. The exiled King James was advised by his
agents that the time was ripe for a combined French invasion
and Jacobite rising. Louis XIV, anxious to end a punishing war
at a blow, started to assemble men and ships for the invasion.
The snag was that both parties to the plan wanted the other to
make the first move. James even sent his talented bastard son,
the Duke of Berwick (his mother was the Duke of Marlborough's sister Arabella Churchill), to England to try to persuade
the Jacobites to rise first. They refused, and privately Berwick
thought them wise so to do.

To break the deadlock, a group of conspirators led by the
Scots professional soldier, Sir George Barkley, decided to elimi-
nate William first. Berwick was given to understand the plan
was to kidnap William. In fact the aim was always to assassinate
him. Jacobite officers had been infiltrated into the London area.
They were to ambush William's coach as he moved from Ken-
sington to Richmond for his regular Saturday afternoon hunting
party.

Security amongst the conspirators was poor. The French preparations could not be concealed and gave rise to general apprehension that some sort of coup was in the wind. The conspiracy
was penetrated by a spy, and its nature and murderous objective
alienated several late and unenthusiastic recruits to the plot,
Roman Catholic and Jacobite though they were. Once discovered, the plot proved a massive political and propaganda asset
for William. Englishmen, from Surrey to New York and Rhode
Island were mobilized politically by an anti-Jacobite surge of
zeal. Since Jacobites needed at least acquiescence from most
Protestant Englishmen for a coup to succeed, Louis XIV was
justified in dispersing his fleet and troop concentrations. Here is
the official account of the sentencing of two of the conspirators,
Sir John Friend and Sir William Parkins, along with the final
statement of the latter at his Tyburn execution. (Both were in
fact allowed to die by hanging before being butchered).

(i) *A Williamite View: Verdict and Sentence*

About Six of the Clock, the Lord Mayor, Mr Common Serjant,
and several Justices of the City of London returned into Court, and
Proclamation being made for attendance, the Prisoner was brought
to the Bar.

Cl. of Cr.: Sir William Parkins, Hold up thy Hand. Thou standest Convicted of High-Treason, for Conspiring the Death of our Sovereign Lord King William III. What hast thou to say for thy self why Judgment should not pass against thee to dye according to Law?

Sir William Parkins: I have nothing more to say.

Cl. of Cr.: All Manner of Persons are commanded to keep Silence while Judgment is giving, upon pain of Imprisonment.

Then Sentence was Pronounced against Sir John Friend, and Sir William Parkins together.

Mr Com. Serj: You the Prisoners at the Bar, Sir John Friend and Sir William Parkins, have been Indicted for High-treason, in conspiring the Death of the King; for Tryal thereof you have put your selves upon your Countrey, which Countrey have found you Guilty.

The Crimes you are Convicted of, are the greatest a Man can commit. Murder and Robbery are Injuries but to private Persons: But to contrive the Destruction of the King, is letting in Ruin upon Thousands of People. For Robbery and Murder there may be something pleaded for Justification, as for private Revenge &c. But to Set, Conspire, and Debate the Destruction of a Prince, the best of Men, the Father of his Countrey, no Man ever had any colour of Excuse for that. I would not add to your Unhappiness, I am sorry for the severe Judgment that you have brought upon your selves. All that remains for me to do, is, to Pronounce on you the Sentence. And the Court doth award,

That You, and each of You, be carried to the Place from whence you came, and from thence be drawn on a Hurdle to the Place of Execution, and there be severally Hanged, but cut down while you are alive; that your Privy Members be cut off; that your Bowels be taken out, and burnt before your Faces; that your Heads be sever'd from your Bodies, and your Bodies be divided into four Quarters, and your Quarters to be at the King's Dispose: And the Lord have Mercy on your Souls.

(ii)   A Jacobite *Scaffold Statement: Truth from Dying Lips or Propaganda?*
Sir William Parkins's Paper

It hath not been my custom to use many words, and I shall not be long upon this Occasion, having Business of much greater Consequence to employ my thoughts upon. I thank God I am now in a full disposition of Charity, and therefore shall make no Complaints, either of the Hardships of my Trial, or any other Rigour put upon me. However one circumstance I think myself obliged to mention;—as for any Commission particularly levelled against the Person of the Prince of Orange, I neither saw nor heard of any such.

It's true I was privy to the Design upon the Prince, but was not to act in it; and am fully satisfied that very few, or none, knew of it, but those who undertook to do it.

I freely acknowledge, and think it for my Honour to say, that I was entirely in the Interest of the King, being always firmly perswaded of the Justice of his Cause, and looked upon it as my Duty, both as a Subject, and an English-man, to Assist him in the Recovery of his Throne, which I believed him to be Deprived of, contrary to all Right and Justice; taking the Laws and Constitutions of my Country for my Guide.

As for my Religion, I Dye in the Communion of the Church of England, in which I was Educated. And as I freely Forgive all the World, so whoever I may any ways have injured, I heartily ask them Pardon.

William Parkins

The Tryal and Condemnation of Sir William Parkyns, Kt. For The Horrid and Execrable Conspiracy To Assassinate His Sacred Majesty King William, — (London, n.d.)

III. Reactions to the Assassination Plot

i) *A Londoner's Reaction*
Though there had been a succession of plots to assassinate William on the Continent, all of them abortive, none of these provoked the violent reaction which the 1696 plot roused in the English nation. Clearly, the fact that the deed was to be done in England, came so close to being carried out; and involved not only treason in high places, but also infiltration into the London area of Roman Catholic Jacobite ex-officers, who were to supply the "hit men" for the assassination, made the whole affair first-class news. We have the letters which passed between a wealthy

country squire, Richard Coffin of Devon, and the Londoner he retained as book-buyer, and general retailer of metropolitan gossip, Richard Lapthorne of Hatton Garden. Coffin was an old Devon name. (By the nineteenth century it had mutated to the form Pine-Coffin which was borne by at least one distinguished Victorian bureaucrat). Here, what concerns us is the spreading of detailed news about the trials and executions of captured conspirators against William. Note the thoroughly ambiguous nature of the reports as to the role of the exiled King James. All the letters cited are written by Lapthorne and sent to Coffin in Devon.

a) *March 22nd 1696*

On Wednesday last the 3 Conspirators, viz: Charnock King and Keys were hanged drawn and quartered at Tyburne. they did not deny the facts in the Indictment only would not own that the late King James gave them a Commission for the assassination but that it was contrived here. they say that Sir William Perkins is writing a great and ample discovery but others say it will scarce save him but hee wilbe tryed. Sir John Freind wilbe tryed the next weeke by a London Jury. They say now that all in the proclamation are seized saving the Duke of Berwick and Sir — Berkclay[1] who escaped into France. Mr Ferguson and Sir Roger Lestrange are in Newgate. Newgate is very strictly guarded with the Trayne bands the prison being almost filled with the Conspirators. the Parliament hath not yet setled the busines touching Guinieas. Wee are now expecting the Venetian Ambassidors coming from Holland: things are in a very good posture here and very quiet notwithstanding the late great intended villainy and wee hope it is so with you in the Cuntry.

b) *March 28th 1696*

Blessed bee God the late horred conspiracy is at length so layd open that wee doe assure ourselves the neck of it is broken. Sir John Frend and Sir Wm. Perkins who were last tryed and condemned are to bee executed on Wednesday next. There was one Harris a preist who was in the proclamation hath lately surrendred him selfe and discovered two others which were seized in the two prisons called the Counters and another was lately taken in the prison of the Marshalsey, they running into these prisons for Sanctuary. Its sayd that Harris declares King James was privy to that contrivance of the assascination.

c) *April 11th 1696*

The quarters of the two last executed conspirators are put over Temple barr. Fower more wilbe tryed in Westminster Hall Fryday next. Wee have no certaine Intelligence where Admirall Rooke is. The King passed a great many bills yisterday but the Association bill was not ready.

From *The Portledge Papers being extracts from the letters of Richard Lapthorne, Gent, of Hatton Garden London, to Richard Coffin Esq: of Portledge, Bideford, Devon*, ed. Russell J. Kerr and Ida Coffin Duncan (London, 1928).

ii) *The Response of Englishmen, and Others, in the Americas*

Though the racial composition of the American provinces of the English nation was already mixed by the end of the seventeenth century, outside New York it was English norms, values, and identity which dominated. Most immigrants rapidly assimilated to them, even if not themselves originally English. This was even true of the significant element of Scottish settlement in East New Jersey, which had infiltrated the English Empire through the patronage of King James in the days when as Duke of York and an ardent naval imperialist, he had had a special interest in the middle colonies. The Chesapeake settlements were at this point making a transition from a field work-force of mixed black slave and white bondsmen to a purely black chattel slave force, but the views of black slaves on politics were as irrelevant to contemporary calculations as those of European peasants. New York was something of an exception in that it included a large Dutch segment in both New York city and the Hudson Valley. This was hardly surprising, given the fact that the English grip on what had been a possession of the Dutch West India Company had only been finally confirmed in 1674. Here are documents from the Association Oath Rolls of the British Plantations showing how similar was the response in two such different settlements as Virginia and New York. In the latter case, of course, the signatories with Dutch names were pledging their loyalty to a fellow-Dutchman.

(a)

Virginia

October 20th 1696

Forasmuch as it is notoriously manifest that there hath lately been an horrid and detestable conspiracy of Papists and other barbarous and bloody traitors in ye Kingdome of England, to take away his Maties life by assasinateing his Royall Person, to the end of an intended Invasion from France for the subversion of the Religion Laws and Liberties of that Kingdom and in that of this and all other his Maties Dominions might be thereby the better facilitated

We whose names are hereunto underwritten the Burgesses assembled at James City in his Maties Dominion of Virginia do heartily sincerely and solemnly profess testifie and declare that his present Ma^ty King William is our Rightfull and lawfull King and we do hereby mutually promise and engage to stand by and assist each other to the utmost of our Power in the supporting defending and keeping this Governmt for his Ma^ty against the late King James and his adherents and if it should so happen that his Ma^ty should come to a violent or untimely end (which God forbid) we do hereby protest and declare that we wil be enemies to all persons that have been his Enemies and also that we will unite associate and assist each other in the defending and keeping this Dominion for such Successor of his Ma^ty as the Crowne of England shal belong to according to an Act made in the first year of the Reign of King William and Queen Mary. Entituled an Act declareing the Rights and Liberties of the Subject and setling the Succession of the Crown.

Robert Carter	John Thorowgood
William Byrd	Wm. Leigh
Wm. Bassett	Joshua Story
Gideon Macon	Jas. Benn
Ben. Burrough	John Giles

To the King's Most Excellent Majesty

We yor Ma'^ts most Loyall and dutifull subjects the Burgesses now assembled at James City in yor Maties most ancient Colony and Dominion of Virginia, having taken into our serious Consideracon how much yo'r Ma'^ts Subjects here stand obliged for yor Royal care from time to time extended to this yor Dominion and in a more particular manner for those signall Tokens and Marks of yor Maties Grace and favour lately received, in a fresh supply of ammunition and Stores of War for great Guns, in yor Maties gracious acceptance of the money given by the Assembly for the Assistance of New york and thereupon dispenceing with the Quota of men commanded for that service, in the informacon wee have had of the timely and most happy discovery of the late horrid conspiracy against yor Sacred

Person and Intended Invasion of yor Ma^{ts} most Ancient Kingdome of England...and as a Testimony of our Loyall and dutifull inclinations and sincere affection to yor Ma^{ty} (according to the Practice of yor Maties Loyall and good Subjects at home) we have every of us entred into an association, which we have prayed yor Maties governor here to assist us in getting presented to yor Ma^{ty} and in all humility beseech yor Maties gracious acceptance thereof.

October the 20th 1696

By order and in behalf of the House of Burgesses

ROBERT CARTER

Speaker.

(b)

Governor and Councill of New York Province
To the King's Excell^t Maiesty

The humble Address of yr Maiesties Capt. Generall and Govern^r in cheife and the Councill of you Majes^{ties} Province of New Yorke in America

Wee your Majesties most humble most Loyall and most Obedient Subjects deeply sensible of the great and Good providence of Almighty God Lately manifested to all yr Majesties good People in yr most gracious and wonderfull deliverance of your Sacred Person from the horrid and detestable Conspiracy of yr Enemys do heartily congratulate the same and do dayly offer up our Prayers to Almighty God for the Preservation of yr Majesties Person so frequently exposed to Danger for the Preservation of our Religion and Liberty and to Grant unto Your Majesty long Life a Victorious and Happy Reigne.

Newyorke Janry^e 11th 1696.

(c)

Mayor Recorder Alderman and Commonality of the Citty
of New Yorke

Whereas there has been a horrid and detestable conspiracy form'd and carried on by Papists and other wicked and Traiterous Persons for assassinateing his Majest[s] Royall Person in order to encourage an Invasion from France to subvert our Religion Laws and Liberty Wee the Mayor Recorder Aldermen and Commonality of the Citty of New Yorke...In Case his Majesty come to any violent or untimely Death (which God forbid) Wee doe hereby freely and unanimously Oblige our Selves to Unite, Associate and Stand by each other in Revenging the same upon his Enemies and their Adherents, and In Supporting and Defending the Succession of the Crown According to an Act made in the first year of the Reign of King William and Queen Mary Intituled an Act Declaring the Rights and Liberties of the Subject and settling the Succession of the Crown.

Rip Van Dam	)	
J. S. D. Spiegel	)	
Johannes Hardenbroeck	)	Assistants
Martin Clock	)	
Jan Eirwets	)	
Rich Ashfield High Const		

Will. Merrett Mayor
Ja. Graham Recorder
John Tuder Vic. Com.
Will Beechman Alderman

J. S. Cortlandt	)	
Brandt Schuyler	)	
Robert Darkins	)	
Jacob Boeleuz	)	Aldermen
Gerard Bouie	)	
Will. Sharpas Cl.	)	
Ebenezer Willson Chambr	)	
Edw Buckmaster	)	

Printed in *The Association Oath Rolls Of The British Plantations...A.D.1696*, ed. Wallace Gandy (privately printed, London, 1922) pp.30-34.

IV. The Treaty of Ryswick and the Exiled Stuarts, 1697: The End of the First Phase of Jacobitism

By 1693 both Louis XIV and William III had worked out that they could not hope to win a decisive victory against the other. Both wanted peace, but it proved a lengthy process before they could agree on a package which both were prepared to accept.

From 1692 Louis was engaged, usually secretly, in negotiations with at least one member of the alliance facing him, in a sustained attempt to split it.

Another obstacle, however, was the bitter reluctance of Louis to recognize the sovereignty of William in the British Isles. In the 1670s William had helped foil the French attack on the United Netherlands, a state whose very existence under republican institutions roused Louis to fury, for its success belied much of his absolutist creed. Worse still was the ousting of James, for that offended some of the French king's deepest convictions about the sacred nature of hereditary monarchy, especially when the monarch was a fellow Roman Catholic. By 1697 economic and fiscal exhaustion and the need to clear the decks for the coming diplomatic battle over the Spanish succession compelled Louis to accept, in the bland but loaded phraseology of the Treaty of Ryswick, the *de facto* sovereignty of William. To the exiled Stuarts, this was a great defeat.

(i)

Articles of Peace between the most serene and mighty Prince William III. King of Great Britain, and the most serene and mighty Prince Lewis XIV. the most Christian King, concluded in the royal Palace at Ryswicke, the 20th Day of September, 1697.

I. That there be an universal perpetual peace, and a true and sincere friendship, between the most serene and mighty prince William III. King of Great Britain, and the most serene and mighty prince Lewis XIV. the most Christian King, their heirs and successors, and between the kingdoms, states and subjects of both; and that the same be so sincerely and inviolably observed and kept, that the one shall promote the interest, honour, and advantage of the other, and that on both sides a faithful neighbourhood, and true observation of peace and friendship, may daily flourish and increase...

IV. And since the most Christian King was never more desirous of any thing, than that the peace be firm and inviolable, the said king promises and agrees for himself and his successors, that he will on no account whatsoever disturb the said King of Great Britain, in the free possession of the kingdoms, countries, lands or dominions, which he now enjoys, and therefore engages his honour, upon the faith and word of a king, that he will not give or afford any assistance, directly or indirectly, to any enemy or enemies of the said King of Great Britain; and that he will in no manner whatsoever, favour the conspiracies or plots which any rebels, or ill disposed persons, may in any place excite or contrive against the said king; and for that end promises and engages, that he will not assist with arms, ships, ammunition, provisions, or money, or in any other way, by sea or land, any person or persons, who shall hereafter, under any pretence whatsoever, disturb or molest the said King of Great Britain, in the free and full possession of his kingdoms, countries, lands and dominions. The King of Great Britain likewise, promises and engages for himself, and successors, kings of Great Britain, that he will inviolably do and perform the same towards the same most Christian King, his kingdoms, countries, lands and dominions.

Printed in A Collection of All the Treaties, ed. Charles Jenkinson Vol.I (Kelley reprint, New York, 1969), pp.299-300.

(ii)   Even so, an eventual Jacobite restoration of sorts might well now have been arranged had King James' Queen been other than an ultra-devout Catholic with an inflexible will. The source for this episode is in the Duke of Berwick's *Memoirs*.

A little while after the peace of Ryswick, his Most Christian Majesty had proposed to the King of England, that if he would suffer the Prince of Orange to enjoy the kingdom in quiet, he would insure the possession of it, after his death, to the Prince of Wales. The Queen, who was present at the conversation, would not allow the King her husband time to answer, and declared, she would rather see her son dead, than in possession of the crown to the prejudice of his father. Upon which his Most Christian Majesty changed the conversation. It is probable, that what he said had been previously concerted with the Prince of Orange; and it was, if I may venture to say it, a great imprudence to refuse such an offer.

Memoirs of the Duke of Berwick. (London, 1779), Vol.I, pp.157-8.

CHAPTER 5:

THE ORIGINS OF THE '08

I: The Death of King James II and VII

The events surrounding the death of King James in 1701 in a way set the course for the rest of the Jacobite century. The terms of the Treaty of Ryswick had seemed explicit in their renunciation of Louis' support for the exiled Stuart monarchy. So, when James died in the autumn of 1701, Louis' recognition of the former's son as 'King of England' did much to bring Britain into renewed alliance with Holland, Austria and the Empire in war with France, a war which was greatly to weaken France just as it contributed much to Britain's rise as a European and world power. Louis' recognition of 'King James III and VIII' had another consequence which was to be fatal to Jacobite hopes, in that it bound the latter inexorably to Roman Catholicism while England remained resolutely Anglican in her religion.

(i) *Account of the King's Death*
A memorandum made at the time by a French courtier records the drama surrounding King James' death-bed.

Translation

On Monday 11th September 1701, the King went to see the King of England who was very ill. The Queen asked for a private meeting with him, and the King willingly agreed to this. She said to him "You see how I am placed — stricken with grief and about to lose him who is dearest to me. Must I also lose my son? Must the son of a King revert to being a commoner? The King said this needed careful thought; that he had always been well aware of her husband's integrity and indeed looked on him as a saint; that he had the deepest regard for her and a great liking for the Prince of Wales but could not grant him recognition as King without first putting the matter to the Council. He said that he would tell her of the outcome the following day.

The Council duly met the following day. It consisted of the King, Monseigneur, the Chancellor and the Ministers. The Chancellor and a majority of the Ministers were against recognition, but the King and Monseigneur supported the Prince of Wales' right to recognition and the King advanced a number of arguments upholding the view that it would not at all be in contravention of the Treaty of Ryswick. The Prince of Orange was King of England *de facto*, he said, but the Prince of Wales would be King as of right; and that being the son of a King, and that too of a King whose crown was hereditary, this was a right which naturally was his, and could never be taken from him in that he was his father's son. He added that he did not propose to help the Prince of Wales recover his kingdom since that *would* be a breach of the peace-treaty.

On Tuesday 13th, the King went to St Germain, to inform the Queen accordingly. She was delighted and begged the King to be so good as to speak himself to the dying King of England. At that moment the Prince of Wales came into the room, and the King said to him, "I have come here to tell you that I will recognise you as King of England if God takes your father. In so doing I will subordinate all material and political considerations for the sake of true religion. Remember then that it is your religion that makes you King and that it would be quite deplorable if you ever gave up that religion to which you owe so much.

The Queen told her son to throw himself at the King's feet and thank him for all his goodness. He did so, prostrating himself two or three times. They then went to the King of England's bedside, the King saying to him, "Sir, in your present condition, I cannot give you any greater consolation than to tell you that I will recognise your son as King of England if Almighty God calls you to him." At this the dying King raised his eyes and said, "I pray that God will reward you a hundred-fold in this world and the next for all that you have done for me. He alone can make adequate recompense." All the English courtiers who were in the room and had thought that for them all was lost with the King's death, when they understood what had been said, forgetting where they were, began to shout, "Long live the King"; all this with tears of joy and admiration which must have greatly pleased our King.

So perhaps for the very first time ever, in the bed-chamber of a dying King the cry of, "Long live the King" was heard. Surely one of the finest and most moving scenes enacted for a long time in the theatre of the world, and with such a cast!

The King of England died last Friday, the 16th of this month at three in the afternoon. His body was taken to the English Benedictines in Paris at midnight on Saturday. It will rest there until it is known what the English want done with it. Today, Tuesday 20th September 1701 the Prince of Wales received the honours due to a King from the Dauphin.

The King has given the English ambassador a note of the reasons for his action. I do not know how London will look on them but they can only help the Prince of Wales, who once he is recognised by France and (as he will be shortly) by Spain, will some day not be found lacking in powerful friends.

As soon as the King of England was dead, the Papal Nuncio who had been with His Majesty throughout the five or six last days of his illness paid his respects to the new King in accordance with the instructions he had received from the Holy Father. The Abbé Rizzini likewise complimented him on behalf of the Duke of Modena, nephew of the Queen's mother.

On the 21st the new King of England visited the King. The King gave him official recognition in order to make it clear that monarchs can justifiably claim that when crowns are hereditary, succession does not depend on the wishes of their people. So it would be wrong to say that his religion is the reason for the Prince being recognised as King of England. He was born on the 20th June 1688. The King has awarded him the same pension as he gave his father; fifty thousand livres a month, also the same number of guards, the chateau of St Germain etc.

> *Papiers du P.Leonard: Archives Nationales, K121, n35ter.*
> (Reproduced at Appendix XV to *Mémoires de Saint-Simon,*
> ed. A. de Boislisle (Paris, 1892), Tome IX, pp.433-4.

(ii) *Saint-Simon's View*

As compared with the account cited above, the great writer of memoirs of the court of Louis XIV, the Duc de St Simon, echoes much more clearly the doubts felt in influential circles about the decision to recognise James.

Translation

There was general delight at this, but second thoughts were quick in coming, even if they were not voiced. The King had always hoped that his extremely moderate policies in Flanders, the return of the Dutch garrison fortresses, the holding back of his own army when it was in a position to invade with nothing to stop it, would restrain Holland and England (on whom the former was so dependant) from making a breach in support of Austria. That hope was now gravely weakened, but the King was still optimistic and hoped soon to bring to an end both the war in Italy and the whole business of the succession to Spain and all its vast dependencies. The Emperor, he felt, would not be able to stand in his way if the former had at his disposal only his own forces and those of the Empire. But nothing could have been more damaging to the King's policy, and at variance with the recognition he had in all solemnity accorded the Prince of Orange as King of England in the Treaty of Ryswick, which up till that moment he had just as studiously observed. It gave the latter the greatest possible offence and to the whole of England and to Holland. It demonstrated the little trust they could place on this peace treaty, and gave them a splendid opportunity to unite again with all the princes who had been in the Alliance. It also gave them cause to break openly [with France], quite apart from the Austrian question. As to the Prince of Wales, this act of recognition gave him no real help. It only served to highlight the jealousy, the suspicions and the strong feelings of all those who were opposed to him in England; to bind them more firmly in their allegiance to King William and to the Protestant succession on which they were intent. It made them the more vigilant, active and violent against all Catholics and all those suspected of leanings towards the Stuarts. It poisoned them more and more against this young Prince and against France which wanted to foist a King on them contrary to their wishes.

Mémoires de Saint-Simon,
ed. cit. IX, pp.288-92.

II. England's Response

In England, the Act of Settlement of 1701, in response to Louis' recognition of young James as king, now nominated the Electress of Hanover, the elderly grand-daughter of King James VI and I as successor to Princess Anne, old James' staunchly Anglican daughter (known, since her marriage as Princess of Denmark), in the event of the latter succeeding William on his death. War with France when it resumed in 1702 was seen as war in defence of the Protestant Succession and was popular with the

English people in a way that William's involvement of his three British kingdoms in the European war of the previous decade had never been.

Act of Settlement, 1701 (12 & 13 III, C2)

—it having since pleased Almighty God to take away our said sovereign lady and also the most hopeful Prince William, duke of Gloucester (the only surviving issue of her Royal Highness the Princess Anne of Denmark), to the unspeakable grief and sorrow of your Majesty and your said good subjects, who under such losses being sensibly put in mind that it standeth wholly in the pleasure of Almighty God to prolong the lives of your Majesty and of her Royal Highness, and to grant to your Majesty or to her Royal Highness such issue as may be inheritable to the crown and regal government aforesaid by the respective limitations in the said recited Act contained, do constantly implore the divine mercy for those blessings, and your Majesty 's said subjects having daily experience of your royal care and concern for the present and future welfare of these kingdoms, and particularly recommending from your throne a further provision to be made for the succession of the crown in the Protestant line for the happiness of the nation and the security of our religion, and it being absolutely necessary for the safety, peace and quiet of this realm to obviate all doubts and contentions in the same by reason of any pretended titles to the crown, and to maintain a certainty in the succession thereof to which your subjects may safely have recourse for their protection in case the limitations in the said recited Act should determine: therefore for a further provision of the succession of the crown in the Protestant line, we your Majesty's most dutiful and loyal subjects the Lords Spiritual and Temporal and Commons in this present Parliament assembled do beseech your Majesty that it may be enacted and declared, and be it enacted and declared by the king's most excellent Majesty, by and with the advice and consent of the Lords Spiritual and Temporal and Commons in this present Parliament assembled and by the authority of the same, that the most excellent Princess Sophia, electress and duchess dowager of Hanover, daughter of the most excellent Princess Elizabeth, late queen of Bohemia, daughter of our late Sovereign Lord King James the First of happy memory, be and is hereby declared to be the next in succession in the Protestant line to the imperial crown and dignity of the said realms of England, France and Ireland, with the dominions and territories thereunto belonging, after his Majesty and the Princess Anne of Denmark and in default of issue of the said Princess Anne and of his Majesty respectively.—

II. Provided always, and it is hereby enacted, that all and every person and persons who shall or may take or inherit the said crown by virtue of the limitation of this present Act, and is, are or shall be reconciled to, or shall hold communion with, the see or Church of Rome, or shall profess the popish religion or shall marry a papist, shall be subject to such incapacities as in such case or cases are by the said recited Act provided, enacted and established; and that every king and queen of this realm who shall come to and succeed in the imperial crown of this kingdom by virtue of this Act shall have the coronation oath administered to him, her or them at their respective coronations.—

III.   And whereas it is requisite and necessary that some further provision be made for securing our religion, laws and liberties from and after the death of his Majesty and the Princess Anne of Denmark, and in default of issue of the body of the said princess and of his Majesty respectively, be it enacted by the king's most excellent Majesty, by and with the advice and consent of the Lords Spiritual and Temporal and Commons in Parliament assembled and by the authority of the same;

That whosoever shall hereafter come to the possession of this crown shall join in communion with the Church of England as by law established.—

From *Statutes of the Realm*, Vol. VIII, pp. 636-38.

III. France thinks of "playing the Scottish card"

In the opening years of the new century Jacobitism in Scotland was to find a new impetus in national fury at the raw deal Scotland had been and was still receiving from the regal union. The Darien Scheme of 1699-1700 had drained an already impoverished Scotland of money; its collapse, as it seemed to Scots through sabotage by the London government, was a case in point. In 1703 the Scots Parliament passed the Act of Security which threatened to dissolve the regal union on Anne's death unless the sovereignty of Scotland and the freedom of her commerce was secured from English influence. This was followed by widespread anger at the prospect of parliamentary union (an 'incorporating union') with its ending of Scotland's 'thousand years of history' as an independent nation. A separate strand was France's growing need, as the European war progressed, to force Queen Anne's ministers to a general peace; and her growing awareness that this might best be done by staging in Scotland a military diversion from the main theatre of war in Flanders.

This last came about almost by chance. In 1702 a remarkable Scottish Highlander, Simon Fraser who claimed to be the 12th Lord Lovat, came to France, ostensibly on behalf of the Scottish nobility and gentry who were eager (he said) to go to war with England if French help were forthcoming, and secure the restoration of the exiled Stuarts. But he was in fact the loser in a feud with the grasping Murrays of Atholl in the course of which he had sought to retrieve his position by forcibly wedding and bedding the Murray heiress to the Lovat title and estate. Now he sought to recover his position by bringing on a French invasion. It does seem that Louis was taken in by him, though Fraser's account of the meeting is a source to be treated warily.

Fraser's claims as to Scotland's eagerness to rise were soon seen to be exaggerated, but his argument that there was a military potential in Scotland which could be harnessed to France's interests had chimed with the thinking of a senior official in the service of the Marquis de Torcy, Louis' Foreign Minister. This was Colonel Nathaniel Hooke, who had been with Dundee in Scotland in 1689 and come over to France as one of the 'wild geese' of 1691. In a memorandum he read to Louis' *conseil d'en haut* in February 1703 he argued that there was indeed a Scottish card to be played. This memorandum is surprisingly 'modern' in its clarity, presentation and movement towards a conclusion. It reads like many a paper presented to Churchill's War Cabinet of 1940-5.

Fraser's initiative also had important consequences in Scotland and England. When his bluff was called by the lukewarmness of the Scottish Jacobites he then sought to attain his real objective by informing Queen Anne's ministers of the Jacobitic dabbling of, among others, his chief enemy, John, 1st Duke of Atholl. This involved the murky affair, known as 'the Scots Plot', greatly alarming Westminster as it seemed to show the instability of Scottish politics. A wider recognition among English politicians that Union with her volatile northern neighbour was indeed a necessity soon followed.

(i) *The Scottish Act of Security 1704* Passed in 1703 but did not receive the Royal Assent until 1704. It would not have received it at all if the news of Blenheim had reached London a day sooner than it did.

Our Soveraign Lady, the Queen's Majesty, with advice and consent of the Estates of Parliament, doth hereby statute and ordain,—upon the said death of her Majesty, without heirs of her body, or a successor lawfully designed and appointed as above, or in the case of any other King or Queen thereafter succeeding and deceasing without lawful heir or successor, the foresaid Estates of Parliament conveening or meeting are hereby authorised and impowered to nominat and declare the successor to the Imperial Crown of this Realm, and to settle the succession thereof upon the heirs of the said successor's body, the said successor, and the heirs of the successor's body, being always of the Royal Line of Scotland and of the true Protestant Religion. Providing always, That the same be not successor to the Crown of England, unless that in this present session of Parliament, or any other session of this or any ensuing Parliament during her Majesties reign there be such condicions of government settled and enacted, as may secure the honour and soveraignty of this Crown and Kingdom, the freedom, frequency and power of Parliaments, the religion, liberty and trade of the nation from English, or any foreign, influence, with power to the said meeting of Estates to add such further conditions of government as they shall think necessary, the same being consistent with, and no way derogatory from those which shall be enacted in this and any other session of Parliament during her Majesties reign.

[It is further enacted] that the whole protestant heretors and all the burghs within the same [kingdom] shall furth-with provide themselves with fire arms for all the fencible men who are Protestants within their respective bounds...and the said heretors and burghs are hereby impowered and ordained to discipline and exercise their said fencible men once in the moneth at least —

Printed in Gordon Donaldson, *Scottish Historical Documents* (Edinburgh, 1970), pp. 267-68.

(ii) *Simon Fraser's audience with Louis XIV*

The Queen, [Mary of Modena] on her part, unwilling to disoblige him, [Simon Fraser (Lord Lovat)] obtained for him, through the interest of Madame de Maintenon, Cardinal Gualterio, Cardinal de Noailles, and the Marquis de Torcy, a private audience of the Most

Christian King, who had never before granted that favour to any foreigner, let his quality be what it would.

At this audience there was no person present except the Marquis de Torcy, who stood behind the royal chair. Lord Lovat enlarged upon the antient alliances between France and Scotland, observing that the Scotch, assisted by the French, had frequently beaten the English, and that, if they were now honoured with the protection of the greatest King that had ever filled the throne of France, they would not certainly be less successful than they had been in former instances.

His Most Christian Majesty replied, with a look of much benignity, that himself and the whole French nation had their hearts unfeignedly Scottish; and that, since Lord Lovat had been chosen to represent the whole body of loyal Scots, he desired to be understood as from that moment renewing with him all antient alliances between the two nations. The King promised at all times to assist the Scots with troops, money, and everything that might be necessary to support them against the English. He added, that he was perfectly acquainted with the fidelity of Lord Lovat and his family, and that he might depend at all times upon his favourable remembrance.

The Most Christian King then quitted Lord Lovat with a most gracious and engaging air, extremely natural to this celebrated monarch. When Lord Lovat retired at the opposite door of the closet where the King had left him, the Marquis de Torcy and the Marquis de Callières appeared ready to receive him, and had the politeness to say that the King had been highly satisfied with him. Two days after the Queen sent a billet to Cardinal Gualterio, informing him that she had that day received a visit from the King of France, who had the goodness to say, that he did not know whether Lord Lovat were pleased with him, but that he had been extremely pleased with that nobleman: intreating her at the same time never again to demand of him a private audience of any of her subjects, since he had at no other time exposed his person in that manner to any foreigner.

Memoirs of the Life of Simon Lord Lovat,
written by himself in the French language
and now first translated from the original manuscript,
ed. H.K. Fraser (London 1797, London 1902), p.97.

(iii) *Paper by Colonel Hooke Given to the Marquis de Torcy on 18th February 1703 and Read at the Council.*

Although fear of our King's enormous power was the main reason for England's entry to the war, she was so weary of the last war that resumption of the struggle so soon would have been unthinkable if those who had their own reasons for wanting a renewal of war had not been able to persuade their countrymen that the time was ripe for this.

[*In summary*] England's underlying purpose is to damage still further France's financial strength and trade. A paper presented to the English Privy Council in 1701 calculated that while England could stand another bout of war, France could not; and that the time had come through renewed war with France to push for exclusive trading rights in slaves.

France is beset by grasping enemies; globally the prospect is ominous. But she has cards in her hand. England and the United Provinces are uneasy partners. The English aspire to supplant the Dutch as world-wide carriers. They are jealous of the Dutch hold on trade to the Orient, particularly the lucrative trade in spices; and they look with anger on the Dutch herring fleets fishing right up to the mouth of the Humber. In short, the Grand Alliance is vulnerable, and now is the time to break it up before the English Whigs can strengthen their position at Westminster as the party for protestant, Hanoverian succession to the English throne to follow Anne. The prospect of Hanoverian succession is the cement of the alliance, and the dearest hope of the Dutch. In it they see the prospect of a protestant England permanently on their side, at odds with France; and they will spend almost unlimited money to bring it about.

But Hanoverian succession is not inevitable. The Tories are firmly opposed to having a German prince for their future king; at the same time, as the party of the established protestant Church of England, they fear the prospect of a catholic successor in the person of the young Stuart prince. But the succession is not the dominant issue in English politics: for the Tories it is to get the better of France, for the Whigs it is to advance their own interests by whatever means lie to hand.

There is one sure way for France to force English ministers to the conference table before this costly European war goes any further, and that is to bring Scotland into play. The Scots hate the English for their engineering of the Darien disaster of 1699, and with it Scotland's hopes for a new source of prosperity in the Americas.

Likewise they loathe the prospect of Hanoverian succession. English politicans are beguiling the Scots with talk of a union in which Scottish independence would be bartered for free trade; but that could never come about. Scottish animosity towards the English can only grow to new heights in the years ahead.

As to the Scots nobility the Duke of Queensberry, the Queen's Commissioner, has no great following in the country. The Duke of Argyll leads the Scottish Whigs and the Presbyterians who are 'church Whigs'. Lord Lorne, his son, is distributing Hanoverian money among this party to clinch their loyalties. The Duke of Hamilton leads Episcopalians and many others who are opposed both to a Hanoverian succession and to presbyterian rule. All of this party are jacobite in sentiment, more or less. [End of summary].

There are two ways for France to make good use of Scotland.

(1)To cause the Hanoverian succession to be rejected in her Parliament which is due to meet next month. For this, it will not be enough to win over the nobility. It will also be necessary to make sure of the royal burghs of which there are many. Their representatives are so poor that 100,000 francs carefully distributed would suffice. After careful thought and taking advice from others I see the Duke of Hamilton as the only one who can handle this...

The advantages to be derived from all this would be enormous. The [regal] union between the two Kingdoms would be broken and Hanoverian succession would be rejected. Consequently the English would be thrown into alarm seeing the Scots about to break with them and that they were in no state to stop them at a time when the English army is on campaign abroad. This would give the Tories a pretext for joining with the Scots to avoid civil war. It would greatly assist French foreign policy, and it would lead on to the second (and best and most efficacious) way of making Scotland serve the purposes of France.

(2)This is to land a small army with the co-operation of those of the national leadership who would favour such a descent. I have made a study of how this could succeed and of the various landing places proposed, and of what might be expected of the Scots. Although I myself am convinced that this would be a sure way of making England incapable of being a nuisance to France for many years, as everything is not quite ready for this I will say no more about it for the moment.

Correspondence of Col. Nathaniel Hooke,
Vol.I (Roxburghe Club, 1870), pp. 157-249.

IV. Colonel Hooke's 'Negociations'

For the time being, Hooke's proposals fell on deaf ears. Louis and his ministers were confident that French armies would soon end the war by victories in continental Europe. Defeat at Blenheim on the Upper Rhine in 1704 shook this confidence, and the following year Hooke was sent 'over to Scotland in secrecy to report on the prospects for an exhumation of *l'ancienne alliance*. He returned empty-handed, primarily because his efforts had been directed at the Duke of Hamilton who at first cherished the ambition of himself succeeding Anne as monarch in Scotland and then was won over in secret by Queen Anne's Ministers.

Disaster to French arms at Ramillies in Flanders in 1706 made Versailles at last look seriously towards Scotland where Killiecrankie had reminded the French of the survival of a military potential. In 1707 Hooke was sent on a repeat of his earlier mission to Scotland. By now young James, an attractive youth of nineteen, was becoming a focus for Jacobite loyalties; and the imminence of the parliamentary Union with England had enraged both those of the nobility who foresaw a decline in their power and influence, and the mass of the people moved by patriotic sentiment. As George Lockhart of Carnwath, the Jacobite laird who was to chronicle these events, recalled, even the paramilitary Presbyterians of the south-west of Scotland were now prepared to make common cause with the Episcopalian Jacobite nobility and gentry. Hooke, for his part, received from John Ker of Kersland, who professed to be the leader of the militant Presbyterians, an assurance to this effect.

Hooke returned to France in the summer of 1707 with a written undertaking from the Scottish Jacobites that they would rise against England if help were sent from France.

In Paris Hooke now elaborated his proposals for invasion. Scotland was to be the base, but England was the target. The occupation of the Tyne coalfields on which London, the commercial heart of the Grand Alliance, was totally dependent, was the objective. To this French ministers made an important addition. As the Franco-Scottish army swept over the Border there was to be a simultaneous rising in the Flanders towns, lost to France since Ramillies, which would be the signal for the reinvasion of Flanders by a French army, a Flanders, it was hoped, which would have been denuded of British and Dutch troops withdrawn to meet the threat from Scotland. From all this it was confidently expected that a negotiated peace with the Allies would be the outcome.

All this while in London Queen Anne's ministers, obsessed with their mutual rivalries, remained blind to the danger that they might be about to lose the war; this despite increasingly shrill warnings from their 'undercover' agent in Scotland, Daniel Defoe.

In his memorandum Hooke was no doubt over-confident about the prospect of Irishmen and Englishmen joining in the rising. But the strategic kernel of the plan was sound.

(i) *The Scottish Presbyterians Make Common Cause With the Jacobites in 1707.*

(a)—people of all ranks and perswasions were more and more chagrin'd and displeased, and resented the loss of the soveraignty, and were daily more and more perswaded, that nothing but the restoration of the Royal Family, and that by the means of Scotsmen, could restore them to their rights. So that now there was scarce one of a thousand that did not declare for the King; nay the Presbyterians and Cameronians were willing to pass over the objection of his being Papist; for, said they, (according to their predestinating principles) God may convert him, or he may have Protestant children, but the Union can never be good—

George Lockhart of Carnwath, *Memoirs concerning the Affairs of Scotland from Queen Anne's Accession—to the Union*; (London, 1714).

(b)*Ker of Kersland's Memorial for Col. Hooke.*

The Presbyterians are resolved never to agree to the Union, because it hurts their consciences, and because they are persuaded that it will bring an infinite number of calamities upon this nation, and will render the Scots slaves to the English. They are ready to declare unanimously for King James, and only beg his Majesty that he will never consent to the Union, and that he will secure and protect the Protestant religion. The declaration with respect to religion ought to be in general terms.

Those among the Presbyterians who are called Cameronians will raise 5000 men of the best soldiers in the kingdom; and the other

Presbyterians will assemble 8000 more. They beg that the King of England would give them officers, especially general officers, and send them powder, for they have arms already. Whenever his Britannic Majesty shall have granted the preceeding demands, and shall have promised to follow his supplies in person to Scotland, they will take arms against the government, and will give such other assurances of their fidelity as shall be desired. Provided powder be sent them, they engage to defend themselves in their country with their own forces alone against all the strength of England for a year, till the arrival of the king and the succours that he shall bring with him. They leave it to that Prince to bring with him such a number of troops as he shall think proper. They believe, however, that he will not have occasion for a great number. They have a correspondence with the north of Ireland, and they are certain that the Scots who inhabit that province will declare for them—

Hooke's *Correspondence* op.cit. pp. 371-2.

(ii) *Memorial of the Scottish Lords Addressed to the King of France.*

His Most Christian Majesty having been pleased to offer his protection to the kingdom of Scotland, in order to restore its lawful king, and to secure to this nation its liberty, privileges, and independence—

We the underwritten peers and chiefs, having seen the full powers given by his most christian majesty to the said colonel [Hooke], do in our own names, and in the name of the greatest part of this nation, whose dispositions are well known unto us, accept the protection and assistance of his most christian majesty with the utmost gratitude; and we take the liberty most humbly to lay before his said majesty the following representation of the present state of this nation, and of the things we stand in need of.

The greatest part of Scotland has always been well-disposed for the service of its lawful king.—But this good disposition is now become universal. The shires of the west, which used to be the most disaffected, are now very zealous for the service of their lawful king.—

To reap the benefit of so favourable a disposition and of so happy a conjuncture, the presence of the king our sovereign will be absolutely necessary; the people being unwilling to take arms without being sure of having him at their head. The whole nation will rise upon the arrival of its king; he will become master of Scotland without any opposition, and the present government will be entirely abolished.

Out of the numbers that will rise we will draw 25,000 foot, and 5000 horse and dragoons; and with this army we will march strait into England: we, and the other peers and chiefs, will assemble all our men, each in his respective shire. The general rendezvous of the troops on the north of the river Tay shall be at Perth: those of the western shires shall assemble at Stirling; and those of the south and east at Dumfries and at Duns.—

That it may please his Most Christian Majesty to cause the king our sovereign to be accompanied by such a number of troops as shall be judged sufficient to secure his person against any sudden attempts of the troops now on foot in Scotland, being about two thousand men, which may be joined by three or four English regiments at present quartered upon our frontiers.—

We also beseech his majesty to honour this nation with a general, to command in chief under our sovereign, of distinguished rank, that the first men of Scotland may be obliged to obey him without difficulty; and to cause him to be accompanied by such general officers as the two kings shall judge proper.

The peers and other lords, with their friends, desire to command the troops they shall raise, in quality of colonels, lieutenant-colonels, captains, and ensigns: but we want majors, lieutenants, and serjeants to discipline them.—

The great scarcity of money in this country obliges us to beseech his Most Christian majesty to assist us with an hundred thousand pistoles, to enable us to march strait into England. We stand also in need of a regular monthly subsidy during the war.—

We likewise beseech his Most Christian majesty to send with the king our sovereign arms for twenty-five thousand foot and five thousand horse or dragoons, to arm our troops, and to be kept in reserve, together with powder and ball in proportion, and also some pieces of artillery, bombs, grenades, etc., with officers of artillery, engineers, and cannoniers.—

And whereas several of this nation and a great number of the English have forgot their duty towards their sovereign, we take the liberty to acquaint his most Christian majesty, that we have represented to our king what we think is necessary his majesty should do to pacify the minds of his people, and to oblige the most obstinate to return to their duty, with respect to the security of the Protestant religion, and other things which it will be necessary for him to grant to the Protestants. We most humbly thank his Most Christian majesty for the hopes he has given us by colonel Hooke, of having our priveleges restored in France, and of seeing our king and this nation included in the future peace: and we beseech your majesty to settle this affair with the king our sovereign.—

And, in the pursuit of this great design, we are resolved mutually to bind ourselves by the strictest and most sacred ties, to assist one another in this common cause, to forget all family differences, and to concur sincerely and with all our hearts, without jealousy or distrust, like men of honour, in so just and glorious an enterprise. In testimony whereof we have signed these presents, the seventh day of the month of May, of the year one thousand seven hundred and seven.

(Signed) ERROL.   N. MORAY.
     PANMURE.   N. KEITH.
     STORMONT.   DRUMMOND.
     KINNAIRD.   THO. FOTHERINGHAM.
     JAMES OGILVIE.   ALEX. INNES.

The Secret History of Colonel Hooke's Negociations in Scotland in favour of the Pretender in 1707—written by himself. [Editions in London, Edinburgh and Dublin, 1760] pp. 69-75, in which Hooke states that these men signed on behalf of very many others.

(iii) *Colonel Hooke's Proposals for the Invasion of Scotland and England.*

The Scottish Lords oblige themselves, to make all their nation take arms for the restoration of their king and to raise an army of 25,000 foot, and 5,000 horse and dragoons, the regiments to be formed of chosen men, and also to furnish them with accoutrements, provisions and carriages for all their marches, and to cause them march directly for England. They have given in a particular account of the means by which they can accomplish this, and as they have much to lose, the first and the richest Lords of the nation being engaged in the design, they may safely be trusted.

They affirm that they will be joined in England by a very considerable party of English, with whom they keep a correspondence; and, as England is at present destitute of troops, without one single fortress, and full of all kinds of provisions, they will draw from thence, besides their necessary supplies, considerable contributions, after the example of their forefathers, who, in 1639, (besides provisions for the subsistance of their army) drew 12,000 livres a day from the three northern counties of England, which are the poorest of the whole kingdom.

Nothing could hinder them from making themselves masters of the city of Newcastle, and of its coal mines, which are so necessary for firing in London, that the inhabitants of that place could not be deprived of them for six weeks without being reduced to the greatest extremity.

As the Scots advanced in England, their army would be augmented by the English malecontents, who are very numerous, and by the faithful subjects of the lawful King so that they hope to make themselves masters of the greatest part of the kingdom, and even of the city of London, which would be a decisive stroke, before the Princess Anne could transport her troops over from Flanders; and even although she should bring them over, as more than one half of them are Scotch and Irish, it is not doubted but these would join the Scottish army if it were commanded by their lawful King—

The Scots are certain that Ireland waits only for their example to take arms, and the inhabitants alone of the north of Ireland, who are Scots, will directly furnish 20,000 men compleatly armed under a commander of great reputation among them, who has thereto engaged himself.—Even although the Princess Anne should be in a condition to measure her forces with those of her brother, which is not in the least probable, and that she should be so successful even as to drive the Scottish army into their own country, as it is inaccessible, she will still be obliged to keep the same number of troops to watch the Scots, which will render it impossible for her to send troops to Flanders or elsewhere.

As the Scots are at present wholly united, they will be strong enough to restore their King, first in Scotland, and afterwards in England, excepting that it will be necessary to have a body of troops for his protection upon his arrival, till the national army shall be assembled in the field, when they consent to send back the troops if the King should desire it, or an equal number of their Countrymen. They require, if his Majesty pleases, that their King should be accompanied with 5000 men. They would prefer the Irish troops that serve in France, as being most accustomed to their manner of living and speaking the two languages of their country.—They desire a general of noble birth, that the first peers of their nation may make no scruple of obeying him. They would wish to have the Marshall Duke of Berwick, or any other whom his Majesty pleases. They require likewise some general officers, and as many half-pay officers as possible to be sent them. Besides 600,000 livres to put them in a condition to begin the war.

They have demanded arms for 30,000 men, but they will be content with 15,000 stand of arms for the foot, and 5,000 for horse or dragoons, with a promise that the other 10,000 shall be sent them in a short time; gun-powder necessary for 30,000 men, because they have at present almost no powder in Scotland; but a smaller quantity of balls will be sufficient, as they have plenty of lead in the country. A train of field-pieces, with six battering cannon, four mortars, bombs, bullets, and grenadoes will also be needed. They likewise demand a subsidy, but this they leave to the King's pleasure: but as the expedition will not be of long continuance, there need not be any difficulty as to this point.

The most sure and secret means of transporting these supplies to Scotland, is to equip twenty frigates from 20 to 40 guns, at Brest, Rochfort, Port Louis, Havre, and Dunkirk and under pretence of a long voyage, to put six months provisions on board, which will be sufficient for the troops during their passage to Scotland, and to cause the arms and ammunition to be put on board at different ports distributing them equally on board each frigate according to their burthen.—

A little reflection will clearly shew, that it is the most glorious undertaking, the most useful, and even the most necessary that his Majesty, in the present juncture, could form. This single diversion will infallibly overturn all the schemes of the enemy. It will force the English instantly to recall the troops and ships which they employ in different countries against his Majesty, and will put it out of the power of that kingdom to furnish the large sums to its allies, who are thereby enabled to support the war. It will entirely destroy the credit of the exchequer-bills, and of the commerce of the city of London, upon which all the sums employed against his Majesty are advanced: And as the principal strength of the enemy consists in the credit of the city of London, when England shall be attacked at home, it will be out of her power to support her allies abroad, which will soon force the Dutch, upon whom alone the weight of the war will fall, to ask a peace of his Majesty.

—For these reasons it is concluded, that if the expedition to Scotland should be much more expensive than is proposed, it ought to be looked upon as necessary, and as a certain means of getting quit of all embarrassments, of preserving the King of Spain upon the throne, and of putting his Majesty in a condition of making a glorious peace this winter.—

In a further elaboration of the invasion plans

In case of misfortune, the Scots may lay waste the country on the south side of the Firth of Edinburgh, and retire to the north side of that river, where they will have provisions in abundance, and so oblige the English to return for want of subsistence. This conduct has always succeeded with them these 400 years past. It was the council which their King Robert I. gave them on his death-bed, and which they have since always practised with success in the issue.

Hooke's *'Negociations'*; op. cit, pp. 5-68.

(iv) *Daniel Defoe's Reports from Edinburgh to the Secretary of State (Robert Harley) in London.*

(a)   9 August 1707

Sir

I am in hopes myne Come Constantly to your hand and Therefore I Repeat Nothing of what I have wrott;—

I am Not to be Discourag'd Either with Dangers or Difficultys in This work. I kno' That the more Disordred they are here, The more Need of what I am Upon; and Therefore when I give his Ldship a Very Mellancholly Account of Things, it is Neither to Enhance his Opinion of my Services nor to Suggest that I am Either weary Or Affraid of the Undertakeing; — and I speak This Now because I Really am going to give you a Very Mellancholly Account of Things —

The Ferment Runs Every Day higher here, and the ill blood of This people is So much Encreased that There is No speaking among them but with the Uttmost Caution — Not but that I am apt Freely Enough to speak, but if I should give way to Talking in Cases which would Move the patientest Man On Earth to lose his Temper, I should Deprive my Self of the Opportunity of Doeing Good Another Time.

I Therefore hear all Their ill language, and Onely Desire them to have Patience, till they see the End of things, and to Moderate as well as I Can, but 'Tis a Fitt of Lunacy Just Now and when the spirits Are Evaporated it will Cool Again.

I hinted to you a Sermon Preached at a Communion by Mr John Anderson of St Andrews — last Sabbath he preached Again at the Gray Fryers Kirk in this City — his Text Hosea.7. v.8. *Ephraim is a Cake Not Turn'd. Strangers have Devour'd her strength and she knew it Not.* Here he Railed at and Abused the English Nation, Denounc't Gods Judgemt Against the people for Uniteing with a Perjur'd and a Godless people as he Call'd them — and In short flew in the Face of The Union and of the Governmt in Such a Manner as Really is Unsufferable —

He has in Conversation the Same stile, and Goes up and Down Enflameing and Enrageing the people — He is a bold, popular Man, and thereby the more Mischievous.—

I shall not Trouble you with the Artifices of the Jacobites to Enflame these things, How Men were Employd to Go about the streets and Crye Out Upon scotland, and Call the Brewers Men scotch Rogues, and scotch Dogs, just as passing in the streets, and so make the people Believ it was the English Excise men, and such like Methods to Exasperate the people Against them, which makes the poor Fellows afraid to go About their business.—

My Fear of it is its Encreaseing and Refounding a Nationll Aversion, which is the Great thing we hoped the Union would have worne off — and which the Ministers in perticular do now Especially strive to spread in the Minds of the people, and which if it goes On will be past Cure.

I must Confess I Never Saw a Nation So Universally Wild and so Readily Embraceing Everything that may Exasperate them. They Are Ripe for Every Mischief, and if Some Generall step to their Satisfaction is not Taken, *I do not yet foresee how*, they will Certainly Precipitate themselves into some Violent thing or Other On the first Occasion that Offers.

It Seems a perfect Gang-green On the Tempers, And like the Genll Method of Such Exasperations, it Reconciles smaller things to promote this Greater — Different Intrests, Differing partys, all Joyn

97

in a Unsiversall Clamour — and the Very whiggs Declare Openly they will Joyn with France or King James or any body Rather than be Insulted as they Call it by the English — Tis the Happyest thing in the World that the Union is finisht. Were it to act Now it would be all Confusion and Distraction.—

I Thot my Self Oblig'd to give you This Account. I ask your Pardon for its Length, and am

Your Most Obedt Servt
DF

(b)   18 September 1707

Sir

My Impatiuence Urged me to Write a Long and Importunate Letter Two Posts Agoe. I would Not be Construed that I Doubt your Concern for me, but fear you Are Not Sencible of my Incapacity of Waiting As I am Circumstanc'd in This Remote place. [Defoe was in want of cash]—

We are Taken Up with a Discourse of Severll people Landed in the West of scotland From France, and Capt Murray is Apprehended. The Council Are Sitting On it to Day and I Doubt not you Will be Rightly Accquainted with the perticulars. I hope There is Nothing Dangerous in Agitation yet, But I Must Own and have Often Thought to hint it; The humors of That party Are at present Undr Such fermentation, So Encouraged by the successes of The French, and So Unhappily Back't by the Common Disgust, that should the K of France but support them, *Not with Men for they Need them Not*, but should he send About 200 Officers, Arms and Ammunition, Artillery &c. to furnish them, & about 100000 Crowns in Money, he might soon Get Together 12 or 15000 stout fellows & Do a great Deal of Mischief. Nor is it so Much the Inclination of the Men As the Money Disperst among the Landlords, the Lairds, & Jacobite Gentry That would bring them in and The Men Follow of Course.

I Confess this would be a Very Fatall Diversion As things stand here Now, and I hint it because tis a juncture in which it would be of Worse Consequence than Ever with Respect to Other parts of the World.

I am, Sir, Your Most Obedt Servt
DF

Letters of Daniel Defoe,
ed. G.H. Healey (Oxford, 1955), pp.236-8 and 243-4.

CHAPTER 6:

L'ENTREPRISE D'ECOSSE: THE ATTEMPT
ON SCOTLAND

I: The Attempt on Scotland

Not until the late autumn of 1707 did Louis consent to the mounting of *l'entreprise d'Ecosse*, and then only after Mme de Maintenon, close friend of young James' mother, Mary of Modena, had been moved by Louis' ministers to intercede on its behalf. There was however dismay at Versailles at the Scottish Parliament having signed away its independence in the Treaty of Union. Perhaps Louis' initial reluctance also stemmed from his remembering La Hogue, the abortive attempt of 1696, and Simon Fraser's duplicity of five years past.

By the beginning of March 1708 the invasion force, as proposed by Hooke, had been assembled at Dunkirk; and young James had travelled from St Germain to join it. He had received a letter from Louis which illuminates the thinking of *le grand monarque* about the invasion project. Now in his old age Louis for his part seems to have looked on it as, primarily, a crusade in the cause of 'true' religion.

But Louis had made a poor choice of commanders for the invasion. The naval commander was the Comte de Forbin, an outstanding if ebullient *chef d'escadre* of the French navy, but unable to see the strategic merits of the invasion plan. As military commander, the obvious choice was James' half-brother and Louis' youngest marshal, the Duke of Berwick. Louis passed him over in favour of the Comte de Gacé, a pliant nominee of Chamillart, his war minister, who was eager that his friend should win the *bâton* of a *maréchal de France*.

On the 6th March the invasion fleet sailed from Dunkirk, an easterly storm enabling them to get clean away, two days ahead of the hastily assembled opposing English squadron which the same storm had blown down Channel. Scotland seemed open to the invaders; greatly to their consternation Queen Anne's ministers in London who, having ignored Defoe's warnings, had by now learned what was afoot too late to send troop reinforcements to Scotland. January and the first half of February had been passed in a crescendo of ministerial intrigue ending in the dismissal of Harley, Queen Anne's Secretary of State; this had blinded them to all else.

The invasion fleet failed to land its 6000 troops and munitions of war as was planned at the harbour of Burntisland in the Firth of Forth. Forbin took too long to get there. Why this was so is still unclear, but sabotage is a possibility.

With the failure of the '08, Louis and his ministers recognised that their opportunity to 'play the Scottish card' had passed. For four more years the European war dragged on, ruinously for France, to the detriment of Britain's Dutch ally, profitably in the longer term for Britain herself. At Westminster, Queen Anne's ministers had had the fright of their tortuous lives, but brazened out the subsequent Opposition onslaught on their lack of readiness to meet 'the alarm from Dunkirk'.

(i) *The French View of the Invasion Project*

(a) *The Union of Scotland and England as Viewed from Versailles.*

Translation

It was at this stage that the English succeeded in making the great change in affairs for which they had been angling for so long, and which the Prince of Orange had failed to bring off. This is what they termed the Union with Scotland and which the Scots more truthfully described as the reduction of Scotland to an English province. Her independence from England depended on the continued life of her parliament. By intrigue, bribes, and sheer persistence the Scottish parliament was brought to agree at the beginning of this year to abolish itself, and that there should be only one parliament for the two Kingdoms.—Thus there were no more difficulties from Scotland in matters of commerce, nor for government of which the English had complete control. It passes understanding how a nation so proud, so much the traditional enemy of England, a nation which had learned from bitter experience down the years and was so jealous of her freedom and independence could bend her neck to receive this yoke.

Mémoires de Saint-Simon, ed. cit., Vol.XV, pp.280-1.

Translation

You are at present, Sire, a foreigner in my Kingdom. I received you from the hands of a king who was such a good Christian that he preferred to abandon his own Kingdom rather than that of Jesus Christ. God now calls you back to your own country. I am the instrument he deigns to use so that you may return. I have already prepared everything that lies within my power, and I hope that Providence itself will lead you. I have prudently kept completely secret and impenetrable my designs on those who are your enemies and mine. I know that Europe will be stirred and that your embarkation begins to make heresy tremble.

In former times England was the theatre of Religion. To restore all that must be your first object. What I propose to you by my example [is]: give preference always to the interests of God, as did that great King your father, over that of all worldly things, make up your mind about what first to do when you mount the throne which God himself gives you. Remember that he can just as easily take it away from you.

I can claim that I have never relented in matters of Religion, nor have my enemies been able to prevail. The God who has protected my arms will also bless yours. It matters little or nothing to be a King, unless one is a Christian King. I speak to your Majesty as a father. King James, whose memory will be eternal, commended you when dying to me warmly, and my heart has always loved you; indeed I promised God, seeing you still in your cradle, if my life was prolonged, to restore you to your Kingdom. I give voice for the last time, Sire, to all my tenderness for you. Remember this: I have always loved you as my own son. I can say to your Majesty that you could never have caused me the least displeasure.—All is ready at Dunkirk for your departure, nor can you not be astounded at the efforts which I have made.

Love me and love also the Princes my sons, with whom you have been brought up. I know well how great is their tenderness towards Your Majesty. My grandson, the King of Spain in the midst of all his concerns, feels such joy on the occasion of your departure as I cannot describe. If I had consulted only with my heart, you would not now be leaving my kingdom, but it is for the supreme importance of establishing Religion. Be protector of it in your country. Begin to rule with actions worthy to be registered in the Book of Life, and remember that all the pomp of the Earth is less than nothing in comparison with the happiness that God promises us.

You will follow the advice which I will take the liberty of giving Your Majesty, insofar as should be heeded. I am already aware of what is possible at London, and great is the change which I foresee for you. Keep yourself united to the Holy See. Never be separated from it, and if its ministers are sometimes lacking in the respect due to Kings, you must never be lacking in the reverence due to him who takes on earth the place of Jesus Christ. Be always tender and ready to pardon your subjects whom fear or some other reason has detached from your crown. Treat lords and nobility well. See that the people can breathe, and show yourself to them, because they want to see you, and you will be much loved. Win over their hearts with the pledge of your natural goodness; punish advisedly; listen to as many views as you can in your Council; deliberate with the most wise; never execute an affair of which you have not foreseen the outcome.—

Remember me, Sire, after my death in the persons of my Sons. Maintain peace between our two crowns. You will read from time to time the memorials regarding the good order of your Monarchy, all written in my hand, but share them only with your most intimate subjects. Go now. I wish never to see you again.

Scottish Catholic Archives, Edinburgh
SM/3/24/8. From a copy in Italian in a contemporary (i.e. early 18th century) hand which was rescued from the Scots College in Rome when that city was occupied by a French army in 1798. (This document has not been brought to light previously).

(ii) *The Attempted Invasion*

(a) *The Comte de Forbin's Narrative*

I knew the situation in Scotland, and realised clearly that there was no hope of success in that quarter. It is true that Queen Anne had recently brought about the union of England and Scotland under a single Parliament, and that that innovation had caused a good deal of discontent, whence it might appear that those who were opposed to the measure would not fail to rise in favour of James III. But none the less, there seemed very little prospect of a revolution in his favour. And besides, the Minister did not mention any port which was in a condition to receive us, and I could not refrain from telling him—that the project of invasion was entirely without grounds of encouragement; that Scotland was calm and tranquil; that not a single district had risen in Arms; that we could not count on any port where our Fleet might anchor, or where the King of England and his Troops could disembark in safety; and finally, that to land six thousand men without an assured means of retreat was, in fact, to sacrifice them and to send them to certain destruction.—

On the eve of my departure for Dunkirk, I waited on the King to take my leave. 'M. le Comte,' said his Majesty, 'you realise the importance of your Commission; I hope that you will acquit yourself worthily in it.' 'Sire,' I answered, 'you do me great honour; but if your Majesty would vouchsafe to me a few moments, I would venture to represent certain matters in regard to the commission with which I am charged.' The King, whom the Minister had informed of the objections which I had already urged, replied, 'M. de Forbin, I wish you a successful voyage; I am busy and cannot listen to you now.'

The next day I set out, and having arrived at Dunkirk, I strove with all possible diligence to equip thirty Privateers and five Men-of-War. There were many difficulties in the way, but at length I surmounted them.—Every thing was ready so far at least as I was concerned.—A few days later our Sailors arrived; the Ships put out into the Roads; the Soldiers were summoned, and all went on board.

The King of England arrived two days after. Whether from fatigue or some other cause, the King fell ill of measles and for two days was in a fever. The delay which his illness caused to the sailing of our Fleet allowed the Enemy time to reconnoitre our position. Thirty-eight English Men-of-War anchored off Gravelines, two leagues from Dunkirk. Having viewed them closely myself and made out that they were actually Men-of-War, I sent a letter to Court, pointing out that the Enemy's strength was too superior to ours to allow us to set sail under their observation; that to endeavour to do so would mean the total loss of the expedition; that the Enemy, being ready to follow us, would not fail to seize the opportunity to attack us, and since we had no Port of safety in Scotland, it was obvious that they had but to attack us in order to cut off from us any part of our force they pleased; and that in my opinion we ought to dismiss our forces and postpone the expedition to a more fitting opportunity.—

From the intrigues of those who pressed the King so strongly to embark I saw, that beyond their own private interests, they were anxious to foist upon the Department of Marine the whole responsibility for the enterprise.

I was by no means blind to the jealousy which existed between the Ministers of War and Marine. The Emissaries of the former merely hastened the embarkation of the Troops in order that if the expedition proved abortive after the King and the Generals were on board, the Minister of War might be able to charge the failure to the dilatoriness of the Department of Marine, and to represent to the King, 'Sire, I have done all that devolved upon me. The Troops with their Generals have embarked, and I have punctually executed Your Majesty's Orders. If the project has not succeeded, the fault is attributable solely to the Sailors.'—

The King of England and all the General Officers went on board, and I was obliged to set sail.

I was risking the whole expedition, since they would have it so, and was forced to anchor among the shoals. That very night a gale of Wind put the whole Fleet in peril. The King, young as he was, faced the danger with a courage and coolness beyond his years; but his suite were thoroughly frightened.

The Comte de Gacé, who had been proclaimed the previous evening on board my Ship as Marshal of France, under the title of Maréchal de Matignon, was not a bit less frightened than the English. All of them were exceedingly sea-sick, and begged me to put back into the Roads.

It gave me considerable satisfaction to see them so very unwell, having fulfilled their desire to put out to sea. 'I can do nothing,' I told them, 'the wine's drawn and you must drink it. Suffer, feel as uncomfortable as you please; I'm quite content, and don't pity you at all. You have your wish. Why are you dissatisfied?'

Three of our best Ships were nearly lost; they broke their Cables and were saved only by a miracle. Two days later, the wind becoming favourable, we set sail, and on the third day were off the Coast of Scotland, in sight of Land. Our Pilots had made an error of six leagues in their bearings. They altered our course, and the Wind and Tide becoming contrary, we anchored at night-fall at the mouth of the Edinburgh River, about three leagues from Land.

In vain we made Signals, lit Fires, and fired our Cannon; nobody appeared. On the stroke of midnight I was informed that five

Cannon-shot had been heard from the South. I had not taken off my clothes since we sailed from Dunkirk, and rising hastily, I concluded that the five Cannon-shot must be the signal of the Enemy, who had followed our Fleet.

I proved right in my conjecture; for at day-break we discovered the English Fleet anchored at four·leagues distance from us. The sight of them caused me considerable uneasiness. We were shut in in a sort of Bay, with a Cape to be doubled before we could gain the open sea.

I saw at once that considerable coolness was necessary if we were to extricate ourselves from our critical position. So, rapidly making all sail, I bore down on the Enemy as though I designed to attack him. The English ships were under sail, and seeing me manoeuvre as though I was coming up to them, they put themselves in battle-order and so lost a good deal of way. Profiting by their lack of judgment, I signalled to the Fleet to clap on all sail and follow me, and changing my direction, thought only of getting away as fast as possible.—

Meanwhile, to lose no time, I was still pressing on towards the Cape, with the object of doubling it and gaining the open. The Enemy gave chase, and had I had those heavy Transports, as had been at first arranged we must infallibly have been lost. That I succeeded in saving the Expedition was due to no other cause than, that having swift-sailing Privateers recently docked, we soon gained considerably upon our pursuers.—

The English, getting more and more alarmed, proposed to the King that he should go on board the Frigate which had returned from reconnoitring, and should land at a Castle on the sea-coast belonging to a Lord of whose fidelity the King was well-assured.—

The King, who had reluctantly acceded to the importunity of the English, was quite satisfied; but the whistling of Cannon-Shot so much augmented the fears of those cowards, that they returned to the charge, and represented to the King the danger to which my rashness was exposing him, and their anxiety lest it were already too late for him to extricate himself from it. They again urged him to land at the Castle which they had named, and so successfully convinced him that no other course was open to him, that the King told me he would have the Boat prepared at once and without argument.

'Sire,' I answered — I am naturally hasty and impatient — 'I have already had the honour to assure Your Majesty that you are perfectly safe here. I have received orders from the King my Master to take such precautions for your safety as I should for his own, and I will never consent to Your Majesty leaving this Ship to expose yourself in a Castle far away from succour, where Your Majesty may to-morrow be delivered up to your Enemies. I am charged with your safety, and my head will answer for any harm that may befall you. I beg you, therefore, to trust me implicitly and to listen to no one else. Those who venture to give you other advice than this are either traitors or cowards.'—

The result soon justified my opinion; for the Enemy, despairing of overtaking us, hove to, intercepted the Chevalier de Nangis[1], and attacked him. Seeing myself no longer pursued, I despatched four swift Frigates to instruct the rest of the Fleet to crowd on all sail at night-fall, and to steer East-North-East.

[1] Captain of *Le Salisbury*.

Mémoires de Claude, Comte de Forbin, (Paris, 1731).
Memoirs of Claude Comte de Forbin, (London, 1731).

(b) *Hooke's View of the 'Error' in Landfall*

General Hooke told Dr King at Paris, that in the year 1708, when the French fleet made a show as if they intended to land in Scotland, he being one night not disposed to sleep, when about midnight on the deck, and as he was bred to the sea, saw they were stiring on Newcastle Bay[1]; when he challenged the man at the helm, he answered he was going the course ordered; upon which the General went to the Commander to know the meaning of it, who came immediately on deck, reprimanded the stirsman severely, and ordered him to keep the proper course; being unable to rest, the General soon after returned to deck, and found they were again got upon the wrong course, and being told it was by direction, went instantly to the K...'s apartments, and telling him the story, said they were betrayed.

[1] 'Newcastle Bay' is the bay of the New Castle of Slains (as distinct from Old Slains on the Aberdeenshire coast) which is known today as Cruden Bay. Hooke knew it well: Slains had been his point of entry to and departure from Scotland in 1705 and 1707.

Printed in *The Jacobite Lairds of Gask (Grampian Club, 1870),*
pp. 15-16.

Forbin's memoirs, written in his old age, have been recognised by naval historians as not altogether trustworthy in regard to his previous exploits against allied warships and commerce. His account of the failure of the '08 has however been accepted unquestionably by historians from Voltaire and Sir Walter Scott onwards. But it has to be approached with caution and some scepticism.

The use of privateers seems to have been Hooke's idea, not Forbin's. The voyage to Scotland took a crucial day longer than he states, four days not three, and it was this and the faulty landfall which lost another day of his advantage that gave Sir George Byng's pursuing squadron its chance to catch up. As to the 'error' in landfall this was a full 100 miles north of the Forth, not 18 as Forbin says. Nor is there any mention that one of the big frigates which became separated in the storm of 7th-8th March, sailing from Dunkirk on the morning of the 9th was sailing up the Forth by noon on the 11th to an enthusiastic Scottish welcome. The anecdote, given above, of Hooke's view is important because it is all that survives of his testimony. When he died in 1737, though a much honoured figure, the French government, significantly, impounded his 1708 papers!

Forbin's memoirs do bring out his obtuse conviction that he better than anyone knew the state of opinion in Scotland. Nor could he recognize that James wanted to be put ashore on the Angus or Mearns coast, not from fear of being taken prisoner by the British navy, but because he knew he would be among friends there.

Hooke's copy of the log kept by Forbin's pilot survived the impounding of his papers and, thanks to a search made by the archivist at the Ministère des Affaires Etrangères at Paris in 1988, has come to light. This, intriguingly, seems to have been 'cooked' to conceal the length of time Forbin took, having landfall (on 'la terre d'Aberdein') on the 10th of March when it was in reality the 11th. Confusion or conspiracy? Further research, particularly in the *Archives de France* is needed.

(c) *The Cover-Up*

In France the army and the navy blamed each other. Versailles (quite wrongly) chose to suspect the Earl of Middleton, James' Secretary of State, of having betrayed the invasion plan to London. Saint-Simon, with his insider's view suspected collusion between Forbin and the Minister of the Navy to sabotage the invasion project, it being an army rather than a navy initiative; and he rightly deplored the loss of France's great opportunity to bring the war to an end. In Scotland the Jacobites were rounded up or ran for cover. However, as Queen Anne's ministers were forced now to pretend that there had never been any real danger of an invasion the imprisoned nobility and gentry were let go. But the defences of Stirling Castle, key fortress to the control of Scotland, were now strengthened. Next time the Jacobites would not find the authorities so lacking in preparedness. And at Westminster ministers 'toughed it out', as they are ever wont to do, when the storm of recrimination from the Whig opposition descended on them. The following year in the House of Lords Lord Haversham, ever a gadfly to government, upbraided ministers for their lack of preparation as revealed by the parliamentary enquiry that had taken place in the months since March 1708.

"—I will not trouble you farther, I think this matter is now very plain before your Lordships; I could wish I had not said one word of truth in what I have said to you; but the vouchers shew it to be so, and if all this be true, it is a very strange, a very surprizing, and a very astonishing truth.

I shall not move any thing to your Lordships farther in this matter, I believe there has been enough now said, to justify those Lords for moving this enquiry, and shall add but this word, that if there be no greater care taken for the future, than there was at this time of such imminent danger, it will be the greatest miracle in the world, if without a miracle the Pretender be not placed upon that throne."

This is the substance of what was observed by the Lord Haversham, tho' there happened some interlocutories between him and another Lord: And the observations were made upon the papers as they were read: The Duke of Buckingham and several others spoke to the same effect: Upon which it was ordered, that that important affair should be considered the Tuesday following in a full house.

On the 8th of March the Commons took into consideration the papers relating to the designed invasion of Scotland, and the proceedings thereupon, and against the Lord Griffin and others taken in rebellion; and relating to the persons taken upon suspicion, as also to the garrisons of Scotland. Whereupon the house resolved, First, 'That orders were not issued for the marching of the troops in

England until the 14th day of March, it being necessary for the security of her Majesty's person and government, that the troops in this part of the kingdom should not march into Scotland, till there was certain intelligence that the enemy intended to land in that part of the united Kingdom. Secondly, That timely and effectual care was taken by those employed under her Majesty, at the time of the intended invasion of Scotland, to disappoint the designs of her Majesty's enemies both at home and abroad, by fitting out a sufficient number of men of war, ordering a competent number of troops from Flanders, giving directions for the forces in Ireland to be ready for the assistance of the nation, and by making the necessary and proper dispositions of the forces in England.'

A Collection of the Parliamentary Debates in England from the year MDCLXVIII Vol.V. Printed in 1741, pp. 247-8.

If, in the words of Lord Dacre, history is not merely what happened, but also what happened in the context of what might have happened, the '08 might well have been a climacteric in the history of England, and of Europe, as well as of Scotland.

CHAPTER 7:

THE '15

I: Expectations of Change 1710-1714

The politics of Queen Anne's England were dominated by radical polarization between two powerful and cohesive political parties, Whig and Tory. There were, however, sub-groups within both parties, and there is no question that within the Tory party the most significant example of this phenomenon was a bloc of Jacobite peers and MPs. Historians have long debated how powerful and numerous this group really was, but their investigations have always suffered from the fog of contemporary doubt created by the anxiety of contemporary Whigs, especially after 1714, to smear all Tories as Jacobites. As the War of the Spanish succession ground on, and hard-line Whig policies aiming at total victory over the Bourbon powers became less realistic, the pace of political conflict became frantic. The Tories won a decisive electoral victory in 1710. They then embarked, with the support of Queen Anne, on the negotiations which led to the highly controversial Peace of Utrecht of 1713, and their two leaders, Robert Harley Earl of Oxford and Henry St John Viscount Bolingbroke, became locked in a furious power-struggle in which Bolingbroke sought to appeal to the atavistic impulses of the Tory backbenchers.

The latest scholarship suggests that the Jacobite bloc at Westminster was never very large, but that in the period 1710-1714 its 50-60 members were capable of exploiting an extremely unstable situation to their exiled master's advantage, if he had been prepared to let them manoeuvre freely. James was tragically out of touch with the realities of British politics. He failed to grasp that even Bolingbroke did not think a non-Anglican could succeed Anne. Refusing to convert, James fell for ambiguous approaches from Harley, and indirectly Anne, neither of whom wished him well, and told his supporters to back the Harley-Bolingbroke government which, in its dying days, prepared the way for the peaceful succession of George, Elector of Hanover, as George I.

(i) *Bolingbroke's View of the Chevalier*

Given the fantasies which Jacobite-inclined historians have woven round the intentions of Bolingbroke, it is salutary to read this report from a senior French diplomat in London to Louis XIV.

Iberville to Louis XIV. London, Feb.5, 1714 (enciphered).

—It would be difficult to summarize to Your Majesty the various indications which Bolingbroke gave and on the strength of which I believe I can flatly assure Your Majesty that this minister knows well the Elector of Hanover and the interest of England, but is persuaded that nothing can be done for the Chevalier as long as he is Catholic, not even if he should marry a Protestant princess.

Printed in "Extracts from Jacobite Correspondence, 1712-1714" presented (but hardly edited) by L.G. Wickham Legg, *English Historical Review, Vol.XXX (1915), p.508.*

(ii) *A French Agent's Advice to the Chevalier*

The Abbé Gaultier was a French agent originally sent to London to negotiate what became the Peace of Utrecht of 1713 with the Harley ministry. His advice to James clearly reflects the success of Harley's manipulation of Franco-Jacobite perceptions of English politics.

Gaultier to James Francis Edward Stuart, Feb.6, 1714.

It is absolutely necessary that you either conceal the nature of your religion or change it entirely for the one established by law in England.—

You must be careful to make no move which might disturb your sister the queen during her lifetime, or cause any trouble for her ministers. You must on every occasion underline the love you have for your fellow-countrymen, despite their coolness towards you. You must promise them much, and keep your word better than the king your father kept his. Without affectation you must praise their conduct and manners, and make it clear to them that you will never meddle with their religion, laws, or privileges. You must skilfully manipulate the Scots, making them hope for more from you than you mean to give, and never think of using them to conquer England for you, because the English would never tolerate this. Remember that you were born in England and have as a result a great advantage over your competitor, a German quite ignorant of the English language who has made it only too clear to the English that he means to rule them with a rod of iron.—

Your patience, wisdom and discretion, together with the stupidities and instability of the Whigs and the princes of the House of Hanover, and the careful management of your affairs by your friends, will certainly lead to your restoration to your native land.

ibid., p.508-9.

(iii) *James and Harley*
In the spring of 1714 the hopes of the exiled James were understandably, if unrealistically, high, and he wrote to Queen Anne, Bolingbroke, and Harley in the sort of language exemplified by this letter to Harley:

James III to the Earl of Oxford, March 3, 1714

My being frequently informed of your constant good intentions for me is my greatest comfort and next to the confidence I have In the Queen my sisters kindness; It is also what I shall never think I can sufficiently acknowledge, persuaded that you only want an occasion to serve me effectually. You have it now in your hands and time is precious, for this seems to be the critical conjuncture upon which all depends. What would have become of us had my sister failed in her last illness? and what must still happen should she dye without first settling matters? her recovery has given new life to me as her illness cast me into the last anxiety. but after all she is mortal, & cannot too soon provide for her own, her family's & her country's happiness.

It is to facilitate, & promote her good inclinations that I here declare to you that I am willing she remain in quiet possession during her life provided she secure to me the succession after her death; this is too reasonable for you not to enter into it & I am persuaded you love both her & our country too well not to promote as much as possible what alone can secure their quiet & happyness. It would be a sensible satisfaction to me to hear from yourself, & with which alone I can concurr In the most proper measures to attain to the same good good (sic) end wee all aim at. I need not I am sure represent to you how much your interest, & advantage is linked to mine, I know 'tis not private views that govern you, but your country's welfare alone, which must be involved In perpetual warrs and divisions, till the succession is settled in the right line, for tho I willingly yield to my sister, t'is to her alone, & I shall sooner depart from my life, then from my just right to any other,—now you know my sentiments, you see there is no time to be lost, go therefore heartily to work, In securing the Queen my sister's happyness, my just right & our country's welfare: In making yourself the greatest man of ye age, and in deserving from me all that your heart can wish.

Ibid., pp.515-16.

(iv) *The Gentlemen of the Lovat Frasers sense a Coming Storm*

The Frasers of Lovat, whose territories lay near Inverness at the north end of the Great Glen, that mighty transverse fault-line which divides the Highlands, were dominated by a clanned gentry loyal to the holder of the lordship of Lovat. They did not recognize Lord Saltoun, the head of the Aberdeenshire Frasers, and technically the chief of his name, as their chief. When they spoke about their name, they meant the Frasers of Lovat. Around 1714, however, the succession to the lordship of Lovat was violently disputed. To cut a long story short, Clan Mackenzie, under its great chief Lord Seaforth, had made a bid to take control of the Lovat country through its own nominee for the Lovat inheritance. He claimed by female descent, but the Lovat peerage seems to have been one of the few Scots peerages which could only be inherited by direct male descent, which made Simon Fraser of Lovat, the man acceptable to the Fraser gentry, the true heir. He had unfortunately tried to assert his claim against the Mackenzie candidate by marrying the widow of the last Lord Lovat, a lady of the mighty ducal House of Atholl, but the marriage was indistinguishable from kidnapping and the subsequent rape charge led Simon to depart for exile at the French court where his fertile mind contributed the strategic insight behind the '08 invasion bid; it also earned him a reputation as a compulsive double-crosser which placed him eventually in preventive custody. Then in 1714 the despairing Fraser gentry saw welcome signs of impending instability and decided to recall their devious chief, as a sort of crooked Moses to lead them forth from bondage in the House of Seaforth. Despite his lack of French, Major Fraser succeeded in his mission.

—Phopachy and the Major called four gentlemen of the name that they could trust to, and concerted measures what should be done. They swore fidelity and secrecy; the method condescended upon was—since they were informed that Queen Ann was dangerously ill, who was a mortal enemy to Lord Simon and his family, that one of the six should go off to see if their Chief was in life, and that they were persuaded upon King George's accession there would arise some disturbance in Britaine, and if Simon could be stolen out of France, he might come to fish in drumly[1] waters.

This being concerted on betwixt Alexr. Fraser of Phopachy, Major James Fraser, Alexr. Fraser of Culduthall, Hugh Fraser of Foyers, Hugh Fraser of Struy; in the beginning of March 1713 Major Fraser and Alexr. Fraser of Phopachy went off clandestinely, to meet with Sir Peter Fraser of Doors,[2] who was very well known to King George the first,—

Sir Peter asked those gentlemen if they were sure that the whole clan of Frasers were Protestants and that they were for the succession of the family of Hanover.

They assured him they were, whereupon he answered that upon their credit he would write to King George to Hanover,—

Major James Fraser being cousin german to Brigadeer Mackintosh of Borlum,[3] he drew up strongly with him, and pretended to be in the Jacobite interest, he knowing his cousin to be a great man with the Pretender.—Whereupon the Brigadeer immediately jumt to the baite, and gave his cousin, Major Fraser, such credentials as was proper for that occasion,—

[1] troubled or turbid.
[2] Sir Peter Fraser of Durris in Aberdeenshire.
[3] Brigadier William Mackintosh of Borlum was to be the best Jacobite commander in the '15.

Printed in *Major Fraser's Manuscript*,
ed. Alexander Ferguson (Edinburgh 1889),
Vol.1, pp.159-64.

II: The Great Jacobite Rising: The 1715

Though those who have written about Jacobitism tend to be obsessed with the personality of Prince Charles Edward Stuart ("Bonnie Prince Charlie"), and the admittedly dramatic events surrounding the 1745 rising, which he led, the fact is that of all the Jacobite risings, the one which posed by far the most serious threat to the ruling regime in London was the one which broke out in 1715 under the leadership of the Earl of Mar. That rising occurred when the new Hanoverian dynasty was barely established on its thrones, when there was a great deal of political discontent in England as well as widespread national restiveness in Scotland; and was the only Jacobite rising in which the Scottish rebellion, which was always their central feature, was reinforced by a serious rising in the north of England, small in scale perhaps, but rich in potential. Lancashire, with its substantial concentration of Roman Catholics in its south-west corner, had been an area to which the exiled James II had looked for support in the 1690s. It is no accident that during the 1715 the southern Jacobite army was finally brought to bay and forced to surrender at Preston in Lancashire.

The '15 caught the London government entirely off-guard. Unlike the abortive '08, which was a French expedition; the '19, which was a Spanish diversionary attack; or even the '45, which was all about French invasion plans, the '15 owed nothing to foreign sponsorship. It was therefore not "signalled" by a period of diplomatic tension or military preparation abroad. In Scotland it was undoubtedly a massive national rising, at least north of the River Forth, and the government was lucky that the second Duke of Argyll, an extremely experienced general officer, had the presence of mind to take up a strategic position at Stirling, which blocked the southward march of the Jacobite army the Earl of Mar was assembling at Perth. Apart from the formidable obstacle posed by Stirling Castle, the head-waters of the short River Forth were surrounded by extensive mosses and bogs which reduced the route of a southward-moving army to a very narrow compass. Nevertheless, Argyll was heavily outnumbered, and it required remarkable inactivity or rather indecisiveness on the part of Mar to make so little of so promising an initial situation.

The Old Pretender, James Francis Edward Stuart, still a comparatively young man whom it is perhaps better to call the

Chevalier (after his own use of the cover name, the Chevalier de St George), arrived in Scotland too late. The two battles of Sheriffmuir and Preston had been fought, and though the results were tactically ambiguous, they were both decisive strategic defeats for the Jacobites. The rebellion collapsed. James and Mar fled to France in a small ship from Montrose, and the Hanoverian regime was left much more secure than before, for nothing reinforces a government so much as an unsuccessful rising against it.

(i) *The 1715 in Scotland*

(a) *An Overview by a Young Participant of the Start of the Rising*

A very interesting summary of Jacobite hopes and fears on the eve of the '15 can be found in the memoirs of Field Marshal James Keith, the younger brother of the Earl Marischal. James Keith was only nineteen at the time of the rising, and the family, like most Scots Jacobites, was Episcopalian in background. Both brothers were ardent Jacobites at the time of the '15. After its failure they had to go into exile, where both carved out very distinguished careers. James Keith was a soldier who served with the armies of Spain, and later with those of Peter the Great's Russia when he discovered that his Protestantism was an invincible barrier to his advancement in the Spanish service. In Russia there were few religious barriers, and Tsar Peter was used to Scots, for his military tutor when a young man had been the Scots Roman Catholic General Patrick Gordon. From Russia James Keith eventually went to Prussia where his elder brother had established a close relationship with Frederick the Great. James Keith also gained the personal friendship of Frederick. He rose to be a Field Marshal of Prussia, and died at the head of Prussian troops in the well-fought battle of Hochkirchen.

His memoirs are fragmentary. They cover only the period 1714-34, and are incomplete in places even before the final date. Nevertheless they do sketch the situation on the eve of the '15 as he remembered it. Note the stress on English Jacobites, and on hopes that a successful rising would attract open (as distinct from covert) French support. Note also the excellent summary of the reasons why so large a section of the political nation in Scotland was ripe for rebellion in 1715.

—I shall, therefore, begin these at the death of Queen Ann, at which Time, tho' I was young, 17 years old, I was capable of judging a little of the state of the Kingdome of Scotland, and of the inclinations of the people. The long course of prosperity which her reign had been attended with, together with the hopes that she in her lifetime, or at least at her death, would settle the succession on her brother, had kept the Jacobits (who are the prevailing party in that Kingdome)—from giving her any disturbance—

The chief of these in England was the Duke of Ormond, who had been Generalissimo of the forces at the death of the late queen, and in Scotland the Earl of Mar, late Secretary of State,—but who had been both dismissed from their employements on the arrival of King George, to make place for the contrary faction, who now ruled without rivals.—

The Duke of Marr—was bred up to the pen, and was early brought in to bussiness; had good natural parts but few acquired, and knew so little of some of the commonest parts of sciences, that a gentleman of good credit assured me he saw him look for the Dutchy of Deux Pont in a Map of Hungary, Valachia, and Transilvania; but his character is so exactly given in Lockhart's Memoirs, that it's useless to speak more of it here.

To these two the Jacobits adressed themselves on the death of the Queen, but particularly to the Duke of Ormonde, who was then Captain-General of the British forces, but had much more credit with the people then he had with the troopes, who by the negligence of the Earl of Oxford (then High-Treasurer), were still composed of the same Whig officers who had served under the Duke of Marleborough, many of whom having bought their employments, cou'd not well be turn'd out without being reimburs'd, which cou'd only be done by the Treasurer, the Officers who were designed to fill their places not being willing to lay out their own money in purchasing them. The Duke, finding himself not sure of the army, delayed entering into the measures which were proposed to him immediatly after the Queen's death, and an accident which shortly after happen'd convinced him that he cou'd stay no longer in England with safety—

In the beginning of the year 1715, King George call'd a new Parliament, and promises and threats were both made use of to have it to his mind, and in this he very well succeeded; but the corruption was so open in many places, that it exasperated the people to the highest degree, and gave the Jacobits an oportunity of bringing over to their side almost all those who had not as yet taken party.

King James,—was—in Lorrain, yet by his friends in Paris he had got assurances from the King of France that he wou'd assist him in every thing that did not fly openly in the face of the treaty of Utrecht; arms he promised him, and permission to take as many of the Irish troops in the French pay as cou'd be sent without the appearance of formed regiments. But what was most wanted, and most difficult to get was money.—They concerted with the Duke of Marr that he shou'd immediatly go to Scotland, and there declare publickly for King James,—to enable him to prosecute his design, they gave him 7000 pounds sterling to carry with him.—L. Mar brought along with him L. General Hamilton, who tho' an old officer, was not in the least equal to the affair he was to undertake, for tho' he had served long and with very good reputation in the Dutch troops, yet being a man whom only experience, not natural genious, had made an officer, he did not know how to make use of his new troops, who are of a disposition as hot and quick as the Dutch are slow and flegmatick; and this certainly was the occasion of his misfortune at the affair of Dumblain: besides, he having been always used to the regularty of the Dutch, thought all lost when he saw the first sign of confusion among the Highlanders.

With this supply, and many fair promises from the English, did the Earl of Mar arrive in Scotland about the beginning of July, and without stopping at Edenborough went straight to his estate in the Highlands—King George, having clearly discover'd their desseigns, issued out orders that the chiefs of party, to the number of 72 persons, of whom there was above 20 peers, shou'd repair to Edenborough, and there surrender themselves; on which the Earl of Mar assembled all those of them who cou'd conveniently come, and consulted them on the case, where it was unanimously agreed to refuse the summons and take arms.

The Earl of Mar, under pretence of a great hunting, had already assembled about 800 men, and with these he set up the Royal standart on the 3d of September 1715, proclaimed King James, King of Scotland, England, France and Irland, and published a declaration in which he deduced all the misfortunes the Revolution had brought on the Kingdome of Scotland, and particularly the hardships it groan'd under since the fatal union, and concluded that he had taken arms by the orders of their lawfull Souveraign, to free them from a burthen they were no longer able to bear.

Many, indead, thought it an ill omen, and even worse policy, to employ the person who had been one of the principal instruments in building the fabrick, and who had been so well paid for it, in the pulling it doun; but the great imploiments he had been in, his knowlege of the country, and the sincere marks of repentance he gave, made the greater number aprove the choise.

A Fragment of a Memoir of Field-Marshal James Keith
Written by Himself 1714-1734
(Edinburgh, 1853), pp.1-11.

(b) *The Master of Sinclair's Account of the Battle of Sheriffmuir*

It is extremely difficult to find a coherent contemporary account of the Battle of Sheriffmuir, or even a coherent subsequent account by a contemporary who was a participant. As a result, historians have tended to reprint accounts of the battle derived from near-contemporary histories. By using two or three of these it is possible to stitch together a deceptively logical overview of the action; but at the price of somewhat obscuring the confusion, and uncertainty, the bad temper and partial vision, which were the hallmarks of the Jacobite experience on that day. The Master of Sinclair's account has been too often dismissed as sheer retrospective venom, mainly directed at Mar, whom Sinclair blamed for the total mismanagement of the rising, never mind the battle. Yet Sinclair probably saw as much as any other participant though he never actually crossed swords with the enemy. Stripped of the overdone abuse of everyone else, the facts ring true. He also gives a clear insight into the fading political and military hopes which buoyed the Jacobite army.

It is interesting that Jacobite hopes and fears for an English rising and a French invasion were so similar towards the end of both the '15 and the '45. Ironically Sinclair, who was pardoned and who returned from exile after the '15 to wash his hands of the Stuarts, did his best to dissuade David Lord Elcho, a man whose account of the '45 is very like Sinclair's account of the '15, to abandon his commitment to what Sinclair had come to regard as a selfish and ungrateful exiled dynasty.

—While our Generall, as well as we, were thus uncertaine, I went and put Huntley's tuo squadrons in the best order I could, and went afterwards to the head of the Fife squadron, where my Lord Huntlie

119

found me. He took me aside and told me, He was not of opinion we should marche further; because, he said, if we should pass the Forth, the King, who we expected daylie, would be lost, and all communication betwixt him and us cut off, and, for that reason, thought we ought to goe back to Auchterarduch to waite the King's comeing. I told him, I differ'd from him, and had no such apprehension as that of passing the Forth; for the Duke of Argyle's comeing out was the onlie thing could doe our busieness, and the onlie occasion ever we could have to recover our liberties, or force the enemie to give us a peace on our old footing, I mean'd, to get home again, and we were now to think of ourselves; for if we returned to Auchterarduch, the Highlandmen, who were alreadie deserting daylie, would lose courage and goe home, so that inevitablie we must be ruin'd, without haveing another occasion either of serveing ourselves or the King, and bring on ourselves ane eternall infamie; and that we were by no means to go back, if it was possible to attack the Duke of Argyle, and, in that case, to marche straight to him in order of battle; and, in the mean time, if we could think of a way to send some deputees to him, to ask him, If he had full power to give us, and all concerned with us, terms? and if not, to tell him that we would fall upon him that moment, since we had no more left us for our all. What made us believe he had full power was ane intercepted letter of my Lord Townsend's to the Duke of Argyle, which Mr Forrester had sent to Mar, and which letter Huntlie had read. Huntlie sent for my Lord Rollo and Major Balfour his uncle, and told them his proposale; and I told them mine, and both went in to it, and Huntlie seem'd satisfied with it himself, and said he'd goe and propose to Glengarie and Sir John MacClean.

I'm satisfied that many will blame me for such a proposale, but am very easie about it. I knew very well that if we did not get terms with our swords in our hands, we could never expect anie; for it was not to be imagin'd that the Highlanders would stay with us, a great many deserting daylie, or if they did, that we could pay them longe; nor did those who were keenest for Mar's project in the beginning, and before we came out, pretend that we were able to doe our work without England's riseing and the help of France, and without the King's presence, and generalls, officers, armes, and monie; all which, to bringe us out, we were made believe was either readie at our riseing, or alreadie in the countrie. How oftne were we told of the King's being landed with the Duke of Berwick before our riseing? and if all those aides were thought absolutlie necessarie to us, in what condition was it naturale to us to think ourselves in when we had not one of them, and nothing to depend upon but the words of one who we knew all his life to be the worst of men? Who,

because he had now trickt us, had usurped the command which he
was altogether incapable of, and which, before we came out, he
durst not pretend to. Nor was that all, for we had not so much as
heard from the King; and some begun to think that the commission
Boyn brought was forged, since he knew nothing about the King;—

—While I was about this, I saw and heard a gentleman come up
to Generall Gordon, calling to him, with great oaths, To attack the
enemie before they were formed, and was told it was old Captain
Livinston, of Dumbarton's regiment. Gordon excused himself, as I
was afterwards told, till he had spoke to Mar; but on Mar's not being
to be found or seen, he soon consented, Livingston representing to
him that he'd loose his time. The order to attack being given, the
two thousand Highlandmen, who were then draun up in very good
order, run towards the ennemie in a disorderlie manner, always
fireing some dropeing shots, which drew upon them a generall salvo
from the ennemie, which begun at their left, opposite to us, and run
to their right. No sooner that begun, the Highlandmen threw
themselves flat on their bellies; and when it slackned, they started to
their feet. Most threw away their suzies, and, drawing their swords,
pierced them everie where with ane incredible vigour and rapiditie,
in four minutes' time from their receaving the order to attack. Not
onlie all in our view and before us turned their backs, but the five
squadrons of dragoons on their left, commanded by General
Witham, went to the right about, and never lookt back till they had
got near Dumblain, almost two miles from us; while the
Highlandmen pursued the infantrie, who run as hard as their feet
could carrie them, a great manie of whome threw away their armes
to enable them to run the faster, and were sabred by the
Highlandmen, who spared few who fell in their hands.—

The night comeing on, the Duke of Argyll seem'd first to make a
feint as if he was moveing towards us, and inclined after to
Dumblain, and, it being almost dark, we soon lost sight of them. It's
certain that Mar told the gentlemen, That the Highlandmen were so
fatigued they had lost spirits, and would not attack; and to the
Highlandmen, That he could not find in his heart to risque the
gentlemen. If it be allowed to judge, from the regarde he had to both
first and last, it wont seem ane uncharitable construction to say that
Mar had no mind to risque himself; for of all the opportunities at
that time, the gentlemen, who had no bread to expect out of the
countrie missed the favourablest that ever offer'd of getting out of
the danger he had plunged them in, haveing at least ane equall
number of horse, and more than double the number of foot; for I
never heard that he was above eight hundred foot, and it was never

denied we were above two thousand.

From *Memoirs of The Insurrection in Scotland in 1715*, ed. Sir Walter Scott, Abottsford Club, Vol 30 (Edinburgh, 1858), pp. 209-223.

(c) *The Earl of Mar at the Outbreak of the '15*

There is no doubt that, though he exploited existing discontents, John Earl of Mar was the key to the outbreak of the '15, which he organized and launched by raising the Jacobite standard formally on the Braes of Mar on September 6, 1715. It was of blue silk with the arms of Scotland on one side, worked in gold, and on the other a Scottish thistle with the traditional motto "nemo me impune lacessit" (wha daur meddle wi me) and the additional one "No union". Two white pendants were inscribed "for our wronged king and oppressed country" and "for ourselves and liberties". All in all, the standard summed up Mar's political stance as he launched the rebellion. It happens we have a neat pair of documents which between them sum up the harsh underlying realities and the high promise of the early stages.

Mar not only had an indifferent communications network, but he also had a curious knack of losing potentially embarrassing letters. For example he "lost" a letter to Huntly written on September 9, and when it became clear it had gone astray even Mar realized it could do great harm in the wrong hands. However, it was his letter of that day to his baillie "Black Jock" Forbes, on the theme of burning out any of his Kildrummy tenants who were slow to join him in arms which did him most damage. Intercepted by the government, it was gleefully reprinted to the point where copies were available in Paris. Lochiel and other chiefs like Glenlyon did much the same. It was accepted by both sides that ordinary people had to be forced to fight. They could also be encouraged by a political manifesto, and Mar's declaration of September 9 shows the persuasive rather than coercive dimension.

1. "Jocke,

Ye was in the right not to come with the 100 men ye sent up tonight, when I expected four times the number. It is a pretty thing when all the Highlands of Scotland are now rising upon their King and Country's account, as I have accounts from them since they were with me, and the gentlemen of our neighbouring Lowlands expecting us down to join them, that my men only should be refractory. Is not this the thing we are now about, which they have been wishing these twenty-six years? And Now, when it is come, and the king and country's cause is at stake, will they for ever sit still and see all perish? I have used gentle means too long, and so shall be forced to put other orders I have in execution. I have sent you enclosed an order for the lordship of Kildrummy, which you are immediately to intimate to all my vassals; if they give ready obedience, it will make some amends, and if not, ye may tell them from me that it will not be in my power to save them (though I were willing) from being treated as enemies by those who are ready soon to join me, and they may depend on it, that I will be the first to propose and order their being so. Particularly let my own tenants in Kildrummy know, that if they come not forth with their best arms, I will send a party immediately to burn what they shall miss taking from them. And they may believe this only a threat but, by all that's sacred, I'll put it in execution — let my loss be what it will. You are to tell the gentlemen that I'll expect them in their best accoutrements, on horseback, and no excuse to be accepted of. Go about this with all diligence, and come yourself and let me know your having done so. All this is not only as ye will be answerable to me, but to your king and country.

Your assured friend and servant,
Mar."

2. *The Earl of Mar's Declaration, September 9, 1715*

"Our rightful and natural King James the 8th, by the Grace of God, who is now coming to relieve us from our oppressions having been pleased to intrust us with the direction of his affairs, and the command of his forces in this his ancient kingdom of Scotland, and some of his faithful subjects and servants met at Aboyne — viz. The Lord Huntley, the Lord Tullibardine, the Earl Mareschal, the Earl of Southesk, Glengary from the Clans, Glendarule from the Earl of Broadalbine and Gentlemen of Argyllshire, Mr Patrick Lyon of Auchterhouse, the Laird of Auldbar,[1] Lieut. General George Hamilton, Major General Gordon and myself, having taken into consideration his Majesty's last and late orders to us, find that as this is now the Time that he ordered us to appear openly in arms for him, so it seems to us absolutely necessary for his Majesty's service and the relieving of our native country from all its hardships, that all his faithful and loving subjects and Lovers of their country should, with all possible speed, put themselves into arms.

These are therefore in his Majesty's name and authority, and by vertue of the power aforesaid, and by the King's special order to me there anent, to require and impower you forthwith to raise your fencible men with their best arms, and you are immediately to march them to join me and some others of the King's forces at the Inver of Braemar on Monday next, in order to proceed on our march to attend the King's standard with his other forces.

The King intending that his Forces shall be paid from the time of their setting out, he expects as he positively orders, that they behave themselves civilly and commit no plundering nor other Disorders upon the highest penalties and his displeasure, which is expected you'll see observed.

Now is the Time for all good men to show their zeal for his Majesty's service, whose cause is so deeply concerned, and the relief of our Native Country from oppression and a foreign yolk too heavy for us and our posterity to bear, and to endeavour the restoring not only of our rightful and native King, but also our country to its ancient free and independent Constitution under him whose ancestors have reigned over us for so many generations.

In so honourable good and just a cause we cannot doubt of the Assistance direction and blessing of Almighty God who has so often rescued the Royal Family of Stuart and our own country from sinking under oppression. Your punctual Observance of these orders is expected, for the doing of all which this shall be to you and all you employ in the execution of them a sufficient warrant.

Mar.

Given at Braemar the 9th September 1715. To the Baillie and the rest of the Gentlemen of the Lordship of Kildrummie."

Printed in Alistair and Henrietta Tayler,
1715: The Story of the Rising
(London, 1936), pp.43-45.

[1]Nephew of the Viscount Dundee who had led the 1689 Jacobite rising.

(d) *Mar, the Chevalier and the Failure of the '15*

The Earl of Mar appears to have launched the '15 without detailed consultation with the exiled court, which was, understandably, taken by surprise by the raising of its standard on the Braes of Mar. Though the Earl of Mar claimed from the outset to have a commission from the Chevalier, this document has been delicately summed up by historians as "an anticipative draft". In due course Mar received a formal commission from James, who also raised him to ducal rank in the Jacobite peerage. Such phantom ranks were, after all, cheap patronage from the point of view of James. Some of his tougher-minded followers were well aware of their real value. The Earl Marischal, for example, was made a Jacobite Knight of the Garter after becoming an exile in the aftermath of the '15, but he only wore the insignia in the presence of the Chevalier, so as not to hurt the latter's feelings.

Mar's correspondence with the Chevalier, before James contrived to land at Peterhead on December 22, 1715, is partially preserved in the Mar family papers, along with one or two associated documents, including an interesting summary of the Jacobite forces in camp in Perth in October 1715. This list does not include the substantial Jacobite force from the western Highlands under General Alexander Gordon of Auchintoul, a veteran of the Russian service who joined Mar with his men on November 10, and commanded the Jacobite centre at Sheriffmuir. It is piquant to compare Mar's enthusiasm for the Chevalier with his earlier zeal to secure the signature of Highland chiefs to a sycophantic address to George I, which Campbell of Glendaruel touted round on behalf of Mar. However, the revealing letter from Mar to his even more ambiguous brother, the lawyer Lord Grange, goes some way towards explaining the underlying motivation which led Mar to act as he did, though it hardly clears him of the charge that his Jacobitism was rooted in personal ambition (or desperation).

1. *Colin Campbell of Glendaruel to the Justice Clerk*

1714, September 2. Lochiel. — I mett with Glengarie and Lochieall the 1st of September. Both of them hes signed a lettir to the Earl of Mar. Sir Johne M'Lean hes also signed it. It's from the cheifs of the clans to his Lordship; all of them are to signe it as I can gett thorow them. The tutor of M'Leod is readie to signe it; he is fourscoir meils from his place, and a verry ill road, so that it will take near eight days, or I can have his subscription and return this lenth. Then there is the rest of the leading men that is to signe it, lives at such a distans that it will take me six or sevin days more. Then I go straight to Edinbruch and takes post for London, for those gentilmen proposis I should goe with their lettir to London to the Earl of Mar to lay there concerns before him. The contents of their lettir is praying his Lordship may assure the Government of there dutifull and hearty resolutions to serve his Majesty King George, and in all things to concur with his Lordship, and to follow his directions in all things wherein they can be usfull to his sacred Majesty's service. I have sent this by ane express to Edinbruch to Mr Harry Mall, writter there, with a lettir to the Earle of Mar, in which I have inclosed ane doubill of the lettir the chiefs of the clans is to send by me to his Lordship, that by it his Lordship may prevent any ill impressions that may be given of them. They have alowed me to send it, yett they disayr it should be at present known only to such as his Lordship thinks necisarie. Sir James Campbell and Sir Duncan Campbell each of them writts his Lordship a lettir in there oun name, and in the name of others of Argyllshyre, in the same tearms that the lettir from the clans is, and it is in concert with the clans. There lettirs I also carie with me to his Lordship, butt its fitt nothing be said of there lettirs butt to such as my Lord Mar thinks it absolutly necisarie to impart it to.

2. *The Earl of Mar to his brother, Lord Grange*

1714, November 20. London. — The accounts we have had latly from Scotland make people here belive that there is a designe in Scotland of addressing against the Union, and I am told the Court begin to apprehend it a good dale, and perhaps they have some reason for so doing; for if such addresses were universall, heartie, and soon from Scotland, I am apt to belive that the Parliament might go into it. I have reason to belive most of the Tories wou'd, most of the Whigs too who are out of humour, and several others of them who were formerly against it upon account of the Protestant succession not having then taken place. And by the situation of affairs 'tis probable there will never be a time so likly to bring about a dissolution as now, if our country push it heartily. All sides of our peers own that if the matter of our peerage be not sett right they wou'd wish a dissolution, and I am perfectly of that oppinion, tho' I thought the Union as good a thing as ever I did. Now as to that of our Peerage being sett right, I see now little probability of it, and I confess I almost despair of it by what I pick up in my conversation with the English.—

Give my service to my Lord Balmerino. I thought to have wrote to him to-night; I have not now time, but show you him this.

I am very glade of the account you gave me in your last of some peers; pray go on in that way with others of them, all you can.

3. *1715, October 13. — List of the army at the camp of Perth —*

HORSE

Marquis of Huntly	400
Earl Marischal	180
Perthshire	70
Sterlingshire	77
Angusshire	100
Fifeshire	90
	917

Marquis of Huntly	1200
Lord George Murray	230
Earl Pammure	415
Lord Ogilvie	351
Strouan	203
Innernytie	267
	2666

4. *The Chevalier to the Duke of Mar*

1715, November 15. — If the winds had not been contrary Mr Hayes had not found me on this side the sea, for he arrived here but last night, and I have been waiting here these eight dayes. The accounts he gave have increased the desire you know I have long had of going to you, which nothing but cross winds do now hinder, but I hope they will soon turn and that I may still soon join you. I shall go straight to the place you appointed, and from thence join your army with all possible speed. You will maybe be surprised at this resolution after the message I lately sent you that I was resolved to go to England, but affairs have not gone so well there as we hoped, as Lord John Drummond will tell you. However the D[uke] Ormond parts to-morrow to try again what he can do and with some arms wee have gott here and some few Irish troopers, I do not doubt but that he will be able to make a head and make considerable diversion.—

5. *The Earl of Mar to the Chevalier*

1715, November 24. From the Camp of Perth. — Sir, it was but yesterday I had accounts of your being at sea; and I thought myself obliged to do all in my power to let you know the state of affairs in this island before you land in it, so that you may not be disappointed upon your comeing.

I had the certain accounts yesterday of those who had appeared in arms besouth Forth and in the North of England, all being made prisoners at Preston in Lancashire, which I'm afraid will putt a stop to any more risings in that countrey at this time. Your Majesteis army, which I have the honour to command, fought the enemie in the Shirreff-Muir, near Dumblain, the 13th of this moneth. Our left behaved scandalously and run away, but our right routed the enemies left and most of their body. Their right follow'd and pursued our left, which made me not adventure to prosecute and push our advantage on our right so far as otherwayes wee might have done. However wee keept the field of battle, and the enemies retird to Dumblain.

The armie had lyen without cover the night before, and wee had no provisions there, which obliged me to march the armie back two milles that night, which was the nearest place where I could get any quarters. Next day I found the armie reduced to a small number, more by the Highlanders going home than by any loss wee sustained, which was but very small; so that and want of provisions obliged me yet to retire, first to Auchterarder and then here to Perth. I have been doing all I can ever since to get the armie together again,—

Your Majestie's presence would certainly give new life to your friends, and make them do all in their power for your service, but how farr they would be able to resist such a form'd body of regular troops as will be against them I must leave your Majestie to judge.

May all happiness attend your Majestie, and grand you may be safe whatever become of us. If it do not please God to bless your kingdoms at this time with your being settled on your throne, I make no doubt of its doing at another time—

6. *The Duke of Mar to the Chevalier St George*

1715, December 9, Perth. — If the Duke of Ormond be not in England to make a diversion the enimie will send most of their troops here; but that will give them a fine opportunity there to appear for your Majesty if they have any spirit left. Should your Majesties armie in Scotland not be able to fight the enemie it will be in your power to keep them from fighting you, and were your Majestie once arrived I have very good hopes of a good part of their army coming over to you.

Perhaps your Majesty will hear on your arrival that wee had made an offer to capitulate; it is too long to tell you the story here, but I beg your Majestie may not be alarmed at it, for I hope the danger of that is over, and that you shall not want people to stand by you to the last drop of their blood.—

All prosperity attend your Majesty, and may I have the happiness soon to throw myself at your feet, which is the thing in the world I have long'd most for.

Allow me to say that I am with all veneration, sir, your Majesties most obedient, most faithfull, most humble, and most dutiful subject and servant, Mar. (Copy.)

> Printed in *Report on the Manuscripts of the Earl of Mar
> and Kellie Preserved at Alloa House, N.B.*,
> Historical Manuscripts Commission (London,
> for His Majesty's Stationery Office, 1904),
> pp.509-517.

(ii) *The 1715 In England*

Even before the death of Queen Anne, plots had been concocted for a restoration of the exiled James. On the direct orders of Sir Thomas Parker, Lord Chief Justice of England, who had been informed of subversive activity, two Irish officers were arrested in 1714 at Deal and Gravesend for enlisting men with a view to fighting for the exiled claimant. Though the accession and even the coronation of George I went more smoothly than many expected, the coronation did provoke riots and Jacobite demonstrations at Bristol, Norwich, and Birmingham. Then there was another opportunity for political demonstration supplied by the mandatory English general election. As parliament was a manifestation of the royal personality, and the King was much the most important of its three parts (King, Lords and Commons), it followed that any parliament was an embodiment of the living sovereign. With his or her death, it died, so another had to be elected to embody the new sovereign's majesty and sovereignty, in a particular mode. The 1715 general election caused more riots such as the one at Bristol where the rioters shouted for Ormonde, the Tory-Jacobite hero, and damned foreign governments.

Lord Stair, the new British ambassador in Paris had established a spy network which enabled him in July 1715 to warn the London government of plans for a Jacobite rising in the west of England, to be supplemented by an invasion from France. Preparations for the latter had started in the port of le Havre, and characteristically had not been wholly suspended despite French acknowledgement of the Protestant Succession to the British thrones in the Peace of Utrecht. There was therefore some official apprehension of a Jacobite rebellion in mid-1715, but of the wrong rebellion.

(a) *English Responses to the Approach and Outbreak of the '15*

The Westminster government was apprehensive by the summer of 1715 that the Pretender would invade England, assisted by "a restless Party" which had, the Hanoverian regime was sure, promoted widespread and repeated riots against the new Whig administration. The language used in official statements was ambiguous, for the "restless party" could be taken as a general reference to Jacobites, or a more specific implied reference to seditiously disgruntled Tories, or most probably as a phrase which deliberately confused the issue. Though it turned out to be misplaced, there was nothing insincere about the declared concern of the ruling ministry, and it is instructive to see in the following documents that they placed their faith in measures designed systematically to disarm the entire civilian population and in particular to deprive Roman Catholics of surplus weaponry and horses good enough for military service.

King George I was not only the most important part of the King-in-his Westminster Parliament, but also the head of the executive branch of government. It was his job to mobilize the machinery of central and local government against a possible Jacobite invasion, and his principal legal machinery for doing this was his Privy Council. Technically, since the Scots Privy Council had been abolished in 1708, it was the Privy Council for Great Britain. In practice, it functioned efficiently only in

England and Wales, and the lack of any effective local body capable of activating and co-ordinating government officers in Scotland was to remain a major weakness of the Hanoverian regime there right up to 1745. Here are a sequence of documents, mostly from the Privy Council to the Lord Lieutenant of Cumberland, the Earl of Carlisle. Cumberland was to face invasion from Scotland, after the Jacobite rising broke out there, to the consternation of the London authorities, but of course similar communications were addressed to all English Lords Lieutenant.

1. *Order of Council*

20 July 1715

To Lord Charles, Earl of Carlisle, Lord Lieutenant of the County of Cumberland.

After our very hearty Commendations to your Lordship, Whereas his Majesty has received certain advice from abroad[1] yt. ye Pretender is preparing to invade this Kingdom, encouraged thereto by ye Riotous, & Tumultuous proceedings set on foot and Carry'd on at home by a restless Party In his favour. And whereas by an Act of Parliament, made in ye 13th and 14th years of ye Reign of ye late King Charles ye 2d, Entituled an Act for ordering ye forces in the severall Counties of this Kingdom, for the Better Securing the Peace of this Kingdom, the respective Lieutenants for ye severall and respective Countys and Cities and Places in England, Dominion of Wales, and Town of Berwick upon Tweed, or any two or more of their Deputys, were enabled & authoriz'd from time to time, by Warrant under their hands & seals, to employ such person or persons as they shoud think fitt, of which a Commission'd Officer, and ye Constable or his Deputy, or ye Tythingman, or in ye Absence of ye Constable and his Deputy and Tythingman, some other person bearing office within ye Parish where ye search shou'd be were take [sic. to be] two; And in Case of a Peer in ye Presence of ye Lieutenant or one or ye Deputy Lieutenants to search for or Seize all arms in ye Custody or Possession of any Person or Persons whom ye said Lieutenants, or any two or more of their Deputys, shou'd judge dangerous to ye Peace of this Kingdom; and to secure such arms for ye purposes in ye said [Act] directed, at ye times and in ye Manner therein Directed. We do therefore, in his Majesties Name and by his express Command, hereby pray & Require your Lordship forthwith to cause all arms belonging to Papists and Nonjurors, being dangerous to ye Peace of this Kingdom, in your Lieutenancy to be

Siez'd & Secur'd according to ye said act & to encourage, as much as in you lies, ye Seizure thereof; and of your proceedings herein Your Lordship is desired to Returne an exact account to this Court. And so we bid your Lordship very heartily farewell, From ye Council Chamber at St. Jameses ye 20th of July 1715...

[Signed:- (all privy councillors),]

Nottingham,[3] Devonshire, Dorset, Manchester, Orrery, Aylesford, Carleton, Christopher Musgrave.[4]
[Copy]

[1] From Lord Stair, the ambassador in Paris.
[2] A reference to the disturbances at Bristol, Norwich, and Birmingham.
[3] Daniel Finch, 2nd Earl of Nottingham — an old Hanoverian Tory who joined the Whigs. Became Lord President at accession of George I. In 1716 moved an address for mercy to impeached Jacobite lords and was dismissed.
[4] The other signatories are in order the 2nd Duke of Devonshire, 7th Earl of Dorst, 4th Earl of Manchester, 4th Earl of Orrery, 1st Earl of Aylesford, 1st and only Baron Carleton, Sir Christopher Musgrave, 5th baronet of Edenhall.

2. *Order of Council*

20 July 1715

To the Earl of Carlisle, Custos Rotulorum[1] of the County of Cumberland.

After our very hearty Commendacons to your Lordship. Whereas... [an invasion is being prepared...] And whereas by an Act of Parliament, made in the first year of the Reign of the late King William and Queen Mary,[2] entituled an Act for the better Security of the Government by Disarming Papists and Reputed Papists, It was Enacted that it should and might be lawful for any Two or more Justices of the Peace, who should know or Suspect any persons to be a papist or should be informed that any Person was or was Suspected to be a Papist to Tender, and they were thereby Authorized and required to tender, to such person, so known or Suspected to be a Papist, the Declaracon Set Down and expressed in an Act of Parliament, made in the 30th year of the Reigne of the late King Charles the 2nd, Entituled An Act for the more effectuall preserving the Kings Person and Government by Disabling Papists from Sitting in either house of Parliament, to be by him made, repeated and Subscribed; and if such person so required should refuse to make, repeat and Subscribe the said Declaracon, or refuse or forbear to appear before the said Justices for the makeing, repeating and Subscribing thereof, on notice to him given or left at his usuall place of aboad, by any person authorized in that behalfe by Warrant under the hands and Seals of the said Two Justices, he was by that Act prohibited to have, or keep in his house, or elsewhere, or in the possession of any other Person to his Use, or at his Disposition, any Arms, Weapons, Gunpowder or Amunition, other than such necessary Weapons as should be allowed by him, by Order of the Justices of the Peace at their Generall Quarter Sessions, for the Defence of his house and person.—We do therefore, in his Majesties Name and by his Express Command, hereby pray and require you forthwith to Signifye his Majesties pleasure to the Justices of the Peace of the County, that they do with the utmost diligence put the Laws of Execucon against Papists and Nonjurors being Dangerous to his Maesties Government.—And so wee bid your Lordship very heartily farewell, from the Councill Chamber at St James's the 20th July, 1715...

[Signed:- (all privy councillors),]

Nottingham P., Manchester, Dorset, Aylesford, Orrery, Hay, Carleton, Christopher Musgrave.

[1] It is to be noted that, although the Earl of Carlisle was both lord lieutenant and custos rotulorum in respect of the county of Cumberland, separate Orders were addressed to him by the council, bearing the same date, the one having regard to the taking up of arms — a military matter (see No.1) and the other, this present Order, as to the religious test — a purely civil matter.
[2] 1 W & M (1688), cap. 15, sec.ii. Justices were authorised to tender the declaration to papists and suspected papists (by sec.ii), and certify the "subscribers" and "refusers" to sessions (by sec.iii). "Refusers" were then forbidden to keep arms (by sec.iv), which if in fact kept, could be seized (ibid).

3. *Order of Council*

16 Sep. 1715

To the Earl of Carlisle, Lord Lieutenant of the County of Cumberland.[1]

After our very hearty commendations to your Lordship. Whereas there is an open and unaturall Rebellion at this time commenced in that part of his Majesties Dominions called Scotland,[2] and amongst other Hostile Acts the Castle of Edenburrow has been attempted to be Surprized.[3] And his Majestie haveing Received Certaine Information of an Intended Invasion of this Kingdom, by the Person who, dureing the lifetime of the late King James the 2d., Pretended to be Prince of Wales, And, since his Decease, has taken upon himselfe the Style and Tytle of James the 3d, King of England and James the 8th. King of Scotland, being bred up in the Popish Superstititon and Instructed to Introduce a Tyranicall Government into his Majestys Dominions, Encouraged thereto by Diverse wicked and Trayterous Persons here at home. Wee think it necessary that the Kingdom be put into the best Condition of Defence with as litle Inconvenience to his Majesty's Good Subjects as may be. And therefore, wee do, in his Majesties name and by his Express Command, hereby pray and Require Your Lordship forthwith to cause the whole Militia, both Horse and Foot, to be put in Such a posture as to be in readiness to meet upon the first Orders. And alsoe to give the necessary Directions to the proper Officers of the Militia forthwith to Seize, with the Assistance of the Constable, the Person's and Arm's of all Papists, Nonjurors or other Person's that you have reason to Suspect to be Disafected to his Majesty and his Government And may probably be Aiding to such Insurrection or Invasion. And of your proceedings herein your Lordship is desired To Returne an Account to this Board. And so wee bid your Lordship very heartily farewell.
From the Councill Chamber at St James's the 16th Day of September 1715...

[Signed:- (all privy councillors),]

Nottingham P., Sunderland C.P.S., Somerset, Bolton, Marlborough, Grafton, H.Boscowen, Somers, T.Fokes, Oxford.[4]

[1]Another Order in similar terms was addressed to the Earl of Carlisle in his capacity of lord lieutenant of Westmorland.
[2]Mar left London secretly for Scotland on 2nd August. He raised the standard in Braemar, proclaimed James VIII, and published a proclamation dated 9th September, 1715.
[3]The custody of this castle was crucial in 1688, 1715, and 1745. In 1715 the Jacobites suborned three soldiers in the garrison, but the plot was discovered and foiled.
[4]Signatories are, in order, the Earl of Nottingham (Lord President of

the Council), 3rd Earl of Sunderland, 6th Duke of Somerset, 2nd Duke of Bolton, 1st Duke of Marlborough, 2nd Duke of Grafton, Hugh Boscawen (Viscount Falmouth), an unidentifiable name which may be mistranscribed, and the 1st Earl of Orford.

4. *Lieutenancy Minute Book. Correspondence*

22nd Sep. 1715

Letter: Earl of Carlisle to Deputy Lieutenants of Cumberland and Westmorland.

Gentlemen,

The King, haveing Received certaine advice that the Pretender Persists in his Design of Invadeing those Kingdoms has thought fit to Give the Directions which you will find Inclosed in the Letters from the Privy Councill and I must Recommend to your Care and Vigilance a Strickt and Due Execution of them.—

As to the other part of the Directions you will take care to Secure the Horses, Arms and persons of all Roman Catholicks and other Disafected people.[1] The City of Carlisle will be the safest and properest place to send the persons you take into Custody to.

I am, Gentlemen, Your very obedient humble Servant,
Carlisle.

[1]A month after this letter was sent, Lord Lonsdale wrote to the Earl of Carlisle saying that he had refused to release Catholic prisoners in Carlisle on parole for fear they might join the Northumberland rebels.

Printed in
*Cumberland County Council Record Series
Vol.I: The Jacobite Risings of 1715 and 1745*
ed. Rupert C.Jarvis (Carlisle, 1954), pp.142-153.

(b) *The Jacobite Campaign in Lancashire*

Brigadier Mackintosh of Borlum's bold attempt to cross the Forth and seize Edinburgh by surprise had failed only narrowly. Argyll, however, moved enough troops to make the seizure of

Edinburgh impractical, and Mackintosh and his men, with no naval support, could not stay indefinitely in the old Cromwellian citadel at Leith, the port of Edinburgh, in which they had barricaded themselves when Argyll sallied out of Edinburgh against them. Instead, the 1500 Jacobites moved down into the Scottish Borders, in the south-west of which there had been a small Jacobite rising led by Lords Kenmure, Nithsdale, Carnwath and Wintoun. As it happened, those Jacobite peers and their few followers had crossed into England to link up with the Northumberland Jacobites whose brightest spirit was Lord Derwentwater, but whose general was Mr Thomas Forster, MP for Northumberland. After uniting at Rothbury the Border and English Jacobites re-entered Scotland to unite with Mackintosh and his Highlanders at Kelso. Reluctantly, Mackintosh and the bulk of his men agreed to march south into Lancashire in hopes of raising local support from Roman Catholics and High Church Anglicans.

There is one remarkably dispassionate account of the Jacobite invasion of Lancashire, written by a participant, a lawyer's clerk in Westmoreland called Peter Clarke, who appears to have been in the suite of the unfortunate Earl of Derwentwater. Since that nobleman was executed in February 1716, along with the Earl of Kenmure, it is easy to understand why Clarke did not originally write up in retrospect the final stages of the rising, but his account, which starts at Penrith, is in many ways more valuable because of its rather bald nature. Note the evidence it provides of the anxiety of the Scots to see signs of, preferably non-Roman Catholic, English support, and the way the Jacobites, as in 1745, collected state revenue on their march. The comic-opera episode with which the narrative starts on Penrith Fell is a classic illustration of the uselessness of the *posse comitatus* (literally: the power of the county) as an internal security force when a largely disarmed society was attacked by armed rebels. The sheriff still had the right to call out "the Aid and Attendance of all Knights, Gentlemen, Yeomen, Labourers, Stewards, Apprentices and other young men above the age of fifteen within the County". Much good did it do him. The posse, like many traditional English institutions and values, was to survive more effectively in the United States of America.

1. *2nd Novr. 1715. — The Posse Comitatus on Penrith Ffell, Numbr. 25000. — The Posse Com. Runs Away*

Sir,

On Wednesday, the second day of November one thousand seaven hundred and fifteene, the then High Sherriff of Cumbrland assembled the Posse Com. on Penrith Ffell, Viscount Loynsdale being there as Commandr of the Malitia of Westmrland, Cumbrland, and Northumbrland, who were assembled at the place aforesd for pr'vention of rebelion & riots. The Ld Bishop of Carlisle & his Daughtr were there.

By ye strictest observation the numbr were Twenty-five thousand men, but very few of them had any regular armes.

At 11 a clock in ye forenoone of the same day, the High Sherriff and ye two Lds received a true account yt ye El of Derwentwater, togethr with his army, were within 6 miles of Penrith. Upon the recept of this newes, the sd High Sherriff & ye sd 2 Lds, the Posse Com' & ye malitia fled, leaving most of their armes upon the sd Ffell.

There is no doubt, had these men stood their ground, ye sd Earl & his men (as it hath since beene acknowledged by diverse of them) wood have retreated.

2. El Derwentwater's Men, 1700, entered Penrith

Abt 3 a clock in the afternoone on the same day, the sd Earl, togethr with his army in numbr abt one thousand seaven hundred, entred the sd towne of Penrith, where they proclamed their King by the name & title of James ye 3d of England & Ireland, & 8th of Scotland.

In this towne they recd wt excise was due to the Crowne, and gave receipts for the same.

3. The Party Sent to Search for Lord Loynsdale

A small party were sent to Lowthr Hall to search for Ld Loynsdale,[1] but not finding him there (for he was gone into Yorkshire) they made bold to take pvision for themselves & their horses, such as the Hall afforded. There were only at that time two old women in the sd Hall, who received no bodily damage.

4. *3d Novr. Marched for Apleby.*

But pvision being scarce in the sd towne Penrith, they marched betimes next morning for Apleby. — Only one man joined them in their march from Penrith to Apleby. —

[This man stole a horse abt one houre before he joined ym, & diserted from them ye next day, and at Augt Assizes 1716 was found guilty & executed at Apleby for stealing ye sd horse.]

5. *Novr. 3d, 4th, and 5th, at Ap'leby.*[1]

The gentlemen paid their quarters of [off] for wt they called for in both these townes (i.e. Penrith and Apleby] but the Commonality paid litle or nothing. Neithr was there any pson that received any bodily damage in eithr of ye sd Townes. If they found any armes, they tooke them without paying the owners for them. In this towne they made the same pclamacon as they had done in the former, and received the excise. The weathr at this time and some days before was rainy.

[1]Appleby is the modern spelling.

6. *5th Novr. Marched to Kendall.*

—Abt 12 a Clock of the same day [Saturday], 6 Quarter Mrs came into the Towne of Kendall, & abt 2 Clock in the afternoone Brigadeere Mackintoss and his man came both a horseback, having both plads on, their targets hanging on their backs, either of them a sword by his side, as also eithr a gun and a case of pistols. The sd Brigadeere looked with a grim countenance. He and his man lodged at Alderman Lowrys, a private house in Highgate street in this towne.—

They compeled the Belman here to go & give notice to the tanners & Inkeeprs to come and pay what excise was due to the crown, or else they that denyed should be plundred by Jack the Highlandr. They recd of the Innkeeprs & Tanners here the sume of eighty pounds & some od shillings, & gave receipts to each pson.

Abt six a clock this night, the Mayor here was taken into custody for not telling where the Malitia armes were hid; (the sd Mayor was a Leivetent in the Malitia). But next morning Mr Crosby, the minister of this towne, went to El Derwentwater and Tho Ffoster, & got the Mayor discharged out of custody.—

In this towne the Horse Gentlemen paid their quarts of, but the Ffoot Highlands paid litle or nothing; and, abt 8 a Clock this morning, the foot marched out, no drums beating nor collours flying, only the bagpipers playing. Most of the Horsemen waited at Mr Ffosters quarters. I stood close to Mr Simpsons doore, and the six Lds, Brigadeere Mackintosse & Tho Ffoster had their hats on when they mounted their horses, but all the othr Horsemen had their hats in their hands. The Brigadeere looked still with a grim countenance, but the Lds, Ffoster, & most of the othr horsemen were dishartned & full of sorrow.

About 9 a clock the same morning, they marched out of the towne, but not in ranks.

A jorniman weaver joyned them here.

7. *6th Novr, They Marched to Kirkby-Loynsdale.*

They marched this day to Kirkby-Loynsdale. The Horsemen quartered there and the Footmen went to the adjacent vilages & houses. In Kirkby-Loynsdale they made the same pclamation and recd what excise was due.

Esqr Carus & his two sons, Thomas & Christopher, all Papists, who lived at Halton Hall, joyned them at this towne.

8. *7th Novr, They Marched for Lancaster.*

It was this [Esqr] Carus that first brought them word, that the Towne of Lancr[1] had left of making any preparions for a defence, so they marched for Lancr next morning.

[1]Lancaster. The reason why the inhabitants of Lancaster had

abandoned their preparations for defence was that they had wrongly concluded that the Jacobites were marching on Newcastle, not Lancaster.

9. *Novr 7. They Come Into the Towne of Lancaster.*

They came into this towne with swords drawn, drums beating, & collours flying & and in their ranks, with the bagpipes also playing. They went streight to the market place, and made the same pclamacion as before.[1]

After this, one Christopher Hopkins, a stationr, was, by the ordr of Tho Ffostr, taken into custody & put prisonr on the guard, for taking account of the numbr of them.

10. *The Esqrs[2] Who Joyned Them at Lancaster.*

The following Esqrs, who lived some few miles from the towne, joyned them here, viz.:

Hodgson of Leighton Hall;
John Dalton of Thurnham Hall;
John Tyldesley of the Lodge;
— Butler of Racliffe;
— Hilton, who lived near Cartmell.

All these attended with their servt men joyned them, as above, sd and were stiled Capts.

Onely two inhabitants of this town, who were Papists, joyned them, to witt, Edmund Gartside, a Barber, and the othrman, whose name I have forgot, was a joyner. These last two men were stiled Quartermasters.

[1] This appears to have been their grandest entry into any town.
[2] Esquire is here used in its strict sense — armigerous gentleman.

11. *The Prisoners on the Crown Side in Lancaster Castle set at Liberty.*

In this towne in the evening, they recd from the Inkepers what excise was due, but it did not amount but to a very litle. Also this night a great consultacion was held there, whethr or no the prisoners in this castle shood be set at liberty. And, at first, it was unanimously agreed that the debtors as well as those upon the crown side shood all be released from their imprisonment. But, upon a second considracion, that onely those upon the crown side shood be set at liberty, wch accordingly was done.

Amongst those released were the Colonel and Capt[1] of the mob of Manchester, whose names I have forgot.—

[1]The Colonel cannot be identified, but the Mob Captain was Tom Siddall, who had been jailed after leading a High Church riot in Manchester on behalf of Dr Sacheverell during which a Dissenting Meeting House was destroyed.

12. *The Search for Armes at Lancaster.*

This night 6 Highlands, who were appointed searchers for armes, by threats compeled Mr Parkinson, the then mayor of this towne, to go along with them from house to house to search for armes. At evry house they demanded armes, wch, if the owner of them did not delivr, Jack the Highlandr was to plundr him. They got very few small armes here, but those as they took they did not pay for.

During their continuance in this towne, the gunsmiths here were well employed in cleaning guns and pistols, and recd pay for their worke. Some small armes were taken from the minister of this towne, whose name is James Ffenton.

The shopkeeps here had litle or no gunpowder, only one whose name is Samuel Saterthwaite, and he thought it properer to bestow a barrel of gunpwdr in the towne well, raithr than sell it.

13. *Novr. 8th They Examine the Books of the Custom House.*

Also this day Commissonrs were apointed to examine the books belonging to the Custom house here, but found nothing due to the crown, only a part of a large quantity of brandy, which the Custom house officrs had some days before seized, being run from the Isle of Man. The sd officrs had made use of a small part of it, and the new Commissonrs took possession of the remaindr part, of which they drank in this towne, and the rest they carryed away in a cart towards Garstang, but they made an end of it before they came to that towne.

14.   *They Bring up the 6 Ship Guns from Sundrland.*

Also at Lancastr, on the sd 8th day, a detachment were sent to Sundrland to bring up the sd 6 ship guns, which accordingly they did.

The history of the six ship guns on board Mr Lawson's vessel lying at Sunderland, five miles from Lancaster, has been before related (See 9). The Rebels had information of them communicated by a gentleman of influence.

It is related, that the six pieces of cannon, thus seized, were mounted upon new carriages, the wheels of which had belonged to Sir Henry Houghton's coaches. These they carried with them.

15.   *Novr. 8th, Mr Paul Reads Prayers in Lancaster Church.*

At 10 a clock this morning, by the ordr of Mr Paul, a ministr of the Church of England, and who had joyned with the sd El Derwentwater, a little bell hanging on the east end of Lancr church was ringed to warne people to come to prayrs, and, while the sd bell was a ringing, Mr Paul[1] tooke the Common prayr booke, which ye ministr of Lancr commonly made use of, and in the prayr for the Queen, Mr Paul razed out the name Queen Anne, and writ King James, and, [in] the prayr for the Royall Ffamily, he razed out the name of the Princess Sophia and writ the Kings mothr. The said words are writ with such a nicety that many takes them to have been printed.[2]

Abundance of psons went this day to this church, and the sd Mr Paul read the usuall prayrs, only, instead of praying for King George, prayed for his new mastr by the name of King James, and, instead of George Prince of Wales, he prayed thus: To bless the Kings Mothr and all the Royall Ffamily. [The minister of Lancaster does not make use of that book now, but has laid it by in the vestry.]

[1]A product of Rugby School and St John's College Cambridge, William Paul had taken the oath of loyalty to Queen Anne and abjuration of the Pretender in 1709. By 1715 he had embraced

Nonjuring and Jacobite principles.
[2]In fact, other sources suggest that this was the work of another
Jacobite called Mr Guin, who entered churches and thus
surreptitiously amended the Book of Common Prayer.

16.   *9th Nov., the Ffoot March to Garstang and Horse to Preston.*

Next morning, being Wednesday 9th, both Horse and Footmen
marchd out of this towne, carrying along with them the sd six ship
guns & some of the brandy, and their prisoner Chr Hopkins. Him
they tooke abt two miles, & so dismissed him. The Horse came to
Preston this night, but the Ffoot lodged at Garstang, & othr country
houses. One Mr Monkcaster, a Protestant, who was Attorney at Law,
who lived in Garstang, joyned them there.[1] Sevl all poore Papists
joyned them also here. Here also they recd what excise was due.

[1]To be joined by even one Lancashire Protestant of influence
naturally greatly cheered the Scots. Mr Monkcaster was, predictably,
an ardent Tory in politics.

17.   *Novr. 10th, The Ffoot Come Into Preston, and Many Papists
Joyn Them Here.*

Next day came also the Footmen into Preston where the same
Pclamacon was made here as in former towns. They also recd wt
excise was due here.

Esqr Townely, a Papist, joyned them here, and Mr Shuttleworth,
who lived in Preston, as also did abundance of Roman Catholics.

18.   *12th November 1715. Genr' all Wills & His Men Come to
Walton Le Dale.*

Upon Saturday ye 12th Novembr 1715, abt 11 a clock in the
forenoone, the Earl Derwentwater ordred 300 Horsemen to go to
Rible bridge to oppose Genrall Wills passage over it: but abt one
hour after Genrall Wills & his men came into Walton in Le dale,
neare unto ye sd Rible Bridge, the sd El Derwentwaters men retired
into Preston.

19.   *After Retiring into Preston, There They Make Trenshes and
Baracades.*

And there they made a trensh and made a Baracade ovr agt the church in Church Gate Preston, & there placed two of the ship guns charged with small bullet, and at the outends of this towne they made trences.[1]

[1]Other sources tell us that the Jacobites erected four barricades: the one mentioned, a little below the parish church; another blocking a lane leading to the fields; the third was the Windmill barrier, on the road to Lancaster; and the fourth on the Watergate, the route to Liverpool.

20. *General Wills Men Enter the Churchgaate Street.*

Abt 2 a clock this afternoone, 200 of Genrall Wills men entred the Churchgate street, and the Highlandrs[1] firing out of the cellrs and windows, in 10 minuits time kiled 120 of them. The Highlandrs also fired the sd 2 ship guns, but the bulletts flew upon the houses, so that no executon was done thereby.

[1]Here Brigadier Mackintosh commanded the Jacobites.

21. *Three Hundred Men Enter the Back Street.*

Abt 4 a clock, the same day, 300 men were commanded to enter the Back Street called the Back Ween [Wynd?] in Preston, and acordingly they made an attempt, but the Highlandrs[1] placing themselves undr Gardens walles, hedges, & diches, kiled the Capt and abt 140 of his men.

[1]These men were Mackintoshes commanded by Brigadier Mackintosh's kinsman, Colonel Mackintosh.

22. *Novr. 13th, Genrall Carpenter And His Men Come Up.*

Also abt 10 a clock next morning, Genrall Carpenter & his men came up and camped round this towne,[1] but did not burne neithr house or barnes.

[1]They had been converging on Preston by forced marches from Newcastle.

23.   *Preston Surrendered to the Two Generalls Carpenter & Wills etc. etc.*

—abt one a Clock in the afternoone, Generall Wills with his men came up to Rible bridge & from thence proceeded to Preston. Generall Carpenter and his men came to that toune on Sunday morning, and on Monday morning the El Derwentwater surrendered ye sd toune, and he and all his men yt were yn yt town made prisnors of war—

Printed in *Lancashire Memorials of the Rebellion, 1715,*
ed. Samuel H. Ware, Chetham Society,
Vol.V, 1845, (reprinted Johnson Reprint Corporation,
New York, 1968), pp.78-137.

(c) *The Aftermath of the '15*

One of the more unusual sources for the study of the dismal final stage of the '15, is a family correspondence preserved in the papers of the Kennedys of Dalquharran and Dunure. Their two baronies of Dalquharran and Dunure lay in Ayrshire, but the head of the family, Sir Thomas Kennedy, was between 1685 and 1686 Lord Provost of Edinburgh. Sir Thomas had seven sons who were in the prime of life at the time of the '15. They were politically divided. Two were active Jacobites: David and Francis. Another, Magnus, was a Jacobite sympathizer whom another brother described as the only "completely happy man" in London during the early success of the '15, but Magnus took no active part in the rising. The rest of the brothers ranged from militantly to moderately Whig in their views. It is significant that the Jacobite David had been a strong Tory who became private secretary to the Duke of Ormonde in 1711. He later followed him into exile and died in 1723 shortly after being nominated Jacobite agent to the United Netherlands.

The brothers represented in the correspondence below were all Whig. Thomas, the eldest, was a lawyer educated at the universities of Edinburgh and Utrecht. By 1714 he had become Lord Advocate, but this appointment only lasted eight months. Subsequently he became a judge of the Scottish Exchequer Court. William, the fifth son and one of the best letter-writers in the family, was a professional soldier holding a commission in Lord Mark Kerr's Regiment. He soldiered through the '15 in Scotland, almost to the end, for Lord Mark Kerr's regiment was with the forces which pursued the defeated and demoralized Jacobites northwards as far as Elgin. Cornelius, the second son, trained as a lawyer in Utrecht and Edinburgh, and then became a military secretary, first to the Earl of Stair, at one time the Colonel-in-Chief of the Scots Brigade in the service of the United Netherlands and later British ambassador in Paris. Despite having worked for the Duke of Ormonde in 1712-13, like his Jacobite brother David, he was able because of his known Whiggery to make the transition to the Hanoverian regime, becoming secretary to one of its Scottish pillars, the Duke of Montrose.

The letters provide a picture of the bleak conditions in the winter of 1715-16. They also refer to the scorched-earth tactics used by the Jacobite army to cover the start of its retreat. Finally, they showed hard-line Whigs like Cadogan taking control of the final stages and refer to some of the political moves whereby the hard-liners entrenched their unpopular ascendancy in the aftermath of the rising.

1. *William to Thomas*

Touch, January 7 1716.

It gives me some uneasiness to think that every letter I send you must carry disappointment along with it for I know you expect a great deal of news and 'tis very seldom I send you any.

What I wrote you last about the Pretender's being landed seems as yet rather to be confirm'd than contradicted, those who have intelligence from the north don't doubt of it, and rekon he is come to Perth this day, there are others who are ready to wager he is still in France, so that one is in doubt what to belive.

2. *Cornelius to Thomas*

Edinburgh, January 5 1716.

There's nothing I will more willingly undertake than to write to you. For my own part, I have wished a thousand times to be removed from the Clash of this place. We are improven in the practice of lying — so farr as one would think all our trade is converted into that one. We have within these ten days got a subject that occupies us not a little yt is the Pretender's landing and Marr's going off for France. This is problematically disputed. Some have seen people from Perth who came from there Sunday last and made affidavit before the Provost that Marr was *not* in Perth.[1]

Another knew from "a sagacious douce carle" that my lady Marischal at Fetteresso served a certain young gentleman on the knee which this man was witness to.[2] The next thing is about the Earl of Sutherland and the Earl of Seaforth, which of them has defeat the other. Some say Duncan (Forbes of Culloden) who is Sutherland's chief manager, has destroyed a number of men to the Earl of Seaforth by a new invention — others that Old Borlum (Mackintosh) has tricked them out of Inverness.[3] In short we are in absolute uncertainty. I understand that all parties agree that the Pretender has made his public entry into Perth on Tuesday and by some letters come to town this night from ye rebellious side of ye Forth that Southerland is utterly routed and he and all his principal officers are taken prisoners. I ever thought it was a wild notion in the Government to lay any stress on what that Country could do though supported by Simon Fraser whose people were the fillip in our Country to join with the clattering Forbes of Culloden to help on the blast. The foolish jacks were a little uppish to reckon all benorth Perth to join them, and when they have, it will import little against Cadogan who now is our hero. Delvin would say something here from Vergil.[4] We've no reason not to value the D. of A now we've got a General *in propria Iracundus*[5] etc. The Jacks likewise beginn to surmise something of ane humour has taken Stair's dragoons to visit their old Colonel at Perth — Our troops are to march tomorrow towards Stirling and to cross over Fife in order to attack Perth very soon.

[1] He arrived there with James Stuart on Monday 9 January but the latter went on to Scone. Letters and manifestoes "from our Court at Scone."
[2] Lady Marischal was not at Fetteresso, but at Inverugie.
[3] Mackintosh had been taken prisoner at Preston, 13 November 1715 and was in Newgate.
[4] George Mackenzie of Delvine, lawyer and classical scholar.
[5] Cadogan.

3. *William to Thomas*

10 January 1716.

Dear Bror,

I have just got time enough to Stirling to save the post, every body seems now at a certainty about the Pretender, he came to Perth either Saturday or Sunday last, he embarqued at Dunkirk in a small dogger and was attended to Peterhead by a French Man of War, he has brought nobody that wee can hear along with him; (Ormond is still in France) his not coming sooner was owing to the watchful eye Stair had upon his motions, but he has at last given him the slip. There has so much snow fallen that it will be impossible for us to march till it be melted, otherwise our armey was to have been in motion by the end of this week, there are 3000 of the Swiss and Dutch already got the other side of Forth, which straitens the enemys quarters very much. There are several of the Pretender's manifestos found here within these few days wherein he invites the armey to joyn him and seems surprised that so many brave men who have fought so well for the defense of their libertys should now resigne them to the D. of Brunswick and be in arms against their lawful soveraigne (as he thinks fit to call himself). He promises if they'll joyn him, he'll pay the officers all their arrears and give great encouragement to the common soldiers, but it does not look as if one in this armey would take his word for it;—

4. *Same to the Same*

February 28, 1716.

I have just time to tell my dearest Brother that I have not had the least opportunity of writing since I left Aberdeen, the bad weather and the swelling of the rivers with the melting snows has made our march so troublesome that in ten days wee have but marched as farr as one could ride with ease in a summer's day, wee had almost catch'd Huntly at Castle Gordon but he very narrowly made his escape, and has since submitted himself at Inverness to Genl. Wightman, where he remains prisoner, Seaforth has not yet surrendered, there was once ane account of his having obtained his pardon, but now thers little appearance of it, for wee hear he designs to draw his men together again, Mr Cadogan who now commands in chief[1] has a mind to send us a hunting into the Highlands to disperse and disarme the clans, but those who know that country don't think it will be very practicable at this time of year.—

[1]Argyll had returned to London.

5. *William to Thomas*

dated 10 April 1716.

I was this night visiting the Castle prisoners and as they have kept me so late that I must scribble anything I have to say least I lose the post. There's ane express passed this toun today from Genl. Cadogan giving ane account that Glengarry has surrendered himself, Keppoch has done the like, and Lochiel[1] by this time has also submitted, so there's ane end of the Highland warr. The London news bears that there's a designe of reducing the triennial act and bringing in a septennial one in its place, the only reason I can hear of it is that the forreigne powers scruple to make treatys with England whilst the Ministry's measures are in so short while lyable to be canvass'd by a subsequent parliament, which the lengthening of it out to seven years will in a great measure prevent.[2]

My Dear Brother I am entirely
Yours.
W.

[1]John Cameron escaped abroad to Boulogne where he was still living in 1745, when Donald, his son, "came out."
[2]The actual reason was that the Government felt it was a bad moment for an election when it was not too popular. The ruling Whigs were delighted to have an excuse for minimising popular influence on government.

6. *William to Thomas*

Edinburgh, 25 August, 1716.

There's very many melancholly hearts in this toun, upon the orders that's come for sending the prisoners to Carlisle to be tryed, there are 89 of the most considerable who are to beginn their march upon Thursday next under a guard of dragoons and foot, theyr tryals will very soon beginn, and 'tis thought the consequence will be very fatal to many of them; in the meantime even those who lately had great estates, are reduced to such want that they can't get so much money as will bear their charges or support their lives till the Law takes it from them, unless it be by the contributions that's making in this toun for them.

I shall send you the list upon Thursday of those that are sent away, there is not one prisoner in the Castle but what are to goe except Stormont, and his son. People have malice enough to think that the J.C.[1] might have prevented this and that the consequences of it ought to be laid to his door.

149

[1]Justice Clerk. The 80 prisoners went in three parties on 3, 4 and 5 September. The delay was caused by the humanity of General Carpenter who managed to provide transport for the badly wounded, or the old. The rest had to walk. Only the Peers remained in Edinburgh Castle. Their transfer to Carlisle for trial was a breach of the provisions of the Act of Union of 1707.

Printed in *The Seven Sons of the Provost*,
ed. Henrietta Tayler (London, 1949), pp.78-85.

CHAPTER 8:

JACOBITISM IN THE DOLDRUMS

The collapse of the 1715 rising in early 1716 dealt a fearsome blow to the long-term credibility and prospects of Jacobitism. Nothing strengthens an unpopular regime more than an unsuccessful rising against it which can be used to blacken the reputation of its principal opposition. The Hanoverian dynasty and its Court Whig servants were in a position after 1716 to denounce all opposition as Jacobite and to drive the once-great Tory party into the political wilderness. The regime was also in a position to benefit from unusually favourable international circumstances.

The '15 owed little or nothing in its inception to international intrigue, though by the time of the Battle of Sheriffmuir some of its supporters were desperately looking for French intervention to turn the ebbing tide of their fortunes. They were never likely to see such intervention, and after 1716 it became very clear that there was an Anglo-French entente in position, based on the fact that both countries were ruled by rather insecure, and by no means popular, new regimes. In France Philip Duke of Orleans had set aside the will of Louis XIV to establish himself as sole Regent. Given the shaky nature of a succession dependent entirely on the life of the boy Louis XV, there was a real possibility of a succession crisis which would see Philip of Orleans fight Philip V of Spain for the throne of France. Philip of Orleans no more wanted the hazards of Anglo-French war than George I and his minister Charles Stanhope, who had by 1717 contrived to link the British realms, France, and the Netherlands in the Triple Alliance.

Bourbon support for Jacobitism was therefore transferred to the new Bourbon dynasty seated on the Spanish throne by the War of the Spanish succession. Although, like France, Spain had a Counter-Reformation culture which guaranteed the exiled Stuarts, seen as martyrs for and paladins of the Faith, a good deal of sympathy at all levels of society, it also had a government desperately strapped for cash, and a tradition of self-interested realpolitik which, combined with acute Anglo-Spanish tension in the Mediterranean, led to perhaps the most humiliating of all Jacobite débâcles, the 1719, which saw Spanish troops in action on Scottish soil.

After that futile but fascinating rising had been most efficiently nipped in the bud, the Westminster government was free to apply its mind to the possibilities of permanently taming those areas of the central and Western Highlands of Scotland which had emerged both in the '15 and in the '19 as the likeliest cradles of future rebellion, and as the Jacobites' main reservoir of fighting men. Though experienced Hanoverian military men knew full well that only the Highland aristocracy had the power to permanently defuse the Jacobite threat in the region, it proved possible for astute manipulators like Simon Fraser Lord Lovat to help nudge the authorities into spending significant sums of money in the Highlands, creating a military road system, building forts, and raising irregular military units which would hopefully be loyal to the House of Hanover. It all failed miserably to stop the last rebellion, but it prefigured even larger and more effective state intervention north of the Highland Line.

I: The Break-Down of the French Connection

Though Louis XIV was sincere in his outrage at the deposition of James VII and II from his three thrones, and genuinely anxious to support an exiled family which to him embodied the divine principle of indefeasible hereditary monarchy, he was also a political realist whose first loyalty was to the French state. Despite his costly decision to acknowledge "James III and VIII", he had, after the abortive '08, offered to abandon the exiled dynasty as part of the feelers he was extending in search of a much-needed negotiated peace. There was little likelihood of any London ministry accepting a peace treaty which did not embody such a renunciation. As it was, the Peace of Utrecht provoked violent political controversy at Westminster and was pushed through by a Tory ministry as a distinctly partisan measure, despite the fact that the French, in order to split the Grand Alliance against them, had even before the peace conference at Utrecht agreed to a long list of territorial concessions to British imperial ambitions.

Although most leading British politicians in the early eight-eenth century, including Marlborough and Godolphin and even so firm a Whig as Lord Somers, exchanged private civilities with the Jacobite court, one of the main motives behind the war in England had been the defence of Queen Anne against the Pretender. When the young James refused suggestions from the British government that he abjure publicly the Church of Rome, he ceased to be politically viable at Westminster and the Treaty of Utrecht, negotiated as it was by a Tory government, commit-ted France to uphold the Protestant Succession as established by the Act of Settlement of 1701, itself passed by a Tory majority. As the interests of the new French regime, especially after the failure of the '15, corresponded with its pledged support for the House of Hanover, James Francis Edward Stuart needed a new patron.

Treaty of Peace and Friendship between the most serene and most potent Princess Anne, by the grace of God, Queen of Great Britain, France, and Ireland, and the most serene and the most potent Prince Lewis XIV. the most Christian King, concluded at Utrecht the 31 day of March 1713—

Reprinted from the copy published by the Queen's special command.

I. That there be an universal perpetual peace, and a true and sincere friendship, between the most serene and most potent Princess Anne, Queen of Great Britain, and the most serene and most potent Prince Lewis XIV. the most Christian King, and their heirs and successors, as also the kingdoms, states, and subjects of both, as well without as within Europe; and that the same be so sincerely and inviolably preserved and cultivated, that the one do promote the interest, honour and advantage of the other, and that a faithful neighbourhood on all sides, and a secure cultivation of peace and friendship, do daily flourish again and encrease.

II. That all enmities, hostilities, discords, and wars, between the said Queen of Great Britain, and the said most Christian King, and their subjects, do cease and be abolished, so that on both sides they do wholly refrain and desist from all plundering, depredation, harm-doing, injuries, and annoyance whatsoever, as well by land, as by sea and fresh water, in all parts of the world, and chiefly through all tracts, dominions, and places, of what kind soever, of the kingdoms, countries, and territories of either side.—

IV.   Furthermore, for adding a greater strength to the peace which is restored, and to the faithful friendship which is never to be violated, and for cutting off all occasions of distrust, which might at any time arise from the established right and order of the hereditary succession to the crown of Great Britain, and the limitation thereof by the laws of Great Britain, (made and enacted in the reigns of the late King William III. of glorious memory, and of the present Queen) to the issue of the abovesaid Queen, and in default thereof, to the most serene Princess Sophia, dowager of Brunswick-Hanover, and her heirs, in the Protestant line of Hanover. That therefore the said succession may remain safe and secure, the most Christian King sincerely and solemnly acknowledges the abovesaid limitation of the succession to the kingdom of Great Britain, and on the faith and word of a king, on the pledge of his own and his successors honour, he does declare and engage, that he accepts and approves the same, and that his heirs and successors do and shall accept and approve the same for ever. And under the same obligation of the word and honour of a king, the most Christian King promises, that no one besides the Queen herself, and her successors, according to the series of the said limitation, shall ever by him, or by his heirs or successors, be acknowledged, or reputed to be King or Queen of Great Britain. And for adding more ample credit to the said acknowledgment and promises the most Christian King does engage, that whereas the person who, in the life-time of the late King James II. did take upon him the title of Prince of Wales, and since his decease, that of King of Great Britain, is lately gone, of his own accord, out of the Kingdom of France, to reside in some other place, he the aforesaid most Christian King, his heirs and successors, will take all possible care, that he shall not at any time hereafter, or under any pretence whatsoever, return into the kingdom of France, or any the dominions thereof.

Moreover, the most Christian King promises, as well in his own name, as in that of his heirs and successors, that they will at no time whatever disturb, or give any molestation to the Queen of Great Britain, her heirs and successors, descended from the aforesaid Protestant line, who possess the crown of Great Britain, and the dominions belonging thereunto. Neither will the aforesaid most Christian King, or any one of his heirs, give at any time any aid, succour, favour, or council, directly or indirectly, by land or by sea, in money, arms, ammunition, warlike provision, ships, soldiers, seamen, or any other way, to any person or persons, whosoever they be, who for any cause, or under any pretext whatsoever, should hereafter endeavour to oppose the said succession, either by open war, or by fomenting seditions, and forming conspiracies against such Prince or Princes who are in possession of the throne of Great Britain, by virtue of the act of parliament aforementioned, or against the Prince or Princess, to whom the succession of the crown of Great Britain shall be open, according to the said acts of parliament.—

Printed in *A Collection of All the Treaties,*
ed. Charles Jenkinson, Vol.II,
(Kelley reprint, New York, 1969), pp.5-7.

II: The Spanish Labyrinth: Philip V and the Jacobites

Louis XIV had pledged his public word to support the Protestant Succession in the British kingdoms by the Treaty of Utrecht. He needed peace, and his government was in poor financial shape. When, therefore, the Duke of Ormonde, who had just recently fled from England, approached him with a request for troops and money to aid the forthcoming Jacobite rising in Scotland, he refused both, but he added that he would write to his grandson Philip V, now King of Spain, asking him to provide financial assistance for the Jacobites. Philip V's government was in if anything worse financial shape than his grandfather's, but Spain did in fact supply significant financial resources to help mount the '15, though not all the money promised was delivered, and some of the bullion sent fell into Hanoverian hands when the vessel carrying it ran aground off St Andrews.

Thereafter, there was pressure on the Spanish government to try to reach an understanding with the regime of George I, in the hope that it would either support or tolerate the Italian territorial claims advanced by Philip V and his Italian wife Elizabeth Farnese. The chief exponent of this view was Guilio Alberoni, the Parmesan envoy to Spain, who due to support from Elizabeth Farnese became powerful within the Spanish government. Of course, even Alberoni meant to keep a Jacobite option up his sleeve, but his preferred strategy was to bribe the government of George I into benign neutrality by means of an advantageous commercial treaty, whilst Spain attacked the possessions of the Hapsburg Emperor in Italy. He rejected a proposal from the Pope that Philip V and the Emperor submit their disputes to papal mediation and then join in a joint effort to restore the exiled Stuarts. James Francis Edward Stuart, the proposed beneficiary of this abortive papal plan had had the good sense to continue to cultivate Alberoni by, for example, throwing his real if limited influence in the Sacred College in Rome behind the successful drive by Alberoni, now recognized as first minister of Spain, for a cardinal's hat. Nevertheless, it was only when Alberoni's first strategy collapsed that he decided the Jacobites might be politically useful to Spain. Late in 1718 a British fleet commanded by Admiral Byng destroyed off Cape Passaro the Spanish fleet which was shielding a Spanish invasion of Sicily. By early 1719 the Duke of Ormonde was in Spain preparing to lead a major Hispano-Jacobite invasion of the west of England. There was also to be a small diversionary invasion of Scotland. James Stuart was urged to make his way to Spain to be available to sail for England. His arrival in Spain coincided with an incredibly bad run of luck for the Jacobite cause, as the main expedition evaporated in a storm and the subsidiary one turned into a debacle. Ormonde's correspondence before he sailed with the main force illuminates these events.

(i)

To PETER
(Received at Rome January 26, 1719)

Peter,	The Chevalier.		
14/a,	Alberoni.	165,	England.
21/l,	Sir Patrick Lawless.	475,	Scotland.
507,	The King of Sweden.	9/m,	The Earl Marischal.
496, 497,	The King of Spain.	14/e,	Brigadier Campbell.[1]
249,	The Elector of Hanover.	23/b,	Bagenal.
289,	The King.	508,	Sweden.
Elmore,	The Emperor.	Morpeth,	James Murray.[2]

[1]Brigadier Campbell of Ormidale. He went to Scotland at the time of the '15, and was one of the Jacobite prisoners taken to Carlisle, but escaped.
[2]The Hon. James Murray, second son of the fifth Viscount Stormont, and brother of Lord Chief Justice Mansfield. He was admitted to the Faculty of Advocates in 1710, was for some time M.P. for the Elgin Burghs, and under Queen Anne was one of the Commissioners for settling the trade with France. In 1718 he joined James at Urbino,

and became one of his confidential advisers. He negotiated the marriage with Princess Clementina, and acted as the Prince's proxy at the marriage ceremony at Bologna. James, in 1721, created him titular Earl of Dunbar. He died at Avignon in 1770.

VALLADOLID, DECEMBER 17TH, 1718.

—14/a came to me privately and informed me that he had sent 21/l to 507 to engage him to enter into an Alliance with 497, that the Chief Article was to endeavour to dethrone 249 their common enemy, that he carryed Bills with him to enable 507 to make the attempt with promises of an Annual Subsidy provided he enter'd into the Allyance.

The next time I saw 14/a he asked me what I demanded as necessary to make an attempt to restore 289. I told him seven or eight thousand men with 15,000 arms and Ammunition proportionable. He answered that 496 wou'd be willing to grant that number if he were in a condition, but considering that the greatest part of their Troops are in Sicily, and that they are threatned with an Invasion from France in two Places, that is, by the way of Roussillon and Navarre, they cou'd not spare a man, but that they wou'd give 15,000 arms and Ammunition proportionable, and that money shou'd not be wanting to enable 507 to invade 165.—

I made 14/a another visit at his desire, and after some discourse he told me that 497 wou'd give five thousand men, of which four thousand are to be foot, a thousand Troopers, of which three hundred with their horses, the rest with their Arms and Accoutrements, and two months pay for them, ten field Pieces, and a thousand Barrels of Powder and fifteen Thousand Arms for foot, with every thing necessary to convoy them.

I told 14/a that it wou'd be necessary to have a Diversion made in 475, and since he cou'd not spare any more men I desired him to let us have two or three thousand arms to send thither. He asked me if there was any man of consideration, to go with them. I told him of 9/ m who was in Paris, and he desired me to write to him to come with all despatch and as privately as possible. I will write to 14/e to come hither as soon as I know where he is. As to the Gentlemen at Bordeaux they shall have timely notice.—

23/b will have Instructions to propose to 507 to send two Thousand men to 475 with five Thousand Arms.—

14/a seem'd very uneasy at your Situation in Italy.—Upon what he says, and the letter I received from Morpeth of the ninth November, it is my humble opinion that you ought to come to 497 with all expedition, that you may be out of Elmore's power, and your presence is necessary here either to Embark with the Troops if you can arrive in Time, or to follow as soon as possible, for 14/a is of opinion that the Opportunity must not be lost tho' you shou'd not arrive in due time, and if it be possible you ought to be here to go to 165 with the Troops.

14/a desires that this design may be the Strictest Secret, and I beg of you not to acquaint Cardinal Aquaviva[1] with it, and when you come away to give it out that it is for your own Safety.

[1]Cardinal Acquaviva was in charge of Spanish affairs at Rome.

(ii)   *To Cardinal Alberoni. Valladolid, December 25, 1718.*

Sir, — Last night I had the honour to receive your letter, with its enclosures. I am delighted to hear that you have decided to send for Mr. Peter as soon as possible. I confess that I fear much for his safety, as he is in a country where he is surrounded by enemies.—

You have been good enough to tell me that you intended that M. de Cammock[1] should bring him. There are only two ways of making the voyage, either to come in a ship of war or to take a little vessel which is neutral. There is some risk in either way. A naval officer would be the best judge, and as I do not know the whereabouts of Byng's[2] fleet, I should have all the more difficulty in giving an opinion.

You see in the account of the news from London how it is that so many of the Tories have absented themselves from Parliament; but when the taxes come on for discussion, I am sure that they will be assiduous in their attendance, and that with the discontented Whigs they will embarrass the Court so much that they will have great difficulty in raising money to meet the expenses of the war.

[1]George Cammock, or Camocke, had been a captain in the British navy, from which he was dismissed in 1715 for gross breaches of discipline. He entered the Spanish service, and was made a rear-admiral. At the battle of Cape Passaro he tried to bribe both Byng and Walton to take their ships into a Spanish port. It may be recorded to his credit that he was kind to James Keith when the

latter was in great poverty in Madrid in 1720.

[2]Admiral Sir George Byng, the victor of Cape Passaro, created Viscount Torrington in 1721. He chased the French fleet out of the Firth of Forth at the time of the Jacobite attempt of 1708. He was the father of the Admiral who was shot at Portsmouth in 1757, 'pour encourager les autres,' as Voltaire said.

(iii) *To Cardinal Alberoni, by the same courier. Valladolid. January 27, morning. [1719]*

Sir, — I have just received this morning the honour of your letter of the 25th, with the sad news of the death of the King of Sweden, which, in the present state of affairs, is a very great loss, but notwithstanding this misfortune we must follow out our enterprise. If anything could increase the discontent in England, it would be the news which you send me of what has taken place in Parliament, at the instance of your friend Stanhope,[1] about the Nonconformists and the Universities, which will not only enrage the Anglicans, but also displease the Moderates.—

[1]James, first Earl Stanhope, who in 1717 succeeded Lord Townshend as First Lord of the Treasury and Chancellor of the Exchequer. He had commanded the British army in Spain from 1708 to 1710; and when a prisoner at Saragossa, after the disaster of Brihuega, had befriended Alberoni, then a humble attendant of the Duke of Vendome. On December 13, 1718, Stanhope introduced into the House of Lords a bill for the relief of Protestant Dissenters, which was carried by narrow majorities after important concessions had been made to the High Church party.

(iv) *To Mr. Robinson, by the Earl Marischal. Astorga, February 13, 1719.*

Sir, — The Earl Marischal found me here last night. I am very glad that you are giving him two thousand muskets and the powder which you mentioned. He will propose that you should give him three hundred men. If you are pleased to agree to this, I am sure that it will have a very good effect, for when these few men have arrived, the talk of the country will make them three thousand, which will oblige the enemy to keep a large number of troops in that country, and the rumour of the regular troops being in that country will have a very good effect. The number is inconsiderable in this country, but will be of great importance in Scötland.—

(v)*To the Duke of Gordon. Astorga, 13th February 1719.*

My Lord, — I am so much convinced of yr Grace's zeal and readyness for the King's Service that I make no doubt of your Grace's joining yr interest with my Lord Marischall's for endeavouring the restoring of his Majesty. I hope in God to Land in England with a body of regular Troops, which will draw most of the Enemie's to oppose us, but yr Grace and Lord Marischall's taking up Arms, with as many of yr friends and well affected people, will make a great diversion, and contribute greatly to the hoped for Success, which the justice of our cause gives us reason to expect, and with the Blessing of God I do not doubt of. My Lord Marischall go's to you with Arms, and Ammunition. The King designs to go to England, his presence there being absolutely necessary.

[1]Alexander, second Duke of Gordon. He succeeded his father in 1716, and died in 1728. He was out of the '15, and was present at Sheriffmuir, but took no part in the 1719.

(vi)   *To the King, Pr express. Corogne, 17 March 1719.*

This day I receiv'd a letter from the Cardinal of the 13th Instant, with the agreeable news of your being landed at Roses, for which I do most heartily thank God, and do with all the sincerity and respect imaginable congratulate you on your safe arrivall into this Country,—

I came to the Marqs de Risbourcqe's this afternoon, to be ready to embarque but I have no news of the Fleet's being seen on the Coast, tho' I do expect every moment to hear of it's being seen off of the Cap Finisterre. It is very unlucky that the designe is discovered but it was almost impossible it shou'd not, the winds and weather having kept the Fleet from sailing after it had been ready to go to sea for some weeks.—

(vii) *To the King. Corogne, the 11th Apl 1719.*

—we have not heard of any more Ships, but expect to see some arrive every hour. God grant that the rest of the Fleet come soon, and that they may be in a condition to put to Sea in a little time. The Cardinall has sent Orders to the Marquis de Risbourg to give me 40000 Crowns, and has promissed me three score thousand more.

This Embarkeation has been so unfortunatly delayed that I hope you will not think of going on board if that the ffleet shou'd be in a Condition to put to Sea in a short time; if my Opinion be of any consequence I shall be against your Embarking.—

printed in *The Jacobite Attempt of 1719*,
ed. William Kirk Dickson, Scottish History Society
Vol.XIX (Edinburgh, 1895), pp.15-109.

III: The 1719 in Scotland

The Scottish part of the rising was always intended as a diversion. It had no strategic purpose if the main Jacobite force failed to land in England as planned. The Earl Marischal sailed from Spain on March 8, accompanied by a force of Spanish infantry amounting to 307 officers and men. However, the leadership of the small Jacobite force eventually assembled in Scotland was partially drawn from a group of exiles in France, whom the Earl Marischal's gallant young brother James Keith had been sent to alert and organize, with the help of 18000 crowns provided by Alberoni. This party left le Havre on March 19 in a cockleshell ship of twenty-five tons and eventually joined the two frigates carrying the Earl Marischal and his force in the harbour of Stornoway in Lewis on April 4. Apart from James Keith, the second party included three important men, Campbell of Glendaruel, the Earl of Seaforth the chief of Clan Mackenzie, and the Marquis of Tullibardine the dispossessed heir of the Duke of Atholl. Not only were all these men identified with the faction of Mar in the much-divided politics of the Jacobite exiles, and therefore suspicious of Marischal and of his military adviser Brigadier Campbell, but, unknown to Marischal, Tullibardine was carrying a commission from the Chevalier, drawn up two years before and making him commander of all Jacobite forces in Scotland.

From the start the leadership split. Tullibardine and Glendaruel wanted to stay in Lewis until they heard news of Ormonde's landing in England. Marischal insisted on landing on the mainland with a view to making a quick dash for a weakly-garrisoned Inverness. Superseded by Tullibardine in the military command, Marischal retained command of the Spanish frigates because of an express commission from Alberoni. By April 13 the Jacobites had made landfall on the mainland at Loch Alsh, where chiefs like MacDonald of Clanranald and Cameron of Lochiel came to meet them. Tullibardine and Glendaruel, supported by Clanranald, remained advocates of delay, or even re-embarkation. To prevent this, Marischal sent the Spanish frigates home, thereby ensuring that they were not sunk by a massively superior British squadron which reached the coast only days later. What the squadron did achieve was the destruction of the main Jacobite magazine which had been established in the old Mackenzie castle of Eilean Donan, situated just where Loch Alsh divides into Loch Duich and Loch Long.

While the Jacobite leadership bickered, General Wightman led the reinforced garrison of Inverness down Loch Ness and across by Glenmoriston to Glenshiel, where the two forces finally met on June 10 in a fierce fire-fight. Wightman's battery of four light bronze cohorn mortars (called after their inventor the Dutch field engineer Baron van Cohorn) gave him the edge in the action which ended with the disintegration of the Jacobite force and the capture of all the Spaniards.

Two problems remained. One was the disposal of the Spaniards. The London government at first refused to pay for either their subsistence or their repatriation, so they had to borrow money from the officers who captured them, and then relied on credit from Jacobite sympathisers when marched to Edinburgh, where they were eventually saved by funds sent there by the Spanish ambassador to the Netherlands. The second problem was the much more intractable one of pacifying the Jacobite Highlands and securing the loyalty of such slippery rogues as MacDonnel of Glengarry. To his credit, Wightman, a veteran of Sheriffmuir, could see that this was easier said than done.

(i) *The Marquis of Tullibardine to the Earl of Mar*

My Lord, — Since what I write by Mr Douglas, there has been no means untryed to get people together so as to keep life in the affair till we should have some certain accounts of the expedition from Spain, or else the Kings commands, which would enliven every body and make things go right, in expectation of that with a great deal adoe a few of the Clans were prevailed on to send some small assistance, which was gathering, that we might be able to keep together when their came accounts of the Enemys march from

Inverness with above twelve hundred horse and foot. On the fifth Lochiel came first up with near one hundred and fifty men, and finding others could not soon enough join us, so as that we might be in a condition to fight the Ennemy, we went about three miles from Glenshell to view the narrow passes in the little Glen, hoping to maintain the Rough Ground till people that were expected should come up on the seventh. My Lord Seaforth met us and told me he had brought to the Crow of Kintaile about five hundred of his men who, it was thought, would heartily defend their own Country. On the eight Rob Roy's son brought a Company of men who, with some volunteers, made up near Eighty. That night we got accounts the enemy were removed from Gilly whining[1] to the Braes of Glenmoriston,—The first attack they made was on our men with Lord George on the Right, by a small detachment of Reed coats and there Highlanders, who fired several times at other without doeing great damage, upon which they sent a second and third detachment that made most of those with Lord Geo. run to the other side of a steep Burn where he himself and the rest were afterwards obliged to follow, where they continued till all was over, it being uneasy for the enemy to pass the hollow Banks of that Burn. When they found that party on our Right give way there Right began to move up the Hill from thence, to fall down on our left, but when they saw my Lord Seaforths people, who were behind the steep Rock, they were oblig'd to attack them least they should been flank'd in coming to us, upon which the Laird of Coul (most of whose men began to goe off on the seing the enemy) mov'd up with his Battalion to sustain the rest of the McKenzies.—next morning we had hardly any body togeither except some of the Spaniards. I then proposed to my Lord Marshall, Locheill, Brigadier Campble and all present, that we should keep in a body with the Spaniards and march thro' the Highlands for some time till we could gather again in case of a Landing, or else should the King send instructions, the Highlanders would then rise and soon make up all that was past. But every body declar'd against doing any thing further, for as things stood they thought it impracticable, and my Lord Mairshall with Brigadier Campble of Ormondell went off without any more adoe or so much as taking leave. The Spaniards themselves declared they could neither live without bread nor make any hard marches thro' the Country, therefore I was oblig'd to give them leave to Capitulate the best way they could, and every body else went off to shift for themselves; so that all we could make of My Lord Marishalls ill concerted expedition is to be now shamefully dispers'd at last.—It is not to be imagin'd how much people are dispirited at the manner of our Coming and there has not been as yet so much as one word sent us from any that have the manadgment of affairs. But hopeing there

163

will be ere long good accounts I'le say no more, being,

> My Lord,
> Your Graces most Humble and most Obedient Servant,
> > TULLIBARDINE.

Glen G(arry), 16th June 1719.

¹Cill Chuimein, 'the church of Cuimmein,' the Gaelic name of Fort Augustus.

(ii) *The Earl of Seaforth to James*
(Received at Rome Dec. 22, 1719)

—I am sorry I am forc'd to acquaint your Majtie that your affairs here are brought to so low an ebb (by whose fault I wont say) that there nothing remains but every one to shift for him self, and yt by ye advise of him you honour with your commands, I still made it my studdy (upon which account I suffer most of any) to serve your Majtie to ye utmost of my power, and tho I be once more oblig'd to leave my native country, as in all probabilty I must, to wander abroad, in what ever place fortune alots my abode, I shall always beg leave to subscrive my self, with the proudest regret,

> Sir,
> Your Majties most dutifull subject
> > and most Obedient humble servant,
> > > SEAFORT.

Aug. ye 10th, O.S., 1719.

(iii) *General Lord Carpenter, commanding in Scotland, to Charles Delafaye, Secretary to the Lords Justices.*

> Edinburgh, 27th June 1719.

Sir, — Last night at 9 I received yours of the 23d, with their Excellency's orders to send the Spanish prisoners under a sufficient guard to Plymouth, and I write by this opportunity to Mr. Treby, for appointing guards to receive them on the Borders, my routs being good no farther, whose answer will be here before those prisoners can come to this place.

Lord Justice Clerk and I are endeavouring to discover what persons of note, being his Majesty's subjects, were engag'd in this Rebellion. I suppose you have writt the same to Mr. Wightman in your letter, that I have this morning early forwarded to him; however, I have writt to him to the same purpose. — I am,

Sir,
Your most humble Servant,
CARPENTER.

Charles Delafaye, Esqr.

(iv) *Lord Justice-Clerk Cockburn[1] to Charles Delafaye.*

Edinbr., 27th June 1719.

Sir, — As has been done hitherto, so shall it be continued to give the Clergy all encouragement to come in and take the oaths, tho' they had not the opportunity before the first of June; Shirreffs have been written to, that they should admit the Clergy to qualifie whenever they applye, and severalls have appeared before the Court of Session and taken the oaths. As to the Recusants, who is to put the laws in execution? I'm affrayed without a special direction for that effect, there shall be no prosecution either of these of the established Clergy or these for the Episcopall meeting houses. What their Excellys. comand as to the procuring ane exact List of all his Majys. subjects of any note who are engadged in the present Rebellion, wt the proper evidence to convict them, My Lord Carpenter and I had both of us written North to the same purpose, but in Regard there are so few prisoners, we apprehend ane exact List will be very difficult, and will require some time. But nothing shall be omitted to give yr Excellys satisfaction is in the power of him who is in great truth,

Sir,
Your most obedient and most humble Servant,
AD. COCKBURNE.

[1]Adam Cockburn of Ormiston, appointed Lord Justice-Clerk in 1692, dismissed from all his offices on the accession of Queen Anne, reappointed in 1705. He was superseded as Lord Justice-Clerk in 1710 by James Erskine of Grange, but retained his seat on the bench as an ordinary Lord of Session till his death in 1735. In the papers of 1719 he is frequently referred to as 'Lord Justice-Clerk,' though not actually holding the office at the time.

(v)*General Lord Carpenter to Charles Delafaye*

Edinburgh, July 7, 1719.

Sir, — On Sunday night late I rec'd your favour of the 2, with the Lords Justices orders to keep the Spanish Prisoners here, and to let them have money on the chief Officers bill if he shall desire itt nott exceeding their Pay.

Their Excys. do me great hon. in leaving to my discretion the making dispositions for preventing Robbery's, Seizing Rebells, and disarming the Highlanders;—but we could nott forme any scheme that would answere those ends. It is impossible to catch any Rebell Highlanders with Party's of Regular Troops, and any sort of orders from the Civill or Military here to bring in their Armes would signify nothing. Such orders by proclamation or otherwise must come from those who have Power to promise that all Common People who will bring in their armes by a day prefixt and returne home to live peaceably shall nott be molested; and for the others who pay nott obedience to that order, their houses shall be burn't and their stocks taken away; which last may be putt in execution in the Winter, butt in this season they are on the mountains with their Cattle, and will be able easily to avoid any Parties of the Troops that might be sent to take them or their Cattle.

Whatever orders the Lords Justices are pleas'd to send me I will put them in execution, and use my best endeavours to make them answere the purposes they are designed for.

I am, Sir, Yr. most humble and obedient Servant,
CARPENTER.

Charles Delafaye, Esq.

[1]Robert Dundas of Arniston, who was raised to the Bench as Lord Arniston in 1737, and in 1748 succeeded Duncan Forbes of Culloden as Lord President.

(vi) *Major-General Wightman to Charles Delafaye*

Edinburgh, Sept. 1st, 1719.

Sir,—The Spaniards begin to grow very sulky under their Confinemt, and the money advanc't by Ld. Carpenter for subsisting of them is almost expended (wch I have already acquainted His Grace of Roxburghe with), and shou'd be glad to know what their Excellencies the Lords Justices designe to do with them. All things in these parts Remain perfectly quiet.

> I am with great Truth,
> Sir,
> Yr most humble Servt,
> J. WIGHTMAN.

(vii) *Major-General Wightman to Charles Delafaye*

Edinburgh, Sept. 17th, 1719.

—I have advanc't the Spaniards fifty Pounds to Subsist them, and keep their men from starving, and have drawn my Bill on Ld. Lincoln[1] (the money which Ld. Carpenter advanc't them being all exhausted).

> I am with great Truth, and Sincerity,
> Sir,
> Yo. most obliged humble Servt,
> J. WIGHTMAN.

Honble. Chas. Delafaye, Esqre.

[1]Henry Clinton, seventh Earl of Lincoln, was Paymaster-General of the Forces from 1715 to 1720.

(viii) *General Lord Carpenter to Charles Delafaye*
(Home Office Papers, Scotland, Bundle 14, No. 79)

Bath, Sept. 12, 1719.

Sir, — By the last post I rec'd here the enclos'd from Glengary, in answere to that I writt to him of the 29 of July, by order of the Lords Justices, of which I sent you a Coppy.

I had also a letter by last post from the Earl of Ffindlater,[1] with the enclos'd paper of Intelligence, and another from Glenbucket, which I send you. I had desired he would write to me hither, and tho' I find he has a ffriendship for Glengary, yett have a very good opinion of his gratitude and duty to His Majesty. He is chief Chamberlain to the Duke of Gordon, and has very great power with all the Dukes ffollowers and Tenants; he came to me soon after I gott to Edenburgh, and offer'd his Service, assuring me he had taken such care that nott one of the Dukes People would joyn or in any manner assist the Rebells, which wee found to be true; he will constantly lett me know every thing materiall from the Highlands, and being a Protestant, I have great confidence in him; I write to him to encourage his Correspondance, and if he sends me any intelligence of consequence, will enclose it to you to lay before their Excys.

> I am,
> Sir,
> Yr. most humble Servant,
> CARPENTER.

Charles Delafaye, Esq.

[1]James Ogilvy, fourth Earl of Findlater, 1st Earl of Seafield.

(ix) *Glengarry to General Lord Carpenter*
(Enclosed in previous document)

My Lord, — As I had the honour to inform your Ldp formerly of my being upon the road to waite upon your Lop, and my Lord Justice Clerke, being advertised of a partie searching for me, I did returne instantly, having abundantly suffered imprisonments, though most innocent several tymes.

And it is most certaine, as your Lp. very well observes, that our laws are good and our King most clement and just, yet ye subjects does suffer both in person and means frequently, notwithstanding of which, be the being keept in gaole in Nth. Britain by the ruling power of a partie or a great man, and this, my Lord, and not any feare of guilte, and ye dying circumstances of my wife these many bypast months does impede me;—

Printed in *The Jacobite Attempt of 1719,*
ed. William Kirk Dickson,
Scottish History Society Vol XIX,
(Edinburgh, 1895), pp.269-287.

IV: The Chevalier's Successful 1719 Campaign

James Francis Edward Stuart had crossed into Italy in 1717, on his way to long-term refuge under papal sovereignty in Rome. On the way south he was entertained by Duke Rinaldo of Modena, his mother's cousin. James promptly fell in love with Benedicta, the eldest of Duke Rinaldo's three daughters, who reminded him of his mother. After two days, James proposed marriage. The idea delighted his supporters, lay and ecclesiastical, because the continuity of the Jacobite cause was dependent on his begetting legitimate heirs, preferably male. Pope Clement XI was so pleased with the idea of an alliance with Modena that he offered to perform the marriage ceremony himself, but Duke Rinaldo, after some months of reflection, absolutely refused to allow the match. He had, after all, to think of his daughter's possible future life in the strange twilight world of Jacobite royalty, as well as the political implications for Modena of alliance with a possibly lost cause.

Thereafter, throughout 1717-18, a succession of princesses were canvassed as possible matches for James. None seemed greatly to appeal to him, and it was his Irish follower Charles Wogan who, when acting as an itinerant talent scout, finally spotted the eventually successful candidate — the then fifteen-year-old Clementina Sobieski, descendant of Polish royalty, whose wealthy father Prince James Sobieski offered a dowry of 200,000 Polish crowns, plus the fabulous, and eminently pawnable, Sobieski rubies. The Pope also offered a generous marriage portion, and a pension of 10,000 livres to assist the match. By the spring of 1719, however, James had left for Spain, and English diplomatic pressure had succeeded in persuading the Emperor to arrest Clementina at Innsbruck, on her way south to join James.

The security surrounding Clementina was pathetically incompetent in the best Austrian tradition, so Wogan had little difficulty in wafting her away, though he showed determination and she spirit in the journey to Bologna where on May 10 there took place a proxy marriage, with James Murray, later Lord Dunbar, standing in for James. The latter returned to Italy four months later and married Clementina at the eccentric hour of midnight at Montefiascone on September 1, thus consummating the only successful Jacobite campaign of 1719. Here is an account of the more dramatic parts of the episode by a well-informed Irish Jacobite priest.

(i) *A Journal of the Arrest and Escape of the Princess Sobieski:* written by Brother Bonaventure Boylan, in the College of St Anthony of Padua, in Lovain, in the year of Our Lord, 1722.

The Chevalier de St George, having received frequent messages from his faithful friends, humbly begging and praying he would please to marry, in order to propagate the royal family, of which he is the last in the male line, thought fit to give them this satisfaction, and concluded thereupon that he could not make a better choice than that of the Princess Clementine Sobieski, youngest daughter of James Sobieski, Prince of Poland, and of Edwige, Elizabeth, Amelia, Palatine of Neuburg, born the 17th day of July, 1702.

Besides these motives, the Chevalier had others of interest to induce him to think of this alliance. The King [James II.], his father, had been more opposed in the recovery of his kingdoms by the Empire than by any other power in Europe. The son did therefore reasonably hope that, by marrying the said Princess, he might be able to make a party in Germany capable to balance that of King George [of England]. For this end Charles Wogan, an Irish gentleman of known ability and integrity, vested with the power and procuration from the Chevalier, went to Germany in the beginning of the year 1718, on pretence of seeing the several courts of the Empire, and being come to that of the Prince Sobieski at Ohlau, in Silesia, demanded of him the Princess Clementine, his daughter, for the Chevalier, his master; which being graciously granted by the unanimous consent both of the father and mother, the contract of marriage was signed by both parties.

It was also agreed upon that the young Princess, accompanied by her mother, should be conducted with all possible secrecy to Bologna, in Italy, to receive the nuptial benediction. Then Mr. Wogan rode post back to Italy, to give the Chevalier an account of his commission at Urbino, whence the Chevalier went, a few days after, to Rome, to notify the same to the Pope, who was god-father to his spouse. The length of the time taken up in preparing for the journey of the Princess gave the emissaries of King George an opportunity to penetrate into the design. This Prince was exceedingly alarmed thereat, and used all his credit with the Emperor to hinder the conclusion of the marriage. And forasmuch as the Imperial Court had great reasons to keep with him upon account of the alliance with Spain, orders were immediately despatched for the governor of Inspruck to arrest the Princess Clementine Sobieski in her passage, and to keep her confined under a strong guard till further orders; which was accordingly executed.—

The Chevalier, judging there was no room left to hope for the liberty of his spouse by means of any solicitations, gave a commission to the same Charles Wogan, and ordered him to return to Germany, in order to watch for an opportunity to take her away from the place of her confinement. He came to Inspruck in the month of December, 1718, had a conference with a French gentleman, Monsieur Chateaudoux, gentleman-usher to the mother of the Princess, and by his means communicated his commission to the Princess herself. The Princess declared she was immovable in her resolution, and ready to concur in what the Chevalier desired of her, acknowledging the submission she owed to his will and pleasure. She only desired Mr. Wogan would go to Ohlau to consult with her father on the measures which were to be taken, and that on her side she would make all the preparations necessary to dispose matters to the best in her power in order to facilitate her escape.—

So soon as she received the message which Chateaudoux sent her by Konska, she put on her apron, took her hood in her hand, and, after some few prayers that God might protect her, she bid Konska follow her to the inn with the packet in which she had put her jewels, in a few minutes after she should go out.—

When Wogan and Gaydon had taken their places, they gave the Princess their muffs, and prayed her to put them on her legs to keep her warm. Then they took off the wet cloak, and put on her a dry one, and so set out from Inspruck, leaving Toole as the court-steward to pay the bill of their expenses, —

The 28th, by eight o'clock in the morning, they had made but three stages, though the berlin was drawn by six good horses. But the depth of the snow and the ruggedness of the way occasioned that, having gained the summit of the mountain of Brenner,—The descent of this mountain was no less rugged than the coming, so that they were forced to go slowly. Her Royal Highness being very well recovered of her weakness, entertained the company with most gracious discourses, to which it was answered that what she had undertaken for the Chevalier was so great and so worthy the protection of Heaven, that they could not doubt to see an end put soon to her misfortunes.—

Power given to Mr. Murray, when the king [James III.] parted for Spain, to open letters and to solemnize the king's marriage with the princess: February, 1719.

The necessity of our affairs obliging us to set out suddenly from Italy,—we hereby impower him to open such letters as shall come in our absence by any direction for us,
—to return such answers, and to give such lights as from the knowledge he has of our affairs he shall think most conducive to our service.

And whereas we have left in the hands of the said honourable James Murray a procuration impowering him to solemnize our marriage with her royal highness princess Clementine Sobieski, we hereby give him authority to use the said procuration as soon as she, being at liberty, shall desire him to do it, but not during her confinement.

In testimony whereof, we have signed and sealed these presents with our sign manual and privy signet.

Given at Rome, the 2nd day of February, 1719, and in the 18th year of our reign. — By his majesties command.

V: Forts, Roads, and Independent Companies: Government Policy and the Highlands after the '15 and the '19

With the collapse of the '19 and Spain's acknowledgement of her inability seriously to challenge the international status quo, there was really very little chance of any immediate Jacobite rising in the Scottish Highlands. The Highland aristocracy was far better-educated and more cosmopolitan than is often assumed. It also had a shrewd sense of political and military realities, so it knew that without substantial foreign aid a rising was much too risky a game to play, and it understood only too well that the existence of an Anglo-French entente ruled out the possibility of the only foreign aid worth having. Benign neglect allied to the maintenance of an adequate military striking force in Scotland was a defensible option for the Westminster government. However, it hardly suited Simon Fraser Lord Lovat, who had returned from France during the '15, almost certainly with a view to supporting the Chevalier, and had promptly and prudently changed to the side of King George when he worked out that the rebellion was going nowhere. Frustrated by his inability to gain office and financial reward, Lovat sent George I in 1724 a memorial which grossly exaggerated the lawlessness and "barbarism" of the Highlands, and insinuated that any solution would need to ensure that Lord Lovat became a justice of the peace, Lord Lieutenant of Inverness-shire, and commander of an independent (but government-funded) company.

Wisely, the Westminster regime commissioned independent reports on the Highland problem from its principal internal security specialist, the Irish General George Wade. He produced a first report in 1724 and a second in 1727. They are revealing documents, showing how the Highlands appeared to a Hanoverian military hard-liner, laying down plans for both opening up, and holding down the central Highlands, and reporting on progress. Wade's famous roads were built by military construction parties and were designed primarily for the movement of troops, which is why they often proved unsuitable in gradient for the movement of modern vehicular traffic. Wade himself appears to have had oversight over the construction of about 240 miles of military road in Scotland before he relinquished his command there to Lieutenant-General Jasper Clayton in 1740. At its fullest extent around 1780, there were to be over 1100 miles of road in the Scottish military road system.

Functionally, the roads proved more efficient than the forts, few of which incorporated, or due to their sites could incorporate, the latest artillery defences. Whilst Edinburgh and Stirling castles successfully resisted the last Jacobite rebellion, all the Highland forts fell, apart from Fort William. In fact, the roads were more use to the Jacobite army than to anyone else in 1745, when the independent companies were conspicuous by their absence.

(i) *General Wade's First Report, 1724*

—The Number of Men able to carry Arms in the Highlands (including the Inhabitants of the Isles) is by the nearest Computation about 22,000 Men, of which Number about 10,000 are Vassals to the Superiors well affected to Your Majesty's Government; most of the remaining 12,000 have been engaged in Rebellion against Your Majesty, and are ready, whenever encouraged by their Superiors or Chiefs of Clans, to create new Troubles and rise in Arms in favour of the Pretender.

Their Notions of Virtue and Vice are very different from the more civilized part of Mankind. They think it a most Sublime Virtue to pay a Servile and Abject Obedience to the Commands of their Chieftans, altho' in opposition to their Sovereign and the Laws of the Kingdom, and to encourage this, their Fidelity, they are treated by their Chiefs with great Familiarity, they partake with them in their Diversions, and shake them by the Hand wherever they meet them.—

The Highlanders are divided into Tribes or Clans, under Lairds, or Chieftans (as they are called in the Laws of Scotland), each Tribe or Clan is subdivided into little Branches sprung from the Main Stock, who have also Chieftans over them, and from these are still smaller Branches of Fifty or Sixty Men, who deduce their Original from them, and on whom they rely as their Protectors and Defenders.—

On sudden Alarms, or when any Chieftan is in Distress, they give Notice to their Clans or those in Alliance with them, by sending a Man with what they call the Fiery Cross, which is a Stick in the form of a Cross, burnt at the End, who send it forward to the next Tribe or Clan. They carry with it a written Paper directing them where to Assemble; upon sight of which they leave their Habitation and with great Expedition repair to the place of Rendezvous, with Arms, Ammunition and Meal for their Provision.—

The Clans in the Highlands, the most addicted to Rapine and Plunder, are, the Cameron's on the West of the Shire of Inverness. The Mackenzie's and others in the Shire of Ross who were Vassals to the late Earl of Seaforth, the McDonell's of Keppoch, the Broadalbin Men, and the McGregors on the Borders of Argyleshire. They go out in Parties from Ten to Thirty Men, traverse large Tracts of Mountains till they arrive at the Lowlands where they Design to Commit Depredations, which they chuse to do in places distant from the Clans where they Inhabit; They drive the Stolen Cattle in the Night time, and in the Day remain on the Tops of the Mountains or in the Woods (with which the Highlands abound) and take the first occasion to sell them at the Fairs or Markets that are annually held in many parts of the Country.

Those who are robbed of their Cattle (or Persons employ'd by them) follow them by the Tract and often recover them from the Robbers by Compounding for a certain sum of Money agreed on, but if the Pursuers are Armed and in Numbers Superior to the Thieves and happen to seize any of them, they are seldom or never prosecuted, the poorer sort being unable to support the charge of Prosecution.—

To remedy these Inconveniences there was an Act of Parliamt. passed in the Year 1716 for the more effectual securing the Peace of the Highlands in Scotland, by Disarming the Highlanders, which has been so ill executed, that the Clans the most disaffected to Your Majesty's Government remain better Armed than ever, and consequently more in a Capacity not only of committing Robberies and Depredations, but to be used as Tools or Instruments to any Foreign Power or Domestic Incendiaries who may attempt to disturb the Peace of your Majesty's Reign. By this Act the Collectors for Taxes were impowered to pay for the Arms delivered in, as they were Valued by Persons appointed for that Service in the respective Countries, but as the Government was to support the Charge, they did scruple to Appraise them at a much higher rate than their real worth, few or none being delivered up except such as were broken and unfit for service; And I have been informed that from the time of passing that Act, to the time it was put in execution, great Quantities of broken and useless Arms were brought from Holland and delivered up to the Persons appointed to receive the same at exorbitant prices.

The Spaniards who landed at Castle Donnan in the Year 1719 brought with them a great Number of Arms: They were delivered to the Rebellious Highlanders who are still possessed of them, many of which I have seen in my passage through that Country, and I judge them to be the same from their peculiar make, and the fashion of their Locks. These and others now in their Possession by a Moderate Computation are supposed to amount to 5 or 6,000, besides those in the Possession of the Clans who are in Your Majesty's Interest, provided as they alledge, for their own defence.—

I must further beg leave to Report to your Majesty that another great Cause of Disorders in the Highlands, is the want of proper Persons to execute the several Offices of Civil Magistrates, especially in the Shires of Ross, Inverness and some other parts of the Highlands.—And I take the liberty to observe that the want of acting Justices of the Peace is a great encouragement to the Disorders so frequently committed in that part of the Country, there being but one, residing as an acting Justice for the Space of above a hundred Miles in Compass.

Your Majesty's Commands requiring me to examine into the State and Condition of the late Earl of Seaforth's Estate, engaged me to go to the Castle of Brahan his principal Seat, and other parts of the said Estate, which for the most part is Highland Country, and extends from Brahan to Kintail on the Western Coast, being 36 Miles in length and the most Mountainous part of the Highlands; The whole Isle of Lewis was also a part of the said Earl's Estate. The Tennants before the late Rebellion were reputed the richest of any in the Highlands, but now are become poor by neglecting their business and applying themselves wholly to the use of Arms. The Rents continue to be levied by one Donald Murchieson a Servant of the late Earl's who annually remits (or carries) the same to his Master into France.

—The last year this Murchieson travell'd in a Public manner to Edinburgh to remit £800 to France for his Master's use, and remained there fourteen Days unmolested.

I cannot omit observing to Your Majesty; this National tenderness your Subjects of North Britain have one for the other, is great encouragement to the Rebells and attainted Persons to return home from their Banishment.—from the Tops of the Hills which they return without effect, as it happened at the affair of Glenshiels, where the Rebells lost but one Man in the (sic) tho' a Considerable number of Your Majesty's Troops were killed and wounded.—

Printed in *Historical Papers Relating to*
The Jacobite Period 1699-1750 Vol.I,
ed. James Allardyce,
The New Spalding Club (Aberdeen 1895) pp.132-40.

(ii)   *General Wade's Second Report, 1727*

—The Inconveniences arising from the practice of carrying Arms in the Highlands have often been under the Consideration of the Privy Council and Parliaments of Scotland before the Union and Several Rigorous Laws were made to disarm and reduce them to Obedience; Yet they have always fail'd of Success; As I humbly conceive from their being formed with more Severity than Judgment, but I humbly hope the Measures Your Maty is now taking will prove an effectual Remedy to these Evils and will render the Highlands as Quiet and Peaceable as any other part of Your Maty's Dominions.

I also beg leave to represent to Your Maty; That pursuant to the Instructions I recd, from Your Royal Father for granting Licences under my Hand and Seal, to Merchants, Drovers, and others permitting them to carry Arms for the security and defence of their Property; I gave out in the year 1725, 230 Licences for the whole Highlands which were to remain in force for two years and no longer. These Licences expiring in September last were call'd in and 210 were issued out in Your Maty's Name to continue in force for three years, provided the Person possessing the same, during that time, behaved themselves as faithfull Subjects of Your Maty, and peaceably and quietly towards the People of the Country.

I presume further to Report to Your Maty, That the great Road of Communication extending from the East to the West Sea, through the middle of the Highlands, has been successfully carried on upon the South side of the Lakes from Inverness to Fort William, being near 60 Miles in length, and is made practicable for the March of Artillery or other Wheel Carriage, as may appear by my having travell'd to that Garrison the last Summer in a Coach and Six Horses to the great Wonder of the Inhabitants, who, before this Road was made, could not pass on Horseback without Danger and Difficulty.—

In regard to the Fortifications in Scotland, I humbly presume to Represent to your Maty; That till the last year, nothing had been effectually done to Secure them from the danger of a surprize, to which they have been exposed for many years past; And particularly the Castle of Edinburgh, which, I humbly conceive is a place of the greatest Importance to the Safety of that Part of Your Maty's Dominions.

The Parapet Walls of this Castle were so ruinous that the Soldiers after the shutting the Gates had found a Way to ascend and descend to an from the Town of Edinburgh when ever they thought fit.—

The new Fortification erecting at Inverness, call'd after Your Maty's Name, Fort George, is situate on a Hill on the South side of the River Ness, near the place where it falls into the East Sea, as Fort William does on the Western Ocean.—This Fortification is irregular as are all the other Castles and Forts in Scotland, which are generally built upon Eminencies, incapable by their Situation to admit of regular Works.—

The Fort and Barrack proposed to be built at Killihinmen[1] near the West End of the Lake Ness is not yet begun, but Materials are providing to go on with the Work, next Spring, as soon as the Season of the Year will admit. This Place being in the Center of the Highlands equally distant from Fort George and Fort William, will, I humbly conceive, be a proper Situation for the Residence of a Governour, who, if it is Your Maty's Pleasure, may have the Chief Command, not only of the two Forts above mention'd, but of all the Barracks and Independant Companys in the Highlands by which he will be enabled speedily to Assemble a Body of 1000 Men, to March to any part of that Country for preventing or suppressing Insurrections;—

[1]The future Fort Augustus.

PROPOSAL

1st.

That the new Fort and Barrack projected to be built at Killihinmen Adjoining to the West End of the Lake Ness, be carried on the next Spring, as soon as the Season of the Year will permit, and proper Store Rooms built Sufficient to contain Provisions for a Battalion of Foot, with Ovens for baking Ammunition Bread or Biscuit for the use of the Garrison or for Detachments that may be sent into the Mountains. And that all due Encouragment be given for erecting a Market Town on the Ground between the Old Barrack and the End of the Lake (a space of about 500 yards in Length and 400 in breadth) which being situate in the Center of the Highlands will very much contribute to Civilize the Highlanders, who by living separate in the Hills, where there are no Towns, are without Examples to induce them to change their Barbarous Customs.

2d.

That a small Tower of Stone in the form of a Redoute, capable of containing a Guard of an Officer, and Twenty Soldiers, be built at each end of the Lake Lochy, and another at the East end of the Lake Ness, the better to secure the line of Communication between Fort George and Fort William.

3d.

That a small Harbour be made at each [end of] the Lake Ness, for the Security of the Highland galley against Violent Storms which are very frequent [in that] Country.—

8th.

That in order to make the Roads of Communication more perfect, an allowance of £600 p Annum be made for building Stone Bridges and other Torrents of Water that fall from Mountains, by which Passengers frequently Lives, and the Troops are often interrupted Marches for several Days successively.

All which is most humbly submitted to Your Majesty's Royal Consideration.

(signed)   GEORGE WADE.

Printed in *ibid*, pp.161-64.

VI: The Nadir of Jacobitism

Jacobite hopes revived with the birth of an heir, Charles Edward, in 1720, followed by a second son, Henry Benedict in 1725. Unfortunately estrangement grew between James and his wife and a prolonged quarrel ensued, of which Hanoverian propaganda made much. Lockhart of Carnwath was now James' chief agent in Scotland. In the summer of 1727 King George had died and James, informing Lockhart of his intentions, had made a dash from Rome to Lorraine with a view to getting into Britain quickly in the event of a Jacobite rising. Lockhart told him firmly that the time was not ripe, and in forthright terms explained why.

Throughout these years James kept in touch with his Scottish friends. He intervened in 1724 to arrest a feud between the Macphersons of Speyside and the Duke of Gordon which had involved violence against the Duke's factor, an elderly Jacobite laird from Aberdeenshire, Gordon of Glenbucket, a veteran of the '15 and the '19. James also sustained many impoverished Jacobite exiles, striving to contain their many quarrels in the heated atmosphere of his Court at Rome.

'Contingency planning' continued against the day when a further attempt to restore James might become possible. An instance of this were the instructions sent in 1729 by James to 'young' Lochiel, who during his father's exile was acting chief of the strongly Jacobite Clan Cameron in Lochaber. These have to be seen in the light of an Anglo-Spanish confrontation between 1727 and 1729, in the course of which the Madrid government besieged Gibraltar and tried to reactivate the Jacobite card in Scotland. The notorious Rob Roy MacGregor, a Jacobite veteran of the '15 and '19 informed the Westminster government of the tentative plot. It was a good plot to betray.

(i) *Lockhart to James, August 4th 1727 dissuading him from any attempt on Britain, now that George I had died [written from Aix in Provence, Lockhart being temporarily on the continent].*

—I have no intelligence from tother side of the water, but by the publick letters tis plain that the people of England are intoxicated at present, having forgot their late ailments by the (ill-grounded) hopes of a better management, and till they find themselves dissapointed, I can form no hopes from them, especially seing you have no prospect of what you and all your advisers judgd essentially necessary, even under the fairest of views, for your support and others' encouragement. And as for Scotland, they can't possibly do any thing without being provided in many materiall things they want and ere that can be done much time and many difficulties must be surmounted, during which opposite preparations will be made on all hands.

—I belive Scotland is much as I left it, that is, very well disposed, but withall so overrun and oppressd that it is impracticable for them to do anything but jointly and in concurrance with their neighbours of England, and I am pritty well assured this notion is so establishd and fixed in their breasts that they will scarce on any event divert from it, so that all depends on the people of England, and for a certain person to venture over without ane assurance of some support may prove pernicious to him and fatall to all that wish him well.—No man living woud more gladlie see the dawning of a fair day, but when every airth of the compass is black and cloudie, I cannot but dread bad weather, such as can give no encouragement to a traveler, nay cannot well fail to prove his own and his dependents' ruin and destruction. What I have represented is from the very bottom of my heart and soul, which at the same time I submit with the greatest respect to your judgement.

The Letters of Lockhart of Carnwath, ed. Daniel Szechi, Scottish History Society (Edinburgh, 1989), pp.312-13.

(ii) *Letter conveying James' instructions to Young Lochiel from Allan Cameron, his exiled uncle at the Jacobite Court.*

Dear Nephew,   Albano, Oct.3, 1729.

Yours, of September 11th, came to my hand in due time, which I took upon me to shew His Majesty, who not only was pleased to say, that you wrote with a great deal of zeal and good sense, but was so gracious and good as to write you a letter with his own hand, herewith sent you, wherein he gives full and ample powers to treat with such of his friends in Scotland, as you think are safe to be trusted in what concerns his affairs, until an opportunity offer for executing any reasonable project towards a happy restoration,—

You are to assure yourself and others that the King has determined to make Scotland happy, and the Clans in particular, when it pleases God to restore him; this is consistent with my certain knowledge. You are only to touch upon this in a discreet way, and to a very few discreet persons: but all these matters I leave to your own good sense and prudence, for you may be sure there are people who will give account of your behaviour after you return home: but I hope none will be able to do it to your disadvantage: keep always to the truth in what you inform the King, and that will stand: though even on the truth itself, you are to put the handsomest gloss you can on some occasions.

You are to keep in good terms with Glengary,[1] and all other neighbours, and let by-gones be by-gones, as long as they continue firm to the King's interest: let no private animosity take place, but see to gain them with curtesy and good management, which I hope will give you an opportunity to make a figure amongst them, not but you are to tell the truth, if any of them fail in their duty to the King or country.

As to Lovat,[2] pray be always on your guard, but not so as to lose him; on the contrary, you may say that the King trusts a great deal to the resolution he has taken to serve him; and expects he will continue in that resolution. But, dear Nephew, you know very well that he must give true and real proof of his sincerity, by performance, before he can be entirely reckoned on, after the part he has acted. This I say to yourself, and therefore you must deal with him very dexterously; and I must leave it to your own judgment what lengths to go with him, since you know he has always been a man whose chief view was his own interest.—

[1]Ian MacAlasdair Dubh, 12th Chief of the MacDonells of Glengarry.
[2]Simon, 12th Lord Lovat.

John Home, *The History of the Rebellion in the year 1745* (London, 1802), Appendix II.

CHAPTER 9:

THE ORIGINS OF THE '45

I: The First Stirrings of Renewed, Realistic Jacobite Hopes

Hope was a commodity which exiled Jacobites could conjure up out of thin air. They lived on it, and not surprisingly many of their hopes proved wildly unrealistic, like their expectations of trouble for the Hanoverian regime when George I died. The only realistic Jacobite hope by about 1730 was that Britain might become embroiled in war with a major European power, preferably France. James actually urged his supporters in the Westminster parliament in that year to "promote a misunderstanding between the English government and any foreign power, but most especially France". The understanding between the regimes of Sir Robert Walpole in England, and Cardinal Fleury in France was the biggest single obstacle to the revival of Jacobitism as a serious force after the débâcles of the '15 and '19. Deterioration in Anglo-Spanish relations in 1738-40 greatly cheered Jacobites, for there was a reasonable chance that France would be drawn in to support Spain. As late as 1741-43 the French government was reluctant to commit significant resources to the Jacobites, but after the death of the aged Fleury early in 1743, the French and British governments entered a collision course. These documents from the late 1730s show how much the British government dreaded a Franco-Jacobite combination.

All the instructions cited below are addressed to James, Earl Waldegrave, British Ambassador to France 1730-40. His mother was the eldest daughter of James II by Arabella Churchill. He was, despite his Hanoverian allegiance, not only kin to the Chevalier but had also been on close terms with his uncle, the Duke of Berwick, until the latter's death in action at a siege in Germany in 1734.

(i) *To Waldegrave from Whitehall, 8 May 1739.*
  Most private.

—His Majesty observes by the accounts that your Excellency gives of your conferences with the Cardinal that His Eminency seems as ill humour'd as possible in everything that relates to His Majesty and this country;—

You may also, as from yourself, mention the quartering their Irish troops over against our coasts, and without shewing any uneasiness or making any complaint, endeavour to see what sort of intercourse the Jacobites have at present with the Cardinal, and what, if any, encouragement His Eminency has given them.

Upon the whole, the present situation requires Your Excellency's most active attention. The uncertainty of the success of our negotiation with Spain, the probability of their offensive alliance with France, the rumours that are daily spread of the hopes and expectations of the Jacobites, and (as they give out) of their certain dependance upon some assistance from those two Crowns, even for an attempt upon His Majesty's dominions; these circumstances, I am persuaded, Your Excellency will think of such consequence that you will use your utmost care to send the King constant informations of all that you shall be able to learn relating to them—

(ii)   *To same from Whitehall, 8 May 1739.*
       Private and Particular. In Cypher. To be open'd and
       decypher'd by himself.

—Upon the whole, as the present is a most critical situation, and the views of France appear and are universally acknowledged to be very extensive; and as His Majesty has received advices that the interests of the Pretender are mixed with them, and that even the present situation is not thought by the Jacobites an unfavourable one for some attempt to be made upon His Majesty's dominions in which both France and Spain are represented to concur, the King is persuaded, from Your Excellency's zeal for his service and from your attachment to His Majesty's person and government that you will exert yourself with more than ordinary activity upon this occasion, and that you will omit nothing that may tend to procure His Majesty the most perfect informations either from 101[1] or from any other way of what the Court of France is doing. And it is His Majesty's pleasure that you should endeavour to have persons in the several ports of France where ships are fitting out, and to get constant accounts of the preparations that are making, and where design'd; and above all, that you should be very diligent in watching the motions of Obrian[2] and the Jacobites, as well with relation to

183

their proceedings at the Court of France, as to their correspondence here. And, as 101 must be very useful to you in all these inquiries, you will do everything that is necessary to keep him in good humour, and to make him disclose to you all that comes to his knowledge—

[1]"101" is a British agent within the French government.
[2]O'Brian: Col. Daniel O'Brien, Jacobite Agent at the French Court.

(iii) *To same from Whitehall, 7 June 1739.*
   Most private.

—Your Excellency cannot be too alert in this critical conjuncture, and you will therefore have persons in the several ports of France to send you constant advices; and it might not be amiss if you employ'd proper persons all along the coast to be viewing and observing the motions of the Irish regiments.—

—And above all, I must recommend to you the procuring the best information you can of the motions and designs of the Jacobites and those that are employed by the Pretender in France.

There is a report come from Spain, and indeed from many places abroad that one of the French King's daughters is to be married to the Pretender's eldest son. The King looks upon this as a most idle story, but perhaps it may be a pretence for you, as from yourself, to talk to the Cardinal upon the subject of the Pretender.—

Printed in *British Diplomatic Instructions 1689-1789,*
Vol.VI — France, 1727-1744,
ed. L.G.Whickham Legg, Royal Historical Society,
Camden Third Series, Vol.XLIII (London, 1930), pp.217-25.

II: Scottish Initiatives

There had been a separate impetus to the Jacobite cause from the activities of Gordon of Glenbucket. He crossed to France, and from Paris addressed a 'memorial' to James in Rome via Colonel O'Brien, James' agent in Paris.

With it was a covering letter from Father Innes, Principal of the Scots College in Paris which incidentally shewed that resentment of the heavy-handed measures of King George's government against the town of Edinburgh after the Porteous riots of 1737 had put it into some Jacobite minds that Scotland was ready to unite for the Stuart cause. (The riots had been occasioned by the execution of a notorious smuggler who was something of a local hero, excise duties on drink being perceived as a burdensome consequence of the Union.) But Innes himself was sceptical.

In the flurry of Jacobite activity that followed after war broke out between Britain and Spain, the Earl Marischal, the exiled erstwhile magnate from north-east Scotland, was appointed James' 'Commander-in-chief' in Scotland for the Rising whenever it would come. But Marischal though accepting the appointment was too much the realist to surrender to wilder Jacobite enthusiasm. (He was to take no part in the '45).

The leading English Jacobites were sounded in secrecy, the agents employed for this and the Jacobites in Paris wishfully thinking that English revulsion from corrupt Walpolean government was to be equated with enthusiasm for the return of James. In Scotland commitment to James' cause was more robust, though the association known as 'the concert', which now formed itself from Jacobite enthusiasts, was unimpressive in its composition. As the prospect of a general European war became clearer there were protracted discussions between James' representatives in Paris and Louis XV's chief minister, Cardinal Fleury. As regards England, Fleury was reluctant to commit France to an invasion attempt before English Jacobites had given clearer proof of their loyalties. But for Scotland, France now promised arms, money, and the famous Irish Brigade in support of a future Jacobite rising there. For its part 'the concert' committed itself in a letter to Fleury of March 1741. It was this French commitment which, four years later, Louis XV sought (with only partial success) to honour in sustaining the '45.

Meanwhile, at Rome, the lure of Jacobitism could dazzle young Scots noblemen on the Grand Tour, such as Lord Elcho, heir to the Earl of Wemyss.

(i) *Glenbucket's 'Memorial' to King James.*

(a) *The Text*

Your Majesties Loyall Subjects haveing seriouslie considered the Humour, and divisions, presently radges in Brittaine, both in Church and State, Humbly and with all Submissione doe most earnestly and with greatest zeell, beg and pray your Majestie (without loss of tyme) to use yr outmost endeavours to affurd a small fforigne force, if but eight or ten thousand men to land in England and Scotland with your Majestie and prince of Wales. This make ye Restoratione easie. But iff difficultie shall be found in this, your Majestie and Prince landing in Scotland, with arms and Amunitione to ye number of eight or ten thousand stand, a few experiencd officiers, and twentie thousand pounds sterling of money, the affaire will goe on with pleasr. and good success.

And iff your Majestie cannot make effectuall neither of these two proposalls, your Subjects doe disyre and think proper your Majestie ye Prince and some officers land in the highlands of Scotland as the only safe and fittest place in this cace, and ye sooner the better since such ane favourable oppertunitie has not happened since the unhappy Revolutione, and if neglected or Cooll, it is hard to believe, if ever such another may fall. This is the oppinione of all your Majesties subjects I have conversed with, and ye Substance I was disyred lay befor your Majesty. Which is ye occasione of my comeing here and to give your Majestie full assurance of your Subjects fiddletie and how much your Royall presence with ye Prince with great anxietie is disyred And that nothing this syde of tyme can give so much pleesr. nor encouradgement or animate them more. Your Majestie cane expect imediatly on your landing four five thousand men, which will dayly increas as you advance, that befor the South of Scotland is reached your Majestie will have such a considerable body, that it's hoped, how soon your Loyall subjects in England joyns small or no oppositione will happen.

It is true their is fyve or six Regments of foot and Draguns in Scotland a good many of the foot cantuned thorrow the Highlands in barracks ych will be no difficult matter to surpryss imediatly on your Majesties landing. Besydes it is not doubted but a great many both officers and soldiers will come over to your Majestie. I doe know my self a great many weill inclyned Gentlemen in the Armie. Your Majestie may depend this is ye oppinione of your fast freinds and Loyall subjects and those who are most capable to doe service. Which I cane affirm and assure. Therefore in ye nem of God let it please your Majestie to consider the present Juncture and that tyme and opportunitie is not to be neglected. Iff it is (as God forbid) how farr it will discourage and cast down a Loyal people (so firmly resolved to stand in your Majesty's cause and service whyll intrest or blood in their body remains) crying and beseeching your Majestie

to come and possess the throne of your Royal ancessores. God bliss
and direct you.

Printed in *The History of the Rebellion in the years 1745 and 1746;*
ed. Henrietta Tayler (Roxburghe Club, 1944), p. xxvii.

(b) *Father Innes' covering letter to the Memorial*

2 Dec. 1737. Paris.

There arrived here last week another messenger from Scotland —
he goes by the name of Ogilby, but his true name is Gordon of
Glenbucket, known to your Majesty by the figure he made in 1715
when he commanded the most part of D. Gordon's[1] men. He came
straight to me at first but when I found what his errand was, I sent
him to Coll. O'Bryen to whom he says he has given a full account.
He brings no Credentiall in writing, no more than the last Messenger
did, but—he is a gentleman of good family who hath always given
publick proofs of his zeal and fidelity, besides that he is acquainted
with the most considerable of the nobility and gentry of that
kingdom and knows their sentiments and how far they may be
depended upon. He also knows the country well, highlands and
lowlands, having made that his business of late years. What he says
they generally demand is that yr Majesty come in person with what
foreign troops you can get tho' never so few, with some good
officers and a good quantity of arms and ammunition. The great
difference he says between the present disposition that kingdom is in
from what it was in 1715 is that the Whigs and Presbyterians (who
make no small party in that country) were then generally all on the
Government side, whereas now they are all universally displeased
upon the severity of the Government against the Town of Edinburgh
and their obliging all the Ministers to read in their churches the Act
of Parliament relating to that matter. When I asked him what man of
quality and figure there was that could be relyed on that had credit
enough with the Whigs to be at their head and answer for them he
gave no satisfactory answer—

[1]Duke of Gordon

Printed in *Jacobite Epilogue*, by Henrietta Tayler
(London, 1941), pp.166-7.

Translation

—The chiefs of our Highland clans, whose names we have sent at the same time with the number of men that each binds himself to furnish, will without fail keep their engagements, and we venture to be responsible to Your Eminence that there will be 20,000 men on foot for the service of our true and only lord, King James VIII. of Scotland, as soon as it will please His Most Christian Majesty to send us arms and munitions, and the troops that are necessary to guard those arms until we shall be able to assemble.

These 20,000 men will be able so easily to defeat or to destroy the troops that the Government employs at present in our country, and even all those that it may be able to despatch upon the first alarm, so that we feel entirely justified in hoping that with divine assistance and under the auspices of the most Christian King, the loyal Scots will be in a condition, not only in a short time to re-establish the authority of their legitimate King throughout the whole Kingdom of Scotland, and to sustain him there against the efforts of the partisans of Hanover, but also to aid powerfully in the recovery of these other States, which will be all the easier since our neighbours of England are not less wearied than we are of the odious tyranny under which we all equally groan; and we know that they are thoroughly determined to unite with us, and with any power whatever that would give them the opportunity they require to place themselves once more under a legitimate and natural Government. We are at present taking measures to act along with them.

As to the assistance that is necessary for Scotland in particular, we should have preferred that His Most Christian Majesty might have been willing to grant us French troops, who would have renewed among us the lessons of heroic bravery and incorruptible fidelity, that our ancestors have so often learned in France itself, but since Your Eminence thinks fit to send subjects of our King, we will receive them with joy as coming from him, and we will endeavour to make them feel the value that we attach to their devotion to our legitimate Sovereign, and the honour that they have acquired in treading so long in the footsteps of the best subjects and of the bravest troops in the Universe.—

—it is not possible for us to raise a sum that would be sufficient, with the necessary secrecy that present circumstances require. It is this consideration alone that prevents us from raising a fund for the necessary expense, the raising of which would bear further proof of our zeal, which we should give with pleasure, and of the confidence with which we place ourselves under the standard of our natural King; but the good of the service obliges us to restrain our wishes and to have recourse to the generosity of His Most Christian Majesty until it is possible to establish the royal rights in our country in a regular manner.

We are persuaded that it would be possible to accomplish this three months after the arrival of the Irish troops, and we do not doubt that our country, reunited under the Government of its king, so much desired, would make such efforts as would enable Your Excellency to prove to His Most Christian Majesty that the modern Scots are the true descendants of those who have had the honour of being counted during so many centuries the most faithful allies of the kings, his predecessors.—

Subscribed by The Duke of Perth, Lord John Drummond [uncle to the Duke of Perth] Lord Lovat, Lord Linton [heir to the Earl of Traquair], Donald Cameron yr. of Lochiel, Sir James Campbell of Auchinbreck [an elderly Campbell laird], William MacGregor [Drummond] of Balhaldie.

Printed in *Origins of the 'Forty-Five* ed. W.B.Blaikie
Scottish History Society (Edinburgh, 1916), pp. xxxiv-xxxix.

(iii) *The young Lord Elcho's audience with James, and his first meeting with Charles Edward, in Rome in 1740.*

Translation

I was now told by my tutor that I must be presented to the Chevalier, and a request for an audience was made through Mr Hay. He came to fetch me at about seven o'clock in the evening, and we soon found ourselves in a small street besides the Palazzo Muti, which we entered through a little door leading into the cellars. Before saying good bye, Mr Hay pointed out the staircase which I must go up. Having followed his instructions, I found myself in the presence of Mr Edgar,[1] as the secret stairs or ladder led into his room. He opened a door, showed me a suite of rooms and told me I wound find the Chevalier in the fourth. I duly found him there, and after having kissed hands he made me sit close to him before the fire. He was a tall spare man with large features, and he resembled the pictures of his father, James II, and his uncle, Charles II. He told me that he knew that my father was very attached to him, and that

189

this would be taken into consideration should he ever come to the throne. He asked me many questions about my travels and my connections, and he seemed well acquainted with Scotland and Scottish families, more especially with those raised to the peerage since 1688 when his father lost his crown, and whom he described as "Mr" and not "my Lord".

He now rang a small bell and the Princes came in from the next room. I kissed hands and called them 'Your Highness' just as I had called their father 'Your Majesty'. The Chevalier made me stand back to back with the elder, Prince Charles, who was a year older than I and much taller. He now bid me farewell after having showered civilities upon me, and I returned to Mr Edgar's room where I had supper tete-a-tete with him. He told me that of all the British visitors, the Duke of Beaufort was the one who most often climbed that ladder—We were given great dinner parties by the Earls of Winton, Nithsdale and Dunbar, and by Messrs Hay and Irvin; but the food and wine were provided by the Chevalier and brought over by his cooks.

[1]Mr Edgar: James Edgar, James' Secretary.

From Lord Elcho's *Journal*, as yet unpublished.

III: The French Cross-Channel Invasion Project of 1744

This attempt in the early months of 1744 was to set in train events which led directly to the '45. It was intended as a 'Pearl Harbour' strike against King George's England before the outbreak of the (seemingly inevitable) general European war. Support from English Jacobites for Maréchal Saxe's invading army was, however, an essential part of the French plan. Prince Charles Edward, now a handsome twenty-four-year-old arrived on the Channel coast to join the invading army.

As to the prospects of English support, there survives only the reckoning by the exiled court at Rome of how far the English Jacobites were prepared to stake life and property for the Jacobite cause at this juncture. Even by James' own reckoning support would have been thin. The names of the Duke of Beaufort, Lord Barrymore etc are not at all to be equated with the support promised to William of Orange in 1688 before he set out from Holland to invade England.

The cancellation of the invasion attempt after the damage wrought to the French navy by the storms of March was a bitter blow to Charles Edward (though, in the event, the tricky problems of mounting a cross-Channel invasion without a welcoming port — a problem in 1744 as in 1944 — might have defeated it).

The invasion project caused no great stir in Scotland. Lord George Murray, former Jacobite and younger brother to the (Whiggish) Duke of Atholl probably expressed the generally-held view.

(i) *James in Rome to the Duke of Ormond*
(who was to command the Jacobite rising in England).

Rome, Dec. 23d, 1743.

I really cannot tell myself when this may be delivered to you, because you will receive it only at the time when all is ready for the execution of the enterprize. The King of France is resolved to undertake in my favour. His Majesty required so great and strict a secret in the affair, that I was not at liberty to mention any thing of it to you before. He will take care you should have all proper lights and instructions, and I have only time to tell you that the affair has been concerted with people in England, and that your old friends have a great share in it; and I hope you yourself will be in a condition to perform that great part which I have all along designed for you. You have already by you a Commission of Regency, in virtue of which you will act, untill such time as the Prince may joyn the expedition, and then you will remain General under him; for it is absolutely impossible for me to joyn the expedition at first, and I cannot even be sure whether the prince will be able to arrive in time. Whenever he does, you will, to be sure, be of all the help and assistance to him that lyes in your power; and before his arrival, as I conclude, that you will, in all matters of importance, act with the counsel and advice of some of our principal friends. I must particularly recommend to you, for that effect, the following persons, vizt. [*The names which follow are in the Chevalier's own hand, in the original copy.*]—The Duke of Beaufort, the Earls of Barrymore and Orrery, Sir Watkin Williams Wynne, Sir John Hind Cotton, and Sir Robert Abdy, and also the Earl of Westmoreland,

and Lord Cobham. It will be, I think, proper when it is time, that you, Lord Derwentwater, and any others in France, whose presence and assistance you may judge to be of use, that they attend or follow you into England.

James Browne, *History of the Highlands and of the Highland Clans* (Glasgow, 1838), Vol.II, p. 450.

(ii)   *Charles Edward to the Earl Marischal*

The Earl Marischal, a veteran of the '15 and the '19 had been appointed 'commander-in-chief' in Scotland by James. He was lukewarm in his feelings for Charles Edward.

Gravelines, Mar.15, 1744.

Since the misfortune of unlucky weather, and the delay that necessarily brings with it, I am not informed, what change of sentiments it may have occasioned among our friends in England; I hope none, because the sooner they are put in any condition of relieving themselves, they must think it the better: some indeed may be taken up, which will be a misfortune but the suspending the habeas corpus act either a litle before or after our landing would help the Government but very litle. I could wish you had more influence, in which case I would depend on more than can now be expected from it, and will on every thing wherby you can forward the royal cause. It gives me unease, that I have not proper persons to advise our friends both in Scotland and England, of the present state of things, and the part it is wish'd they should act for their own safety and the Kings service. I could then inform them (as I am informed with assurances) that the french King is determined not to give up this expedition untill it is fully executed unless our friends put a stop to it by their not concurring properly. I have been at a loss how to advise them.—

Jacobite Epilogue, ed. Henrietta Tayler (Edinburgh, 1941), p. 85.

(iii) *Lord George Murray to the Duke of Atholl*

[*written c. Feb. 1744*]

All is very quiet at present, and I verily believe if the French have any intentions of making an invasion there are few, if any, in Scotland that now know their design. You know the country better than I can inform you. Whatever the private sentiments of some may be, yet I am persuaded they have neither head nor tail.

Affairs in the Mediterranean and Italy I take to be the great point of view of the French in the first place. If we attack them there and consequently have a war with them, doubtless they will distress us in all shapes they can. But if they ground their hopes upon an insurrection in their favours in Britain, especially in the North part of it, I'm convinced they will be deceived.

[and later]

If there were an invasion, to be sure, there would be single persons and disorderly people that would be glad to fish in muddy waters. But—who is it among them that, were they so inclined, could make any figure in a following or rising? Thirty years has made great alteration in things, in men, and their minds. And were there any disturbances like to be in this country as long as the families of Argyll, Gordon, and your Grace's are united to the Government no commotions can be feared in the Highlands.

Printed in Katherine Tomasson, The Jacobite General
(Edinburgh, 1958), p. 10.

IV: Charles Edward resolves to 'go it alone'.

John Murray of Broughton, a young Peebles-shire laird whose Jacobitism was greater than his financial solvency was now sent to France on behalf of the Scottish conspirators to find out how matters stood. After the '45, while a prisoner in the Tower of London, Murray revealed to the authorities what transpired at his meeting in Paris with the Prince, and how news of the latter's resolve to go it alone was received in Scotland. The rebellion, he showed was the outcome of a tragic muddle in which the Scottish Jacobites had not succeeded in deterring Charles Edward from his obsession. Further information about Lochiel's crucial part in this was contained in Murray's memoirs written eleven years later (while he was universally reviled for having saved his own neck by giving the evidence which brought Lord Lovat to the scaffold). Murray's testimony in this is none the less sound.

(a) *His statement to the authorities while in prison in 1746*

This Examt saith that when he saw the Pretender at Paris, he told this Examt he was determined to come over into this Kingdom if he brought only a single Footman; that this Examt represented the Danger of his coming unless he was sure of assistance. To which the Pretender answered he did not doubt of assistance, but that, however, he would come in all events, and asked this Examt how many men (this Examt thought) might join him. To which this Examt said that at the most he thought there would not be above 4 or 5000, even if all those who were looked upon to be the most attached to his Family should appear for him. That this Examt communicated this Conversation to Lord Traquair, and afterwards to Cameron of Lochiel and Lord Perth[1]; that Lochiel thought it was a rash and desperate undertaking; that Lord Perth thought otherwise.

That Letters were written to the seven Persons of the Concert who had signed the Memorial to apprize them of this Design; that the Laird of McLeod[2] came to Edinburgh in Novr 1744; that McLeod, Lochiel, and this Examt met together at a Tavern, where they talked of this Design, which McLeod thought a very mad one, and said no one would join him; that this Examt asked McLeod what he would do himself, to which he said that tho' it was a rash Design, he would join the Pretender if he came over, but that as McLeod had been drinking, this Examt desired Lochiel to speak to him the next Morning and learn his real sentiments upon this matter, which Lochiel accordingly did, and told this Examt that McLeod continued to say that it was a rash undertaking, but, however, that if the Pretender came, he would join him.

That Lochiel sent one of the Pretender's Letters to Sir Alexander McDonald[3], but he always absolutely refused having anything to do with the Pretender.—

That this Examt wrote a Letter to the Pretender to dissuade him very strongly from pursuing his Design of coming to Scotland; that this Examt delivered the said Letter to Ld Traquair at Edenburgh who undertook to send it from London to Paris, his Lp intending soon to come to London; that Lord Traquair afterwards wrote to this Examt from London by Mr. McLeod,[4] who returned to Scotland in April 1745, acquainting him that his Friends in London were as well disposed as ever, but were against undertaking anything without assistance from France; that Mr. McLeod brought to this Examt from Lord Traquair the Letter which his Ldp had undertaken to send to the Pretender, but had not sent it; that this Examt expressed his surprise to McLeod that Lord Traquair should have neglected to send that Letter, which was of great Importance; that this Examt, at that time, thought no attempt would have been made, and was therefore making Interest to get into the Dutch Service.

That about the latter end of June 1745, this Examt received a Letter from the Pretender which was sent to him by one Cockburn a Merchant at Edenburgh, in which the Pretender acquainted this Examt that he was determined to come to Scotland and desired his Friends might be informed of it;—

That the contents of the Letter were, that he, the Pretender was determined to come to Scotland to the West Coast, the Isle of Ouist or Mull, and hoped to be there in June, appointing Signals, etc.

That the Examt upon receiving this Letter was in great Perplexity but soon determined to go to Lochiel in the Highlands, which he did, and they agreed to persuade the Pretender so soon as he should arrive to go back again. That this Letter from the Pretender, or a Copy of it, was carried to Lord Lovat by Lochiel's Brother; that McLeod was with Lord Lovat when Lochiel's Brother arrived there; that Lord Lovat and McLeod entirely disapproved the Design. That this Examt afterwards sent McDonald of Scotus[5] to McLeod at Glenelg, to desire to know his Thoughts as to what should be done to prevent the Pretender from coming on Shore; that McLeod sent him word in answer that he disapproved the Undertaking, but that if the Pretender came he would join him; however that he thought a Letter should be wrote to dissuade him from landing in Scotland; that this Examt accordingly wrote two Letters and left them in the Hands of Macdonald of Scotus to be delivered to the Pretender upon, or before his Landing, advising him by all means to return to France; that the Examt heard that one or both of those Letters were delivered; that this Examt then returned to his own house.

That about a Fortnight or three Weeks after, he heard the Pretender was landed: that there came with the Pretender, Lord Tullibardine, Sir Thos Sheridan,[6] Sullivan, Strickland, Sir John MacDonald, and McDonald the Banker at Paris.

[1]Lord Perth: the 3rd (titular) Duke of Perth.
[2]Laird of MacLeod: Norman, 22nd Chief of Clan MacLeod.
[3]Sir Alexander McDonald, of Sleat, Chief of Clan Donald in Skye.

⁴ Mr McLeod; Alexander MacLeod, yr. of Muiravonside.
⁵McDonald of Scotus in Knoydart.
⁶Sir Thomas Sheridan was the elderly courtier of Irish descent who was the Prince's chief confidant (and in the eyes of some, the source of future dissension between the Irish and the Scots). 'McDonald the Banker' was a brother of the MacDonald Laird of Kinlochmoidart in Clanranald's country.

From *Memorials of John Murray of Broughton*
ed. R.F.Bell, Scottish History Society
(Edinburgh, 1898), pp. 428-30.

(b)*Murray's Memoir of Consultation with Lochiel in* June 1745

I set out next day to Lochyell's house at Achnacarry, but being known there by all the family, I stopped at an Inn about a mile from the house, and sent a Gentleman, who had gone with me as a guide, to acquaint Lochyell of my arrival.

He soon after met me in his garden, and told me, he had received the letter by express from the Duke of Perth, and sent it by his brother (the Doctor) to Lord Lovat, with whom Macleod then was, and expected he would return the next day.

I then repeated every particular circumstance which had happened from the time of his leaving Edinburgh, in the month of February, especially the fate of the letters sent by Traquair: and argued from thence, that his coming was certain, his letter being so explicit as even to mention the signals he intended to make, and likewise from his having sent Sir Hector Macleane before with dispatches, and orders about the signals.

I also observed, that though Traquair had failed us, yet there was no reason to doubt the English would appear: they had been long engaged in the affair, had given assurances the year before; and therefore it was not to be imagined they had so little regard for their own honour as to sit still, if he was once amongst them: nor was it to be doubted but their agents had informed him of every thing that had passed, though Traquair had said nothing to us. If this resolution to land in Scotland was disagreeable to them, they would most certainly have made remonstrances against it; and would likewise have acquainted us not to depend upon them.

I then freely gave it as my opinion, that considering his Royal Highness had advertised his friends here of his design so many months before, and though they had objected to his coming without troops, yet they nevertheless engaged to join him; so taking things in that light, I did not see how they could in honour excuse themselves—that I looked upon myself as indispensably obliged, though no more bound than any of them, to join, and was determined to do it as soon as I should hear of his arrival, let what would be the event: and conluded by saying, that I would endeavour to influence him nor no man, further than was my duty, though I must be allowed to have my own way of thinking of every one who flinched after having so deeply engaged.—

He [Lochiel] then acknowledged he did not see how any man of honour could get off, especially those who had been the first movers of the whole; for allowing that his coming to France, from whence this expedition proceeded, was owing to Bohaldy's[1] having represented things in a wrong light, and as though he was their agent and might be disowned by them; yet it could be no reason for refusing to join the Prince, especially as he was to throw himself naked into their arms, and thereby shew the entire confidence he had in them: so, for his own part, he would not delay one moment to give him all the assistance in his power.

[1]William Drummond (MacGregor) of Balhaldie

Murray, op.cit., pp. 141-43.

(ii)   *Highland Jacobitism*

With the news spreading among the Jacobite clans that the Prince was coming the high excitement was still further raised by the Gaelic songs written that summer by Alexander MacDonald, a gentleman of Clanranald known to the Gaels as Alasdair Mac Mhaighstir Alasdair. One of several sung throughout the Jacobite 'countries' was his 'Song to the Prince'.

A Song to the Prince

Translation

O, hi ri ri, he is coming,
O, hi ri ri, our exiled King,

Let us take our arms and clothing,
 And the flowing tartan plaid.

Joyful! I am, he is coming,
 Son of our rightful exiled King,
A mighty form which becomes armour,
 The broad-sword and the bossy shield.

He is coming o'er the ocean
 Of stature tall, and fairest face,
A happy rider of the war-horse,
 Moving lightly in the charge.

Like the gales of March his visage
 Or dog-tooth in the wind storm seen;
A slim sword in his hand for battle
 To cut down foes like standing grain.

The music of thy pipes and banners
 Would fill thy folk with reckless fire,
Our proud spirits would awaken,
 And we'd put the mob to rout.

The thundering of bombs and cannons
 With its force will rend the earth,
Hill and dale will answer to it,
 And the echo leave us deaf!

Pity him who on that day then
 Wears the ugly coat of red,
His black hat, bordered and cockaded,
 Split like a cabbage round his ears!

From *Highland Songs of the 'Forty-Five*
ed. John Lorne Campbell;
Scottish Gaelic Texts Society
(Edinburgh, 1984), pp. 48-51.

CHAPTER 10:

THE '45

I: French Complicity

The evidence about French complicity in Charles Edward's descent on Scotland is conflicting. This is a matter of some importance. If the Prince sailed for the Hebrides in June 1745 without any solid expectation of French help he was foolhardy in the extreme. If he had good reason to believe that France would eventually back him by mounting a cross-Channel invasion of England then his initiative was a calculated risk. The letter Charles Edward sent to Louis XV on the eve of his departure for Scotland points one way. But Voltaire (who was close to the French court in these years) believed Cardinal Tencin, one of Louis' chief Ministers, instigated the '45. Colonel O'Sullivan in the narrative he wrote for King James after the collapse of the Rising modified this view and argued that the French government were unaware of what the Prince was about to do. But then there is the matter of the great store of munitions of war put into the line of battleship *L'Elisabeth* which accompanied the Prince until she was intercepted and disabled by the Royal Navy's *Lyon*; also the commission dated 1 June 1745 from the King of France to Aeneas MacDonald (one of the 'seven men of Moidart') authorising him to be supplied with stores from French arsenals; at his trial in 1747 MacDonald said this was signed by the Comte D'Argenson, Louis' War Minister. With *L'Elisabeth* there also sailed a bodyguard for the Prince 'handsomely clade in blue faced with red', a company of about a hundred drawn mainly from the officer cadets of the French navy under command of the Chevalier de Lanzière de Lancize. (The very frigate which carried Charles Edward to Scotland was named after M. du Teillay, the *intendant* at Nantes). However, even if Charles Edward's attempt on Scotland is seen as a 'calculated risk', the fact remains that he, for his part, never viewed it as an attempt on Scotland alone. For him it was ever the *British* crown or nothing; and that depended altogether on the English Jacobites declaring themselves, as indeed did the prospect of a cross-Channel invasion without which the whole attempt on Scotland as on England must fail.

Again, documentary evidence about the readiness (such as it was) of English Jacobites to rise, is hard to come by. With the onset of war, correspondence with the English Jacobites was interrupted (but Charles Edward showed little concern about that, convinced as he was of his heaven-sent destiny). An indication of the rose-coloured spectacles with which James' agents in Paris in the early summer of 1745 viewed the strength of English Jacobitism is given in a letter to James in Rome about a secret visit of Drummond of Balhaldie to England (Drummond, and Sempill, both seemingly being unaware of Charles Edward's embarkation at Nantes).

(i) *The Prince's Letter to Louis XV*

Translation

Dear Uncle,

Having tried in vain by every means to meet Your Majesty in the hope of getting, out of your generosity, the help I need to enable me to play a role worthy of my birth, I have resolved to make myself known by my deeds and on my own to undertake a project which would be certain to succeed with a moderate amount of help. I dare to think that Your Majesty will not refuse it to me. I would certainly not have come to France if the Expedition which was to take place over a year ago had not acquainted me with your Majesty's good intentions towards me, and I hope that the unforeseen events which at the time made that expedition impracticable will not have changed them. Might I not dare to say that the signal victory which Your Majesty has now gained over your enemies (for they are indeed mine too) will have changed matters and that I will be able to benefit from this new and glorious light that shines on you? I beg Your Majesty to reflect that in supporting the justice of my claim, you will put yourself in a position to reach a firm and lasting peace, the final conclusion to the war in which you are presently engaged.

At last I go to seek my destiny which other than being in the hands of God is in Your Majesty's. If you enable me to succeed, you will find a faithfull ally in a relative who has already the honour to be, with the greatest respect, dear Uncle, Your Majesty's most asffectionate nephew.

Charles P.

Navarre
12th June 1746.

Printed in *Memorials of John Murray of Broughton*,
ed R.F.Bell; Scottish History Society
(Edinburgh, 1898), p. 507.

(ii) *Voltaire's View*

Translation

—Meeting one day Cardinal Tencin (who had bought his
nomination for a cardinal's hat from the ex-King, the Prince's
father), Tencin said to him [Charles Edward], "Why don't you try to
get over to the north of Scotland in some ship? Your very presence
there will command support and enable you to raise an army. Then
France will *have* to send you help." This bold advice, in line with
Charles Edward's own brave desires, made up his mind for him—

Voltaire, *Précis du Siècle de Louis XV,
Oeuvres Complètes de Voltaire*, T.15,
(Paris, 1878), Chap. XXIV.

(iii) *O'Sullivan's Version of How the Prince's Venture Began*
[Colonel O'Sullivan, an Irishman who was Quartermaster
General to the Prince's army in the '45, and was also one of 'the
seven men of Moidart', wrote for James in Rome afterwards a
lengthy report on the Rising beginning with Charles Edward's belief
there were encouraging signals from Scotland.]

—This was certainly encouragement enough for a young Prince,
& found no other difficulty but to get a Ship, wch was no easy
matter, without the help or knowledge of the Frinch Court, whom he
had his raisons not to let into the secret of his project, nor even the
King our Mastre, fearing least his Majesty, wou'd oppose it, as I
hear, he already had, when the Cardinal of Tensin propos'd the same
schame to the Prince some time before.

There were only Sr Thomas Sheridan, & Kelly at this time in the
secret; O'Sullivan, who had the honr to be at this time in the
Prince's family, knew nothing of the matter, but imagined by the
frequent questions made to him by Sr Thomas, of the places in
France where the best armes cou'd be found, the prisses of 'um,
several other questions about the regulation of Troops, of an

Embarquation of a Landing, the precautions yt were to be taken upon those occasions, made Sullivan believe yet there was something abrewing.

The Prince had alwaise his object in vew, but cou'd fall upon no means of getting a Ship but by bying one. There was not mony enough to spare for yt & the other expences yt were necessary; Rutledge was then at Paris, who just obtain'd the permission to arme a 60 Guns Ship [*L'Elisabeth*] to Course in the North Seas; Sir Thomas applyed to him to see if the Prince cou'd not make use of yt Ship, wch he agreed upon, the Prince & seven or eight personnes yt was to go aboard as Vollontiers.—Rutledge parted without losse of time for Brest, to get the Ship ready as soon as possible, but finding more difficulties than he foresaw, applyed to Welsh[1] at Nantes, who had then a Brig ready to Seal for the West Indies. Welsh took poast imediatly, came to Paris, where it was agreed upon, yt the Prince wou'd go aboard his Ship, & yt the *Elizabeth* wou'd escort 'em; this was the most reasonable project, as it prouved by the event.—The Prince arrived at Nantes about the 10th of June & embarqued two or three days after, set seal imediatly; but the wind being contrary, cast ancre under the Isleland of Belle Isle, where he waited at least fifteen days for the *Elizabeth*. As soon as the news arrived that the *Elizabeth* had been sent off, H.R.H. decided to start.

[1]Welsh: Antoine Walsh, Franco-Irish Jacobite and wealthy slave-trader.

A & H Tayler, *1745 and After* by (London, 1938), pp. 46-8.

(iv) *English Support: Lord Sempill in Paris to James at Rome, 28th June 1745 [by the British Calendar, 17th June 1745]*

I received a long letter from Balhady written in concert with Mr Erskine, Lord Traquair, and Lord Barrymore's cousin and confidant: they represent the Regency in England to be divided, and so diffident of each other, that there is not so much as the appearance of resolution and harmony, or common prudence in their councils. They say our friends in the administration have yielded to all the Duke of Hanover desired, with no other view than to precipitate his ruin, in which they have in a great measure succeeded, both by exasperating the nation so as to make any revolution desirable, and by giving the Duke of Hanover such high spirits upon the opinion of his having overcome all opposition, that he has not only ventured all himself, but has even drawn almost all the troops out of Britain. They remark that the loss of the battle in Flanders has enraged the middle and lower ranks of people, from all which they conclude that there never was, and never can be, such a favourable opportunity to attempt your Majesty's restoration. They assure that if the Prince landed in the present circumstances with ten batallions, or even with a smaller body of troops, there will be no opposition, but, on the contrary, that his royal highness will be received with blessings and acclamations. They affirm this to be the sentiments of all who observe the present state and disposition of things, but upon Balhady's informing our friends, that the same appearances of harmony and unanimity which have imposed on the Duke of Hanover, have rendered the real state of things doubtful at the Court of France, and that some means must be taken to prove to the King of France what we all believe and know to be true: upon this information of Balhady's they considered the case with all possible attention, and judged it impossible to bring any stranger into England at this juncture, and to make him converse with a certain number of principal persons without raising a suspicion that would deprive your Majesty of many advantages, and perehaps ruin your affairs: they judged it equally impossible to get a sufficient number of the King's friends to subscribe any paper:—-

Printed in, John Browne, *A History of the Highlands and the Highland Clans* (Glasgow, 1838), Vol.II, pp.463-4

II: The Rising Gets Under Way

It was the heady atmosphere created by such as Alasdair Mac Mhaighstir Alasdair's poems of Jacobite incitement which was to tip the balance in favour of this the last Jacobite Rising getting under way. The crucial moment was aboard *Le du Teillay* as she lay at anchor in an Inverness-shire sea loch on 27th July 1745 as recorded by Alasdair Mac Mhaighstir Alasdair himself. The gentlemen of Clanranald were in no mood to be cautious. The next key figure was Lochiel, and he likewise succumbed. From then on it was inevitable that there would be rebellion by the openly Jacobite clans. Nevertheless the '45 could not have happened had there not also been an extraordinary welling-up of enthusiasm for Charles Edward from the common people of the parts of the Highlands. (This measure of popular support for a military campaign was to distinguish the '45 from most other wars of *ancien régime* Europe). Why this should have been so is hard to see, but it seems to have sprung deep from Gaelic culture. There are, unfortunately few documentary sources for this most interesting aspect of the Rising. About all we get is the comment of the Campbell Sheriff at Inveraray writing to the Lord Justice Clerk at Edinburgh on 13th August about Clan Donald in Moidart ". . . truly the inhabitants of these countrys are demented, and from all hands I have it they are quite ready to join . . . ". But surviving local tranditions attest strongly.

Lochiel prudently extracted from the Prince that if the enterprise failed he would be compensated from Stuart funds to the value of his ancestral Lochaber estate. As the Highland Army rapidly moved southwards other gentlemen engaged knowing that ruin was the probable outcome. One such was Lord George Murray soon to become effective commander of the Prince's army.

That support for the Jacobite cause in the Lowlands was deeper and wider than triumphant Whigs, in the years that followed the eclipse of the Rising, would allow it to have been, is indicated in the reminiscences put together many years later by the Rev. Alexander Carlyle, Parish Minister of Inveresk, a leading light of the 'Moderates' in the Church of Scotland during the great years of the Enlightenment in the second half of the century but a student at Edinburgh University at the time of the '45. However, the fact remained that for all the enthusiastic welcome given him by Edinburgh few from south of the Tay joined his standard, and more than half of the Highland clans still held aloof however Jacobite they may have been at heart.

(i) *The Prince Wins Over the Western Clans*

(a) *MacDonald of Clanranald*

July [26]th ane express was dispatch'd for young [Ranald Macdonald of] Clanronald, and next day, being the [27]th, Clanronald, Alexander McDonald of Glenaladale, Aeneas McDonald of Dalily, and I, came to Forsy, a small village opposite to the road where the Prince's vessel lay. We called for the ships boat and were immediatly carried on board, and our hearts were overjoyed to find ourselves so near our long wished for P—ce. We boat and were immediatly carryed on board, and our hearts were overjoyed to find ourselves so near our long wished for P—ce. We found a large tent erected with poles on the ships deck, covered and well furnished with variety of wines and spirits. As we enter'd this pavilion we were most chearfully welcom'd by the Duke of Athole, to whom some of us had been known in the year 1715. While the Duke was talking with us, Clanronald was a-missing, and had, as we understood, been called into the P—ce's cabin, nor did we look for the honour of seeing His R.H. at least for that night. After being 3 hours with the P., Clanronald returned to us, and in about half ane hour after there entered the tent a tall youth of a most agreeable aspect, in a plain black coat, with a plain shirt, not very clean, and a cambrick stock fixed with a plain silver buckle, a fair round wig out of the buckle, a plain hatt with a canvas string haveing one end fixed to one of his coat buttons; he had black stockins and brass buckles in his shoes; at his first appearance I found my heart swell to my very throat.

The Lockhart Papers (London, 1817), ii, 479.

(b) *Cameron of Lochiel*

[Lochiel] was not a little troubled when he received a letter from Charles, acquainting him that he was come to the Highlands, and desired to see him immediately. Lochiel complied—He was no sooner arrived at Boradale, than Charles and he retired by themselves—Lochiel acknowledged the engagements of the chiefs, but observed that they were no ways binding, as he had come over without the stipulated [French] aid; and therefore, as there was not the least prospect of success, he advised His Royal Highness to return to France—Charles refused to follow Lochiel's advice.—'In a few days' (said he), 'with the few friends that I have, I will erect the royal standard, and proclaim to the people of Britain, that Charles Stuart is come over to claim the crown of his ancestors, to win it, or to perish in the attempt: Lochiel, who, my father has often told me, was our firmest friend, may stay at home, and learn from the newspapers the fate of his prince.' 'No,' said Lochiel, 'I'll share the fate of my prince; and so shall every man over whom nature or fortune hath given me any power'.—

John Home, *The History of the Rebellion in the year 1745* (London, 1802), p. 41.

(ii) *Lord George Murray Engages for the Prince*

Tullibardine 3rd Sepr. six in the evening.

Dear Brother,

I wrote to you this morning from Stirling, and I hope Lady Jane and Lady Charlotte got safe to Edinburgh. I was not a little difficulted when you left this place, and gave me the charge of your daughters to bring them to Edinburgh, for to speak the truth, I was at that time resolved to take a step which I was certain you would disapprove of as much when you knew it, as it would surprise you to hear it.

I never did say to any person in my life that I would not engage in the Cause I always in my heart thought just and right, as well for the interest, good, and liberty of my country.

But this letter is not wrote with a view to argue or reason with you upon that subject. I own frankly now that I am to engage, that what I do may and will be reckoned desperate. All appearances seem to be against me. Interest, prudence, and the obligations to you which I lie under, would prevent most people in my situation from taking a resolution that may probably end in my utter ruin.

My life, my fortune, my expectations, the happiness of my wife and children are all at stake (and the chances are against me), and yet a principle of (what seems to me) honour, and my duty to King and Country, outweighs everything. If I err, it is only with respect to you. I owe obligations to nobody else—I mean the Court of London. If you find you cannot forgive me, yet sure you will pity me.

Think of what a weight there is upon my spirits. My wife is in a dangerous state—

—I will not venture to recommend her and my children to your protection. All I shall say on that head is, that a man of worth never repented of doing good-natured offices. After what I have said, you may believe that I have weighed what I am going to do with all the deliberation I am capable of, and suppose I were sure of dying in the attempt, it would neither deter nor prevent me. I shall conclude with declaring that should it ever be in my power to be of use to you, I would embrace the occasion with a grateful heart, and wish for nothing more than to be able to show you that I am, dear brother,

Your most affectionate brother and faithful humble servant

GEORGE MURRAY.

Printed in, Katherine Thomasson, The Jacobite General
(London, 1958), p. 20.

Printed in, Katherine Thomasson, *The Jacobite General*
(London, 1958), p. 20.

(iii) *Lowland Loyalties*

The Commons in General as well as two thirds of the Gentry, at
that period, had no aversion to the Family of Stuart, and could their
Religion have been Secur'd, would have been very glad to see them
on the Throne again.

Alexander Carlyle, *Anecdotes and Characters of the Times*
(London, 1973), p.69.

III: French Support

Elated by news of the Prince's victory on September 21st 1745
at the Battle of Prestonpans, in October the French government
entered into a formal treaty of alliance with Charles Edward.
This, the Treaty of Fontainebleau, left in the air the extent of the
Prince's conquest in the British Isles which was to be supported.
It could be read as applying only to Scotland.

It was in compliance with this that in the first days of December (while the Highland Army was approaching Derby) 800
troops, mostly from the Régiment Royal Ecossais, disembarked
at Montrose, the frigate of Louis XV's navy which had transported them from Dunkirk having eluded the blockade by the
Royal Navy of the Jacobite-held ports of the East of Scotland.
Their commander, Lord John Drummond, brother to the Duke of
Perth, issued a proclamation on landing which, on his own initiative, exceeded the terms of the Treaty of Fontainebleau in that
the conquest of England and Ireland as well as of Scotland was
envisaged. More in accordance with French policy however it
looked forward to the Régiment Royal Ecossais soon being followed by the whole 6000 of the Irish Brigade in the service of
France. (That was not to be: Britain's sea-power prevented it
happening).

France having committed troops in support of the Prince, the
Dutch regiments in Field-Marshal Wade's army, by now at Newcastle, had to be returned to Holland (in terms of an undertaking
the Dutch had given Louis XV that they would not assist any
country at war with France). This was a serious blow to King
George's government. France was known to be massing an army
for a renewed attempt at cross-Channel invasion. In the darkness

of a winter's night with an easterly or a southerly wind blowing, the Royal Navy in the age of sail was powerless to seal the French Channel ports. Of this the Duke of Newcastle, King George's Prime Minister, would be only too well aware, however great the outward composure he maintained in writing to the Government's chief representative in Scotland, however enheartened he was by the northward retreat of the Highland Army, now begun.

For the fifth time a naval-military enterprise from France which would have restored the exiled Stuarts to the British Crowns came to nothing, despite the assembly of an invading army on the Channel coast, shipping to carry it across and the preparation of a resounding manifesto from the pen of Voltaire himself to the people of Britain. Partly it was the adverse weather which was to blame for the cancellation; partly the watchfulness of the British navy; partly a commendable reluctance by Louis XV (unlike his grandfather) to replay the Wars of Religion of the previous century as an attack on Protestant England would imply. Partly it was the character of the chosen commander, the pleasure-loving Duc de Richelieu. Retreating with his army into Scotland the Prince knew nothing of all this.

After defeating General Hawley's army in the fading light of a January afternoon, the Highland Army withdrew to the Highlands to await the French invasion. The exasperation the Prince and his circle felt was expressed in a letter from Sir Thomas Sheridan, probably to O'Brien at Paris.

However, from one point of view the '45 had been a great success for France: it had enabled Maréchal de Saxe to recapture Brussels!

The French court would, however, be mortified by the Prince's plight later that year as a fugitive likely to fall into Hanoverian hands. Both from considerations of policy and from genuine regard for Charles Edward there would be no less than six successive (and ultimately successful) commando-style attempts from France that summer to bring the Prince safely back.

(i) *The Treaty of Fontainebleau: the Text*

Translation

Prince Charles Edward of the royal house of Stuart having been proclaimed at Edinburgh as Regent of the Kingdom of Scotland, and like His Most Christian Majesty being at war with King George, the Elector of Hanover, has asked His Most Christian Majesty to send him assistance in troops to be used against their common enemy and to unite their respective interests by a treaty of Alliance. His Most Christian Majesty having agreed to this proposition, the undersigned, duly authorised, ministers are agreed on the following articles.

Article 1. Between the French Crown and the states which have accepted or will accept the Regency of the Royal Prince Charles Edward Stuart, or subsequently come under his control, there will be friendship, good neighbourliness and alliance so that every endeavour is made to strengthen and augment more and more this good understanding for the common advantage of both parties.

Article 2. His Most Christian Majesty being desirous of contributing to the success of the Royal Prince Charles Edward Stuart and the better to assist him in holding out and striking at their common enemy, His Majesty undertakes to assist him to this end in all possible ways.

Article 3. To this end, His Majesty herewith makes over a corps of troops from the Irish regiments and others to act under the Prince's orders, to defend the states which have submitted or will submit to his Regency against anyone whomsoever who attempts to disturb them, to attack the common enemy and to fall in with whatever courses are judged to be useful or necessary.

Article 4. In accordance with the alliance between the Most Christian King and the royal house of Stuart, the King and the Royal Prince promise and undertake to give no assistance to their respective enemies, to prevent as far as lies within their power all injury and harm which might be attempted against the states and their subjects, and to work together and in harmony for the restoration of peace on a basis which can be of reciprocal advantage of the two nations.

Article 5. To strengthen ever further the union and understanding between the crown of France and the states which have accepted or will accept the Regency of the Royal Prince Charles Edward, or subsequently come under his control, as soon as peaceful conditions return, a commercial treaty will be concluded in the interests of all mutual advantages tending to the well being of the two nations.

Article 6. The present treaty will be ratified by both sides and the ratifications will be exchanged at Paris within two months or sooner if possible.

At Fontainebleau
24th October 1745

De Voyer d'Argenson
D. O'Brien

[24th October by the then British calendar was 13th October]

Printed in, James Browne, *A History of the Highlands
and the Highland Clans,*
(Glasgow, 1838), pp.448-50.

(ii) *Lord John Drummond's Proclamation*

Declaration of Lord John Drummond, Commander in chief of his most Christian Majesties forces in Scotland.

The Lord John Drummond, Commander in chief of his most Christian Majesties forces in Scotland do hereby declare that we are come to this kingdom wt written orders to make War against the King of England, Elector of Hanover and all his adherents and that the positive orders we have from his most Christian Majestie are to Attack all his Enemies in this Kingdom, whom he has declared to be those who will not immediately join and assist, as far as will lie in their power, the Regent of Scotland his Alley and whom he has resolved with the concurrence of the King of Spain to support in taking possession of England, Scotland and Ireland, if necessary at the Expence of all the men and money he is master of; to which three kingdoms the family of Steuarts have so just and indisputable a Title, and his most Christian Majesties positive orders are that his enemies should be used in this Kingdom in proportion to the Harm they do or intend to do his Royal Highness' Cause. Given at Montrose the 2nd day of December, 1745.

Printed in, *Jacobite Letters to Lord Pitsligo;*
1745-6, eds. A. and H. Tayler;
Aberdeen, 1930, pp.46-7.

(iii) *The Duke of Newcastle to Lord Milton* (the Lord Justice
Clerk at Edinburgh).

My Lord,   Whitehall, December 14th, 1745.

I received last night, by express, the honour of your Lordship's
letter of the 9th instant, with the inclosed copies of Lord John
Drummond's letters to Major General Blakeney[1] and Lieutenant
General Guest[2], and laid it immediately before the King; and I have
sent His Majesty's orders to Marshal Wade, to acquaint the French
drummer that he had transmitted an account of this matter to the
King, and could not return any answer to the letter till he had His
Majesty's orders upon it;—

I have the satisfaction to acquaint your Lordship, that His
Majesty is taking the necessary measures for having, in a short time,
such a number of regular troops in Scotland as may, by the blessing
of God, be sufficient to put a speedy end to the present unnatural
rebellion. We are in the greatest hopes that we shall soon have the
pleasure to hear of his Royal Highness the Duke of Cumberland
having come up with that body of rebels which are now retreating in
great confusion towards Scotland; and in that case there is the
greatest reason to hope, that His Royal Highness will have been able
greatly to distress, if not entirely to reduce them.

Our latest advices from Dunkirk assure us, that the preparations
that have been for some time making at that place for an
embarkation, are in such forwardness that we expect soon to hear of
their being actually put to sea. It is generally thought their design is
to make some attempt upon the southern or eastern coast of this
kingdom, though some are of opinion that their destination is for
Scotland. We have had the good fortune to take three or four of their
ships going from Boulogne to Dunkirk with cloathing and bedding
for soldiers; and we have reason to hope, that the great number of
ships we have now cruising will be able to prevent them from
landing any troops in this kingdom. I am with great truth and
respect,

[1] Commanding Stirling Castle.
[2] The octogenarian commander of Edinburgh Castle

Printed in, John Home, *The History of the Rebellion
in the year 1745* (London, 1802), App.XXXII.

(iv) *Voltaire's Draft Manifesto: December 1745*

Declaration by the King of France in Support of Prince Charles Edward

Translation

His Most Serene Highness Charles Edward landed in Great Britain with no other resource than courage. All he has done has won the admiration of Europe and the hearts of all true Englishmen. The King of France is of the same mind as them. He has considered it his duty to help a Prince who is worthy of the throne of his ancestors and a warm-hearted nation of which the wisest part at least summons Prince Charles Stuart to his own country. He has sent across the Duke of Richelieu and his troops only because right-minded Englishmen have asked for this degree of support, and he employs in this no more than the number of troops asked of him, troops who are ready to withdraw as soon as the nation requires.

His Majesty in giving assistance to one who is at one and the same time his relative, the son of a long line of Kings, and a Prince so well-fitted to reign, only does so for the English nation, with the assured purpose of bringing peace to England and Europe, and sure in the knowledge that the Most Serene Prince Edward puts his trust in their good-will, and looks on their liberties, the upholding of their laws and their well-being as the end of all he has in view; and that the greatest Kings of England have been those who, like him, nurtured in adversity, have deserved the nation's love and affection.—

He hopes that an opportunity like this will reunite two nations which ought to hold each other in high esteem, and have a common bond in the requirements of trade.—

The Duke of Richelieu, commanding the troops of His Majesty the King of France addresses this declaration to all faithful citizens of the three kingdoms of Great Britain and assures them of the constant protection of the King his master. He has placed himself alongside the true successor to their former line of Kings, like him to hazard his life in serving them.

Printed in, F.J.McLynn, *France and the Jacobite Rising of 1745* (Edinburgh, 1981), App.III.

(v) *The Duc de Richelieu*

The Paris wits, ever frivolous, spun a rhyme about the Duc de Richelieu at this time. Watteau's '*L'Embarquement pour Cythère*' they thought was more his style!

"Quand je vis partir L'Excellence
　　De Richelieu,
Je prédis sa mauvaise chance
　　Hélas, Mon Dieu!
Ce pilote ignore les vents d'Angleterre,
Il ne sait qu'embarquer les gens
　　Pour l'île de Cythère."

"*His Grace the Duke's invasion fleet I saw,*
Mon Dieu, The sight of it filled me with woe,
This mariner knows naught of Channel gales,
It's for the Isle of Cythera he sails!"

Quoted in *Les Lettres de Marville* (Paris, 1903), Vol. II, pp. 247-8.

(vi) *Sir Thomas Sheridan Writes to France about the Postponement of Invasion*

Translation

Blair Castle in Athol 8th February 1746.

Sir,

You will no doubt be surprised that two weeks after a victory such as that of which I had the honour to tell you in my last letter, we have so soon after decided to retreat, but the disappointing outcome of the siege of Stirling Castle has brought a change to our plans. Yet another victory would not have enabled us to resume it.—

But, Sir, we see only too clearly that this is the second time that the postponement of the invasion project has forced us to retrace our steps when things were going splendidly for us. For the love of God, what do they think they are doing? Do they look on our success as a matter of indifference to France? Do they want us to perish? If such is not what the Court wants, they must really get down to business, and that without wasting any more time. If they do so, all will yet be well. If they don't, we will hold out as long as we can, but we need help of every kind, in artillery and all that goes with it, mortars, bombs, engineers etc, above all we need troops [ie from France] and a lot more money. Had we had two thousand regular troops at the last battle, the enemy would never have been able to make an orderly retreat. Artillery and baggage can always be replaced. Thus their loss is only the thousand men killed in the battle, which is more than I said in my last letter, there being apparently as many wounded and a thousand others taken prisoner or deserted. But the basis of their army is intact, and this will be a threat to us when they reflect on their retreat and that we lack regular troops to profit from a victory.

As to money, it is now essential that we be enabled to maintain our army and augment it. I have said so much about this, as has M. D'Eguilles,[1] that I need not say more. Allow me to say only that among captured papers taken at Falkirk, there was a letter from General Cope to one of his friends, in which he said that it was given out categorically in London that a French invasion was no longer expected. This would be a shattering blow for us and very dishonourable for France after all that has happened with all Europe watching. I make myself believe that it is a false report. However this is the impression that is gaining currency, and as you may imagine, it does nothing for the morale of the army. So it is deeds that are needed, and a lot of support to sustain us — not promises and mere crumbs.—

[1]Monsieur du Boyer Marquis d'Eguilles: The French "ambassador" to the Prince.

Printed in, James Browne, *A History of the Highlands and of the Highland Clans* (Glasgow, 1838), Vol.I, pp.457-8.

IV: The Fatal Dissension in the Highland Army

As soon as France at the turn of the year called off the intended invasion, the Prince's cause was doomed, even though Culloden still lay four months into the future. However it was the fatal dissension in the Jacobite command which ensured that the Rising would end in bloody disaster.

There had been some acrimony between the Prince and his Irish confidants, principally Sir Thomas Sheridan, on the one hand, and on the other, some of the Jacobite leaders, Lord George Murray in particular, from the days of the Highland Army's sojourn in Edinburgh. This was to be recorded in a narrative of the campaign by Lord Elcho who had joined the Prince before he took Edinburgh. The decision to retreat from Derby on 'Black Friday', the 6th of December 1745 was forced on the Prince amidst bitter exchanges between him and his army council which kept day to day control. But, after Derby, the Prince held no more councils. Three times on the forced march back to Scotland the lack of concerted command was potentially or, as regards the garrisoning of Carlisle, actually disastrous. However, for the historian concerned with written sources, Charles Edward's obduracy in this had the merit that when in early January, the Highland Army back in the Scottish Lowlands, tempers boiled over with a demand from Lord George Murray and the chiefs for a resumption of command by council, both this demand and the Prince's furious response were put *in writing*.

But the difficulties continued. The retreat into the Highlands (to wait for French help!) was a military shambles. Nemesis, when it came on Culloden Moor on the 16th of April was assisted by the continuing lack of strategic grip which had made available on the day of battle only two-thirds of the Jacobite strength; had brought about the physical exhaustion of those regiments that were available from an abortive night attack on the Duke of Cumberland's encampment; and had resulted in the choice of a field of battle by Colonel O'Sullivan (and the Prince) which gave every advantage to the Duke's army. The outcome was Cumberland's 'famous victory', won by his army's superior fire-power and discipline. The right wing of the Highland Army charged in something of a muddle to death and glory; the Clan Donald battalions, which that day made up the left wing, did not show their wonted *élan*. In terms of the relationship between Charles Edward and his Jacobite General, the culmination of all this was Lord George Murray's written onslaught on the Prince the day after the catastrophe of battle.

Lord George's thoughts would have been still more acrid had he been aware of the Prince's state of mind during this immediate aftermath of battle. Historians of the '45, from Sir Walter Scott onwards, have tended to cast doubt on the muted criticism of the Prince's conduct at this crisis in Lord Elcho's *Affairs of Scotland in the years 1745 and 1746*. Further evidence, which perhaps may be taken as conclusive, lies in Lord Elcho's private, and less inhibited, *Journal*, which has never been adequately used by historians (only now as we go to press is a biography of Elcho in prospect). Giving as it does a portrait both of the Prince, and of Elcho himself, it strongly reinforces the strictures in the *Affairs of Scotland*. Charles Edward abandoned his army in the immediate aftermath of Culloden. Lochiel's recently discovered narrative of the '45 confirms this.

(i) *The Prince and His Council*

(a) *Edinburgh*

The Prince formed a Council which mett regularly every morning in his drawing room. The Gentlemen that he Call'd to it Were The Duke of Perth, Lord Lewis Gordon, Lord George Murray, Lord Elcho, Lord Ogilvy, Lord Pitsligo, Lord Nairn Lochyell, Keppoch, Clanronald, Glenco, Lochgary, Ardshiel, Sir Thomas Sheridan, Coll. OSulivan, Glenbuckett & Secretary Murray.

The Prince in this Councill used Always first to declare what he was for, and then he Ask'd Every bodys opinion in their turn. There was one third of the Councill who's principals were that Kings and Princes Can never either act or think wrong, so in Consequence they always Confirmed whatever the Prince Said. The other two thirds, who thought that Kings and Princes thought sometimes like other men and were not altogether infallable and that this Prince was no more so than others, beg'd leave to differ from him, when they Could give Sufficient reasons for their difference of Opinion. Which very often was no hard matter to do, for as the Prince and his Old Governor Sir Thomas Sheridan were altogether ignorant of the Ways and Customs in Great Britain, and both much for the Doctrine of Absolute monarchy, they would very often, had they not been prevented, have fall'n into Blunders which might have hurt the Cause. The Prince Could not bear to hear any body differ in Sentiment from him, and took a dislike to Every body that did, for he had a Notion of Commanding this army As any General does a body of Mercenaries, and so lett them know only what he pleased, and they obey without inquiring further about the matter. This might have done better had his favourites been people of the Country, but as they were Irish And had nothing at Stake, The People of Fashion that had their all at Stake, and Consequently Ought to be Supposed to Give the best advice they were Capable of, thought they had a

216

title to know and be Consulted in what was for the Good of the Cause in which they had so much Concern; and if it had not been for their insisting Strongly upon it, the Prince when he found that his Sentiments were not always approved of, would have Abolish'd this Council long ere he did.

David, Lord Elcho, *A Short Account of the Affairs of Scotland in the Years 1744, 1745, 1746*
(1907, reprinted James Thin, Edinburgh, 1973), pp.288-90.

(b) *Carlisle*

The Prince held a Councill at Carlisle, wherein he proposed Going Straight to London. The answere that was made was that the army came up to join his English friends or a French Landing, but could not pretend putting him in possession of the crown of England without either, and that it was better to wait at Carlyle for the reinforcements Colonel Maclauchlan had gone for than to think of taking any Step before their arrival. The Prince said he was sure all his English friends would join him in Lancashire. Mr du Boyer assured every body of a French Landing daily, and Mr Murray, who was tresorer as well as Secretary, said that it was impossible to stay longer at Carlisle for want of Money, so every body agreed to March on. The Prince flatter'd himself every body would receive him with joyfull hearts, and that he would meet with no opposition, and the rest of The Gentlemen were determined to carry him to the utmost bounds of Lancashire, that people might not say afterwards had the army march'd to Lancashire the English would certainly have joined, and the French being sure of meeting friends would have been encouraged to Land.

Elcho; op.cit, pp.323-4.

(c) *Derby*

The 4 of December the whole Army marched into Darby.—The 5 in the morning Lord George Murray and all the Commanders of Battalions and Squadrons waited upon the Prince, and Lord George told him that it was the opinion of Every body present that the Scots had now done all that could be Expected of them. That they had marched into the heart of England ready to join any party that would declare for him, that none had, and that the Counties through which the Army had pass'd had Seemed much more Enemies than friends to his Cause, that their was no French Landed in England, and that if their was any party in England for him, it was very odd that they had never so much as Either sent him money or intelligence or the least advice what to do, but if he Could produce any letter from any person of distinction in which their was an invitation for the army to go to London, or to any other part of England, that they were ready to go. But if nobody had either invited them or meddled in the least in their affairs, it was to be Supposed that their was either no party at all, or if their was they did not chuse to act with them, or else they would ere now have lett them know it. Suppose even the Army march'd on and beat the Duke of Cumberland yett in the Battle they must Lose some men, and they had after that the Kings own army consisting of 7000 men near London to deal with. On the contrary, if either of these armies beat them, their would not a man Escape, as the militia, altho they durst never face the army while in a body, yett they would have courage enough to putt an end to them if ever they were routed. And so the people that were in arms in Scotland would fall an Easy Sacrifice to the fury of the Government. Again, Suppose the Army was to Slip the Kings & Dukes army and gett into London, the success of the Affair would intirely depend upon the mobs declaring for or against it, and that if the Mob had been much inclined to his Cause, since his march into England, that to be sure some of his friends in London would have fall'n upon some method to have lett him Know'n it, but if the Mob was against the Affair 4500 men would not make a great figure in London. Lord George concluded by Saying that the Scots army had done their part, that they Came into England at the Princes request, to join his English friends, and to give them Courage by their appearance to take arms and declare for him publickly as they had done, or to join the French if they had Landed; but as none of these things had happened, that certainly 4500 Scots had never thought of putting a King upon the English Throne by themselves. So he Said his Opinion was they Should go back and join their friends in Scotland, and live and die with them,—After Lord George had spoke he desired all the rest of the Gentlemen present to Speak their sentiments, and they all agreed with Lord George except two, [The Duke of Perth and Sir William Gordon] who were for going to Wales to see if the Welch would join.—The Prince heard all these arguments with the greatest impatience, fell into a passion and gave most of the Gentlemen that had Spoke very Abusive Language, and said that they had a mind to betray him. The Case was he knew nothing about the country nor had not the Smallest Idea of the force that was against him, nor where they were Situated. His Irish favourites to pay court to him had always represented the whole nation as his friends, had diminished much all the force that was Against him, & he himself believed firmly That the Soldiers of the Regulars would never dare fight against him, as he was Their true Prince. For all the Success he had had as yett he attributed more to the mens Consciences not

Allowing them to fight against him, than to The power of the Broad Sword, and he always believed he Should enter St James's with as little difficulty as he had done Holyrood house. He Continued all that day positive he would march to London; the Irish in the army were always for what he was for, and were heard to say that day that they knew if they escaped being killed the worst that could happen to them was some months imprisonment. The Scots were all against it: so at Night the Prince Sent for them and told them he consented to go to Scotland, And at the same time he told them that for the future he would have no more Councills, for he would neither ask nor take their Advice, that he was Accountable to nobody for his Actions but to his Father; and he was as good as his word, for he never after advised with any body but the Irish Officers, Mrs Murray & Hay, and never more summons'd a Councill.

Elcho; op.cit, pp.336-341.

(d) *Stirling*
Lord George Murray's Letter

Jan ye 6th 1746.

It is proposed that His Royal Highness shou'd from time to time call a Council of War to consist of all those who command Battalions or Squadrons; but as severals of those may be on partys, and often absent, a Committee should be chosen by those Commanders, to consist of five or seven, and that all Operations for the carrying on the War shou'd be agreed on, by the Majority of those in His Royal Highness presence, and once that a Measure is taken, it is not to be changed except by the advice of those, or most of them, who were present when it was agreed on.

That upon any sudden Emergency such as in a Battle, Skirmish, or in a Siege, a Discretionary power must be allowed to those who command. This is the Method of all Armys, and where so many Gentlemen of Fortune, not only venture their own and their Familys All, But if any Misfortune happen are sure of ending their lives on a Scaffold should they escape in the field, if this plan is not followed the most Dismal Consequence cannot but ensue.

Had not a Council determined the Retreat from Derby, what a Catastrophy must have followed in two or three Days! Had a Council of War been held the Army came to Lancaster, a Day (which at that time was so precious) had not been lost. Had a Council of War been consulted as to the leaving a Garrison at Carlisle it would never have been agreed to, the place not being tenable, and so many brave men wou'd not have been sacrifized, besides the reputation of his Royal Highness Arms.

It is to be considered that this Army is an Army of Volunteers, and not Mercenarys, many of them being resolved not to continue in the Army, were affairs once settled.

GEORGE MURRAY.

Home's History; also in
Itinerary of Prince Charles Edward Stuart;
by W.B.Blaikie; Scottish History Society, 1897;
Appendix, the Prince and Lord George Murray.
(Reprinted, 1975).

The Prince's Reply

When I came into Scotland I knew well enough what I was to expect from my Ennemies, but I little foresaw what I meet with from my Friends. I came vested with all the Authority the King cou'd give me, one chief part of which is the Command of his Armies, and now I am required to give this up to fifteen or sixteen Persons, who may afterwards depute five or seven of their own number to exercise it, for fear if they were six or eight that I might myself pretend to ye casting vote. By the majority of these all things are to be determined, and nothing left to me but the honour of being present at their debates. This I am told is the method of all Armies and this I flatly deny, nor do I believe it to be the Method of any one Army in the World. I am often hit in the teeth that this is an Army of Volunteers, and consequently very different from one composed of Mercenarys. What one wou'd naturally expect from an Army whose chief Officers consist of Gentlemen of rank and fortune, and who came into it meerly upon Motives of Duty and Honour, is more zeal, more resolution and more good manners than in those that fight meerly for pay: but it can be no Army at all where there is no General, or which is the same thing no Obedience or deference paid to him. Every one knew before he engaged in the cause, what he was to expect in case it miscarried, and shoud have staid at home if he could not face Death in any shape: but can I myself hope for better usage? at least I am the only Person upon whose head a Price has been already set, and therefore I cannot indeed threaten at every other Word to throw down my Arms and make my Peace with the Government.—

Home's History also in Itinerary; op.cit.;
Appendix, the Prince and Lord George Murray.

(ii) *The Battle of Culloden*

(a) *As Seen by the Royal Army*

—When we were advanced within five Hundred Yards of the Rebels, we found the Morass, upon our Right, was ended, which left our Right-Flank quite uncovered to them; his Royal Highness thereupon immediately ordered Kingston's Horse from the Reserve, and a little Squadron of about sixty of Cobham's, which had been patrolling, to cover our Flank; and Pultney's Regiment was ordered from the Reserve to the Right of the Royals....We spent above Half an Hour after that, trying which should gain the Flank of the other; and his Royal Highness having sent Lord Bury forward, within one Hundred Yards of the Rebels, to reconnoitre something, that appeared somewhat like a Battery to us, they thereupon began firing their Cannon, which was extreamly ill pointed: Ours immediately answered them, which began their Confusion. They then came running on in their wild Manner; and upon the Right, where his Royal Highness had placed himself, imagining the greatest Push would be there, they came down three several times, within an Hundred Yards of our Men, firing their Pistols, and brandishing their Swords; but the Royals and Pultney's hardly took their Firelocks from their Shoulders; so that after those faint Attempts, they made off, and the little Squadrons on our Right, were sent to pursue them. General Hawley had, by the Help of our Highlanders, beat down two little Stone-Walls, and came in upon the Right-Flank of their Second Line. As their whole First Line came down to attack at once, their Right somewhat out-flanked Barrel's Regiment, which was our Left; and the greatest Part of the little Loss we sustained, was there; but Bligh's and Semple's giving a Fire upon those who had out-flanked Barrel's, soon repulsed them, and Barrel's Regiment, and the Left of Monro's, fairly beat them with their Bayonets: There was scarce a Soldier or Officer of Barrel's, and of that Part of Munro's which engaged, who did not kill one or two Men each with their Bayonets and Spontoons. The Cavalry, which had charged from the Right and Left, met in the Center, except two Squadrons of Dragoons, which we missed, and they were gone in Pursuit of the Runaways: Lord Ancrum was ordered to pursue, with the Horse, as far as he could; and did it with so good Effect, that a very considerable Number was killed in the Pursuit.

As we were in our March to Inverness, and were near arrived there, Major General Bland had also made great Slaughter, and took about Fifty French Officers and Soldiers Prisoners, in his Pursuit.—

The London Gazette, April 26th, 1746.

221

(b) *Lord George Murray's View*

Ruthven,[1] 17 Apl. 1746.

May it please your Royal Highness.

As no person in these kingdomes ventured more franckly in the cause than my self and as I had more at stake than almost all the others put together, so to be sure I cannot but be very deeply affected wth our late loss and present situation, but I declare that were your R.H. person in safety, the loss of the cause and the misfortune and unhappy situation of my countrymen is the only thing that grieves me, for I thank God, I have resolution to bear my own and family's ruine without a grudge.

Sir, you will I hope upon this occasion pardon me if I mention a few truths which all the gentlemen of our army seem convinced of. It was highly wrong to have set up the royal standard without having positive assurance from his most Christian Majesty that he would assist you with all his force, and as your royal family lost the crown of these realms upon the account of France, the world did and had reason to expect that France would seize the first favorable opportunity to restore your august family.

I must also acquaint your R.H. that we were all fully convinced that Mr. O'Sullivan whom your R.H. trusted with the most essential things with regard to your operations was exceedingly unfit for it and committed gross blunders on every occasion of moment. He whose business it was, did not so much as visit the ground where we were to be drawn up in line of battle and it was a fatal error yesterday to allow the enemy those walls upon their left which made it impossible for us to break them, and they with their front frie and flanking us when we went upon the attack destroying us without any possibility of our breaking them, and our Atholl men have lost a full half of their officers and men. I wish Mr. O'Sulivan had never got any other charge in the army than the care of the baggage which I have been told he has been brought up to and understood. I never saw him in time of action neither at Gladsmur, Falkirk nor in the last, and his orders were vastly confused.

The want of provisions was another misfortune which had the most fatal consequence. Mr. Hay whom yr R.H. trusted with the principal direction of ordering provisions of late and without whose orders a boll of meal or farthing of monie was not to be delivered, has served yr R.H. egregiously ill. When I spoke to him, he told me, the thing is ordered, it will be got etc., but he neglected his duty to such a degree that our ruin might probably [have] been prevented had he done his duty; in shortt the three last days which were so critical our army was starved. This was the reason our night march was rendered abortive, when we possibly might have surprized and defeat the enemy at Nairn, but for want of provisions a third of the army scattered to Inverness etc. and the others who marched had not spirits to make it so quick as was necessary being really faint for want of provisions.

The next day, which was the fatal day, if we had got plenty of provisions, we might have crossed the water of Nairn and drawn up so advantageously that we would have obliged the enemy to come to us, for they were resolved to fight at all hazards, at prodigious disadvantage, and probably we would in that case have done by them as they unhappily have done by us.

In short Mr. O'Sulivan and Mr. Hay had rendered themselves odious to all our army and had disgusted them to such a degree that they had bred a mutiny in all ranks that had not the battle come on they were to have represented their grievance to yr R.H. for a remedy. For my own part I never had any particular discussion with either of them, but I ever thought them uncapable and unfit to serve in the stations they were placed in.

Yr R.H. knows I always told I had no design to continue in the army. I would of late when I came last from Atholl have resigned my Commission, but all my friends told me it might be of prejudice to the cause at such a critical time. I hope your R.H. will now accept of my demission. What command you have for me in any other situation please honor me with them. I am with great zeal

Sir
your R.H. most dutifull and humble servant
GEORGE MURRAY.

I have taken the liberty to keep 500 peices which shant be disposed upon except you give leave.

[1]Ruthven; the former government garrison post in Badenoch.

Blaikie, *Itinerary*;
Appendix, "The Prince and Lord George Murray".

(c) *The Prince's Flight from Culloden as described by Lord Elcho*

The Prince, as soon as he saw the left of his army yielding and in retreat, lost his head, fled with the utmost speed, and without even trying to rally any of his scattered host—The Prince made a halt 4 miles from the field of battle, and I found him in a deplorable state. As he had ever been flattered with false hopes that the army of the Duke would fly before him like those of Cope and Hawley, he believed that all his disaster was caused by treason, and appeared to be afraid of the Scotch as a whole, thinking that they would be capable of giving him up to the Duke to obtain peace, and the 30,000£ sterling that the King had offered for his head. He asked if all the Irish officers had superior grades in his army which might be of use to them on their return to France. He appeared to be concerned only about the lot of the Irish and not at all about that of the Scots, and seeing the number of Scotch officers around him increase, he ordered them to go away to a village a mile's distance from where he was, and he would send his orders thither. I remained after their departure and asked if he had any orders for me. He told me that I might go anywhere I liked; as for himself, he was about to leave for France. I told him that I was surprised at a resolution so little worthy a Prince of his birth, that it was unworthy to have engaged all this people to sacrifice itself for him, and to abandon it because he had possibly lost a thousand men in battle; that he ought to remain and put himself at the head of the 9000 men that remained to him, and live and die with them. I pointed out to him that he came into the country without troops and that he would have an army of 9000 men still in spite of the loss of the battle; consequently his position was better than when he arrived. I represented to him also that all his followers finding themselves without leaders would separate and then fall into the vengeful hands of the Duke of Cumberland. But all these reasons made no impression upon him. He told me that he was determined to seek safety in France: whereupon I left him, thoroughly resolved never to have any more to do with him.

From Lord Elcho's *Journal*, part of which is reproduced in *A Jacobite Miscellany*; ed. Henrietta Tayler (Roxburghe Club, 1948), pp.163-4.

V: After Culloden

Culloden was to take its place in Scottish folk memory not for the Royal Army's discipline in the face of its enemy but for the slaughter of wounded Highlanders as they lay on and around the field of battle. The exhilaration of victory over a greatly feared enemy perhaps may excuse much; the subsequent attempt by the Royal Army's commanders to justify the barbarities that took place (by putting about a doctored copy of the Highland Army's orders for the approaching battle) cannot.

Cumberland's reputation has deservedly suffered for this; as Sir Walter Scott, with carefully chosen words, would write, the Duke was "somewhat implicated in the events of that day." What can be said to put in perspective the other aspect of the Royal Army's conduct, the subsequent wasting of certain Jacobite glens and islands, has however remained unsaid down the years. A full month after Culloden the western clans were still under arms with Lochiel their leader — this despite overtures for peace which, according to Jacobite sources, had been made by the Duke from his army headquarters at Inverness. The Duke saw the wasting of the 'countries' of the clans keeping up the struggle as a necessary last resort. He never expressed the slightest regret for the whirlwind of atrocity he unleashed.

Retribution exacted from the prisoners of the '45 was also severe. Some eighty hangings, some three thousand transported to the Barbadoes (and fortunate indeed if they survived the prison hulks on the Thames to reach their destination). Three rebel peers were executed, one of whom was Lord Lovat. As was the 18th century custom, a man about to die on the scaffold was permitted a last speech, and those of condemned Jacobites were collected and published. These are of enduring value as they reveal the nobler — as opposed to the opportunistic or self-interested — side of Jacobitism. But Scotland did not forget or forgive.

(i) *Lord George Murray's Orders to the Highland Army for the Coming Battle and their Subsequent Falsification as to Denial of Quarter*

(a) *The Actual Orders*

[From the Cumberland Papers in the Royal Archives, Windsor, in Lord George Murray's hand.]

'Orders from the 14th to the 15th Apl. 1746.
[pass-word] Rie James (in Inglish King James).

It is His Royall Highness posetive Orders that Evry person atatch themselves to some Corps of The Armie & to remain with that Corps night & day till the Batle & persuit be finally over; This regards the Foot as well as the Horse.
The Order of Batle is to be given to evry Ginerall Officer & evry Commander of Regiments or Squadrons.
It is required & expected that each individual in the Armie as well Officer as Souldiers keep their posts that shall be alotted to them, & if any man turn his back to Runaway the nixt behind such man is to shoot him.
No body on Pain of Death to Strip the Slain or Plunder till the Batle be over. The Highlanders all to be in Kilts, & no body to throw away their Guns; by H.R.H.'s Command. George Murray.

(b) *The Falsification*

As above, but with the addition of "And to give no quarters to the Elector's Troops, on any account whatsoever" after "until the Batle & persuit be finally over".

A History of the Rebellion in the Years 1745 and 1746,
ed. Henrietta Tayler; Roxburghe Club
(London, 1944), p.xix.

(ii) *The Western Clans Remain under Arms*

(a) *Their Compact of 8th May 1746*

At Muirlaggan, the 8th of May, 1746.

We, subscribers, heads of Clans, commanders and leaders, do hereby unanimously agree, and solemnly promise forthwith, with the utmost expedition, to raise in arms, for the interest of His Royal Highness Charles Prince of Wales, and in defence of our country, all the able-bodied men that all and every one of us can command or raise, within our respective interests or properties.

Item, We hereby promise and agree, that the following Clans, viz. Lochiel, Glengary, Clanronald, Stewarts of Appin, Keppoch, Barrisdale, Mackinnon, and Macleods, shall rendezvous on Thursday next the 15th instant, at Auchnicarry, in the braes of Lochaber.—

Item, To facilitate the junction of our army, with all possible speed, it is agreed, that the Frasers of Aird, and others our friends on the north side of the river Ness, shall join the people of Glenmoriston and Glengary; and that the Frasers of Stratherrick, the Macintoshes, and Macphersons, shall assemble and meet at the most convenient place in Badenoch, on Thursday the 15th current.

Item, The Macgregors, Menzies, and Glenlyon's people, shall march to Rannoch, and join the Rannoch and Athol men; and be ready to receive intelligence and orders to meet the main body in the braes of Mar, or any other place that shall be most convenient.

Item, It is agreed, that Major-general Gordon of Glenbucket, and Colonel Roy Stuart, shall advertise Lord Lewis Gordon, Lord Ogilvie, Lord Pitsligo, the Farquharsons, and the other principal gentlemen of the North, with the resolutions taken at this meeting; and that they shall agree among themselves as to a place of rendezvous, so as to be able to join the army where it shall be judged most proper.

Item, That Clunie Macpherson, and Colonel Roy Stuart, shall advertise the principal gentlemen of the Macintoshes, of our resolutions.—

Lastly, We further promise and engage ourselves, each to the other, to stand and abide by these our resolutions, for the interest of His Royal Highness, and the good of our country, which we apprehend to be inseparable, to the last drop of our blood; and never to lay down our arms, or make a separate peace, without the general consent of the whole. And in case any one engaged in this association shall make separate terms for himself, he shall be looked upon as a traitor to his Prince, and treated by us as an enemy.

John Home, *The History of the Rebellion in the year 1745;*
(London, 1802), Appendix XLVII.

[1]Muirlaggan is on Loch Arkaig-side.

(b) *Lochiel to Cluny (chief of the Clan Macpherson)*
writing on 15 May 1746

—We are preparing for a summer campaign and hope soon to join our forces. Mr Murray [the Prince's erstwhile Secretary] desires if any of the picquets [of the Irish Brigade] or the men of Lord John Drummond's regiment, or any other pretty fellows, are straggling in

227

your country that you convene them and keep them with yourself till we join you.

Home, op. cit., Appendix XLVIII.

(iii) *Last Testaments*

(a) *Lord Balmerino*

The Speech of the Right Honourable Arthur,
Lord Balmerino, faithfully transcribed from his
Lordship's Own Handwrit

I was brought up in true loyal Anti-Revolution principles, and I hope the world is convinced that they stick to me.

I must acknowledge I did a very inconsiderate thing, for which I am heartily sorry, in accepting of a company of foot from the Princess Anne, who I knew had no more right to the crown than her predecessor the Prince of Orange, whom I always look upon as a vile, unnatural usurper.

To make amends for what I had done I join'd the King when he was in Scotland, and when all was over I made my escape and liv'd abroad till the year 1734.

In the beginning of that year I got a letter from my father which very much surprized me. It was to let me know that he had got the promise of a remission for me. I did not know what to do. I was then, I think, in the Canton of Bern and had no body to advise with. But next morning I wrote a letter to the King, who was then at Rome, to acquaint his Majesty that this was done without my asking or knowledge, and that I would not accept of without his Majesty's consent. I had in answer to mine a letter written with the King's own hand allowing me to go home, and he told me his banker would give me money for my travelling charges when I came to Paris, which accordingly I got.

When his royal highness came to Edinburgh, as it was my bounden and indispensible duty, I join'd him, though I might easily have excused myself from taking arms on account of my age. But I never could have had peace of conscience if I had stayed at home when that brave Prince was exposing himself to all manner of dangers and fatigue both night and day.

I am at a loss when I come to speak of the Prince; I am not a fit hand to draw his character. I shall leave that to others. But I must beg leave to tell you the incomparable sweetness of his nature, his affability, his compassion, his justice, his temperance, his patience, and his courage are virtues, seldom all to be found in one person. In short, he wants no qualifications requisite to make a great man.—

I have heard since I came to this place that there has been a most wicked report spread and mentioned in several of the Newspapers, that his royal highness, the Prince, before the battle of Culloden, had given out in orders that no quarters should be given to the enemy. This is such an unchristian thing and so unlike that gallant Prince that nobody that knows him will believe it. It is very strange if there had been any such orders that neither the Earl of Kilmarnock, who was Colonel of the regiment of Foot-guards, nor I, who was Colonel of the 2d troop of Life-guards, should never have heard any thing of it, especially since we were both at the head-quarters the morning before the battle. I am convinced that it is a malicious report industriously spread to excuse themselves for the murders they were guilty of in calm blood after the battle.—

I hope you will have the charity to believe I die in peace with all men, for yesterday I received the Holy Eucharist from the hands of a clergyman of the Church of England, in whose Communion I die as in union with the Episcopal Church of Scotland.

I shall conclude with a short prayer.

O Almighty God! I humbly beseech Thee to bless the King, the prince, and Duke of Yorke, and all the dutiful branches of the royal family! Endue them with thy Holy Spirit, enrich them with thy heavenly grace, prosper them with all happiness and bring them to thine everlasting kingdom! Finally I recommend to thy fatherly goodness all my benefactors and all the faithful adherents to the cause for which I am now about to suffer. God reward them! Make them happy here and in the world to come! This I beg for Christs sake, in whose words, etc. Our Father, etc.

The Lyon in Mourning, ed Henry Paton,
Scottish History Society (Edinburgh, 1895, republished 1975),
pps.32-3.

(b) *Thomas Deacon*

(Deacon was one of the three sons of the non-juring Bishop in Manchester who joined the Prince's army. He was taken prisoner at the surrender of Carlisle Castle).

My Dear Fellow-Countrymen,—I am come here to pay the last debt to nature, and I think myself happy in having an opportunity of dying in so just and so glorious a cause. The deluded and infatuated vulgar will no doubt brand my death with all the infamy that ignorance and prejudice can suggest. But the thinking few who have not quite forsaken their duty to God and their king, will I am persuaded look upon it as being little inferiour to martyrdom itself, for I am just going to fall a sacrifice to the resentment and revenge of the Elector of Hanover and all those unhappy miscreants who have openly espoused the cause of a foreign German usurper and withdrawn their allegiance from their only rightful, lawful and native sovereign, King James the 3d. It would be trifling here to expatiate on the loss of so many brave subjects' lives who have had the courage to appear in defence of their native King; the vast, the immense treasure squandered away in defence of the Usurper; the heavy load of taxes and debts under which the nation groans; the prevalence of bribery and corruption; the preference of strangers to natives, and innumerable other inconveniences which must necessarily attend a foreigner's sitting on the throne of Great Britain, and which must be too obvious to every impartial, unprejudiced Englishman.

Moreover, I think it is very evident that the very mercy of the Usurper is no less than arbitrary power, and the freedom of Parliament, bribery, and corruption; from which unhappy circumstances nothing else can restore this nation and bring it to its former happiness and glory but inviting King James the 3d to take possession of his undoubted right.

I profess I die a member, not of the Church of Rome, nor yet that of England, but of a pure Episcopal Church which has reform'd all the errors, corruptions and defects that have been introduc'd into the modern Churches of Christendom — a church which is in perfect communion with the antient and universal Church of Christ, by adhering uniformly to antiquity, universality and consent, that glorious principle which if once strictly and impartially pursued would, and which alone can, remove all the distractions and unite all the divided branches of the Christian Church.—

ibid., I, p. 22.

(c) *Euan MacVey*

[MacVey was one of Lochiel's men, captured in the August of 1746 as he carried a message, from the two French officers of the fourth rescue attempt from France, addressed to the master of their brigantine skulking in the waters near Loch Broom. Their message was that the Prince had been found. MacVey's interrogation took place in the Tolbooth of Inverness; he died soon after.]

Eavan McKay was taken in the Highlands by a whig teacher with letters in French or cyphers, and was sent into town where he was most barbarously and inhumanly treated. Being asked from whom he had and to whom he was going with the letters, to which he giving no answer, got five hunderd lashes, being ty'd to a stake, and then sent to prison again. Some days after he got five hundered more, and they threatn'd to whip him to death if he would not discover what they wanted. None durst go nigh him while in the pit with any necessary; and when they threw down a pound of meal, which was all the allowance given to any one of the prisoners, it was found untouch'd, he being sickly, full of sores, and most barbarously struck by one of the sogars with the butt of his gun in the breast, of which he complain'd while he lived. At last he was carryed to the Tolbooth. One there said to him that he was a great fool not to discover what he knew, to which he gave a noble return: You are the fool. It signifies nothing what they can do to me (Let them do the worst) in respect of what could be done to those from whom I had and to whom I was going with the letters. Their deaths would be great loss, but mine will be none.—

[The papers of Lord Albemarle, commander-in-chief after Cumberland's departure, confirm this, though a thousand lashes was perhaps an exaggeration.]

ibid., II,p. 300.

VI: The '45 as seen by Lord Chesterfield from Dublin Castle

Westminster politics had been notably unstable in the early 1740s and in 1744, in a bid for stability there was formed "the Broad Bottom" ministry which was essentially a coalition between a powerful Court Whig group of former supporters of Sir Robert Walpole, led by the Pelham brothers and Lord Hardwicke, and malcontent Whigs such as Chesterfield, Devonshire, Bedford and Cobham, to which was added the leader of the Hanoverian To-ries, Lord Gower, and for a time Sir John Hynde Cotton, an active Tory with a history of Jacobite contacts. It proved, predictably, a most unstable regime, because its members had little in common. Lord Chesterfield, who was personally obnoxious to George II, was given the post of Viceroy of Ireland, because it meant he would be removed from the royal presence.

In fact Chesterfield went to the Netherlands in February 1745, rather than Dublin, to act as British Ambassador, charged with the difficult job of keeping the Dutch loyal to the anti-French coalition which was not faring well in the war, and was to fare worse, in the sense that before he left the Netherlands Chesterfield had witnessed the heavy defeat of the Duke of Cumberland's army by Marshal Saxe at Fontenoy on May 11.

By the very end of August, Chesterfield had finally reached Dublin to start fulfilling his duties as Viceroy. Almost at once, he heard news of the start of the '45 in Scotland. His correspondence with the elder of the Pelham brothers, the Duke of Newcastle, is extraordinarily revealing. It brings out three important points. One is the almost completely defenceless state of the Kingdom of Ireland, whose armed forces had been reduced to a risible level, by withdrawal of troops for service on the Continent. The second is the completely relaxed response of Chesterfield to this fact. His celebrated urbanity was put on show. Since he expected any French invasion to be aimed at England, he saw no cause for panic in Ireland. He repudiated with contempt the surge of no-Popery agitation in England, with its persecution of Roman Catholics as a potential fifth column. Chesterfield was positively benign towards the Roman Catholic majority in Ireland. He and Newcastle corresponded mainly on European affairs. Thirdly, the correspondence shows the other side of Chesterfield's urbane mask. Faced with a serious challenge to the Westminster political structure, Chesterfield was savagely angry. In the end he urged that the known food shortage in Scotland might be used as a means of genocide, and he was happy to starve government loyalists alongside the Scots Jacobites.

(a) *Chesterfield to Newcastle.*

Dublin Castle, Sept. 2nd 1745.

My dear Lord,

—By letters from Scotland here the young Pretender's affair seems every day to grow more serious, but, as I can't very well

232

depend upon those accounts, I have sent a trusty smuggler to the north of Scotland for more authentick informations. He is gone to the Macdonalds, with whom he has had frequent dealings, and I am assur'd that I may depend upon his accounts.

The little time I have been here has been employ'd in ceremony and noise, and I am sure I have my drums and trumpets with a vengeance. But by what little inquirys·I have yet been able to make this country appears to be in a most defenceless condition. The forts are extremely out of repair, the militia in the several countys absolutely neglected, and the regular troops, as you very well know, very few.

I suppose the King is arriv'd by this time; and I long to hear the consequences of his arrival. Whatever they may be, you will find me equally in every and any situation,

(b) *Chesterfield to Newcastle.*

Dublin Castle, Oct. 5th 1745.

—I look upon the rebellion in Scotland as crush'd, as soon as our army gets there; the Highlanders will then return to their dens, and trust to their damn'd country for their security. But I hope they will not find it there. And were I to direct, I would have a short Act of Parliament for the transporting to the West Indies every man concern'd in the rebellion, and give a reward for every one that should be apprehended and brought to transporttion. This I think would be a much better way than hanging some of the rascals and letting the others go home for another rebellion.

All my good subjects here are unanimously zealous; but unanimosuly frighten'd too, which I confess I am not. They think themselves of so much importance as to be the principal objects of the designs of our enemies; whereas I rather think that our enemies are well enough inform'd to know that this country must necessarily follow the fate of England, and that their whole force will consequently be directed there, and not divided to do here what would either do of itself, or not do at all. However I take all the proper precautions *à bon compte*, but without encouraging the millions of projects that are every day offer'd me. I believe I shall find no difficultys in Parliament here. I fear you can't say so much of yours. I am with the truest regard and attachment,

(c) *Newcastle to Chesterfield.*

Newcastle House, Nov. 20th 1745.

Most private
My dear Lord,

—I have this moment an account of the surrender of the castle of
Carlisle, pretty soon after the surrender of the town, whereby the
rebels have made themselves masters of several pieces of canon, a
quantity of arms, and a number of horses. Every day shews that this
rebellion is by no means a trifle.

(d) *Chesterfield to Newcastle.*

Dublin Castle, Nov. 25th 1745.

My dear Lord,

—As to the rebellion, I confess I am not under the least
apprehensions of it, nor should I be very uneasy if it were to be
seconded by an invasion from abroad; the regular force we now
have in England and the fleets we have round it being more than
sufficient to crush the rebels and to prevent or repel a foreign
invasion, unless we are doom'd to destruction. If we are to fear now,
when are we not to fear? since from the circumstances (in that
respect only fortunate) of the war abroad we have now at home a
greater land and sea force than we are every likely to have at any
given time hereafter. The number and condition of the rebels is
contemptible, and, should they be joyn'd by any insurrection in
England, they would only be joyn'd by people still more
contemptible than themselves. Our mob regiments (I ask their
pardons) would be still better than theirs, and our regular trooops I
am convinc'd are fully equal to three times their own number of
undisciplined rabble. And I make no doubt but that before your
Grace receives this you will have received a much better letter from
General Wade with an account of the destruction or at least the
dispersion of those Scottish rascals. In short I see an end, and I think
a speedy one, of the rebellion—

(e) *Chesterfield to Newcastle.*

Dublin Castle, Dec. 6th 1745.

My dear Lord,

—I wish the trouble of the rebellion were over, for, as for danger,
I confess I see none. I depend upon my Marcellus, the Duke, for
exterminating those rascals more than I do upon your Fabius [sc.

234

Wade]. Why did he stay a month at Newcastle? Why wait for a train of artillery against such fellows? Why not attack 'em with any numbers? Are they to be consider'd as regular troops, who were never yet attack'd by any number of regular troops without being beaten? Why does not Handaside crush those fellows in Perth? He has more troops than are necessary for that business. You did extremely right to repulse Stair's Scotch regiments, and for my own part I am very sorry to hear that any loyall Highlanders are to be arm'd at all. The proverb indeed says, "set a thief to catch a thief", but I beg leave to except Scotch thieves. And I both hope and believe that those to whom I see money is given to raise loyall Highlanders will put that money in their pockets and not raise a man. Upon my word, if you give way to Scotch importunitys and jobbs upon this occasion, you will have a rebellion every seven years at least. There must be alertness and vigour in crushing of this, and unrelenting severity in punishing it afterwards. Will you upon any sollicitation whatever suffer the notorious treachery of honest Stewart, the Provost of Edinburgh, to pass unpunish'd? I have witnesses here who saw the dog receive the Pretender into Edinburgh and do the honours of the town to him with the utmost duty and zeal. The French feed the rebellion only to hinder it from dying of hunger, but not enough to make it thrive. It is only to incline you to negotiation, to which they think you wholly averse. As soon as they find the contrary, I am persuaded there will be an end of their assistance.—

(f) *Newcastle to Chesterfield.*

Newcastle House, Jan. 6th 1745/6.

private.
My dear Lord,

The continual hurry I have been in from the rebellion at home and the threatened invasion from abroad, as well as the unsettled state of our domestick affairs, must be my excuse for having been so long silent.

The vigour, activity, and courage of the Duke, your young Marcellus, have drove the rebels to the place from whence they came, where I hope General Hawley will not only be able to prevent their return, but entirely to reduce and defeat them there. I own I have a more mean opinion of them than I had before H.R.H. with an handful of men chased them through great part of England. But that which did, and does, alarm me most, is the declared part which France takes in their favour.—And, though I rather think from the condition we are in to receive them and from the number of ships we have at present at sea, and from the Pretender's flight, that their design may be at present suspended, yet I am still of opinion that they keep it up, and shall not be surprized if we hear of them, and that soon, on some part of the coast, tho' perhaps not so near London as was at first apprehended.

I send you out of curiosity Lord John Drummond's declaration. Such an avowed engagement in favour of the Pretender and his family has not been taken by France since King James's time, and may cost us some pains to oblige them to recede from; which brings me to our present political resolution and foreign system, which I hope you will approve.—

(g) *Newcastle to Chesterfield.*
Newcastle House, Feb. 10th 1745/6.

My dear Lord,

I have only time to acquaint you that this day Lord Harrington and I resign'd the Seals to His Majesty. My Brother does the same to-morrow, and Lord Chancellor and probably some others soon after. This resolution was taken upon a firm conviction that the King's dislike of his ministers and disapprobation of them, and unwillingness to give them the necessary support, made it impracticable for us to carry on his affairs with success. Lord Bath has lately had frequent access to the Closet and a favourable reception there, in preference, as we had reason to think, to those who were to be responsible for the success of affairs. Our situation therefore became as dangerous as it was disagreeable. And, as your young Marcellus had by his bare appearance drove the rebels to their mountains, we thought the publick affairs could not suffer with regard to the rebellion at home, and the intended invasion from France is at present laid aside, and I hope we are now so well armed, both by sea and land, that they will not venture to resume it. The Duke of Bedford and Gower, I believe, will resign to-morrow. All friends are perfectly well. I need not put you in mind that I have no longer any power over the Postmaster.[1]

[1]This final remark, though technically true, was tongue-in-cheek, for by their resignation, along with all their supporters, the Pelham brothers, Henry and the Duke of Newcastle, expected to, and did

bring George II to acknowledge that only they could run his government successfully. Resignation was the prelude to ascendancy.

Printed in, *Private Correspondence of Chesterfield and Newcastle 1744-46*, Part II: Chesterfield at Dublin, ed. Sir Richard Lodge, Royal Historical Society, Camden Series, Vol.XLIV (London, 1930), pp.62-123.

CHAPTER 11:

THE AFTERMATH OF THE '45

As a serious threat to King George and his ministers, Jacobitism died on the field of Culloden. Contemporaries were not nearly so sure of this as are modern historians (and indeed, in the early months of 1747 Cameron of Lochiel, in exile, was urging the French government to mount another military expedition to Scotland). This may be held in part to explain the severity of the punitive and repressive measures authorised by Westminster in the twelve months that followed the defeat of the Highland Army.

The Prince's younger brother Henry, Jacobite Duke of York, by accepting a cardinal's hat from Pope Benedict XIV at the July consistory in Rome in 1747, more or less indicated that he thought the chances of a restoration were nil. Charles was furious, for the elevation of the Jacobite heir-presumptive to the purple was, politically, appallingly damaging to his cause in both Scotland and England. It was all the more significant that the Old Pretender was very much the sponsor of his younger son's decision. Indeed, though opinion in the College of Cardinals was rightly impressed by Henry's bearing and piety, Benedict XIV granted the cardinalate out of personal appreciation of the misfortunes James had endured because of his uncompromising Roman Catholicism. There was to be one more serious conspiracy against King George and his government, the Elibank Plot, which was penetrated and exploded in 1753 by the government led by Henry Pelham, heir to Walpole. The debacle cost the life of the last Jacobite martyr, Dr Archie Cameron, younger brother to Lochiel, but really by 1753 Prince Charles, despite an expedient conversion to Anglicanism, was not politically viable.

Resumption of war with France in 1756 saw the beginnings of a change in the way Westminster viewed Scotland, the Scottish highlands in particular. Pitt may have been making a virtue out of the necessity of raising new regiments when in a famous speech at the end of the Seven Years War he spoke of his motives during the war in raising new highland regiments for the army.

"I sought for merit wherever it was to be found; it is my boast that I was the first minister who looked for it and found it in the mountains of the north. I called it forth, and drew into your service a hardy and intrepid race of men, who, when left by your jealousy, became a prey to the artifice of your enemies, and had gone nigh to have overturned the State in the war before the last. These men in the last war were brought to combat on your side; they served with fidelity, as they fought with valour, and conquered for you in every part of the world."

But it was all a far cry from the sentiments of the national song, 'God Save the King' as sung in 1745; that had invoked the aid of the Almighty "rebellious Scots to crush".

By 1764 the young and popular George III was on the throne, and Jacobite sympathisers such as Samuel Johnson had transferred their loyalties to the House of Hanover.

I: Repressive and Remedial Legislation

While London rejoiced (Handel's *Judas Maccabeus* with its resounding *"See the conquering hero comes"* was composed to honour the Duke of Cumberland) the punishment of rebellion began within a framework of due process of law. A decision of the Privy Council of 15 May 1746 had required that all rebel prisoners in Scotland be sent to England for trial, so that convictions might be the better assured. There were close to three and a half thousand Jacobite prisoners. Three of the four captive peers, including the octogenarian Lord Lovat were beheaded on Tower Hill; the Royal Army hanged nearly fifty deserters from its ranks to the Jacobite cause (as any army would have done); about the same number of officers and men, highland and lowland, from the Prince's army were also hanged. The severest retribution fell on the Manchester Regiment; of the hundred and thirty taken prisoner at Carlisle, twenty-seven, including all the officers and sergeants, died on the scaffold. Out of the total number of prisoners remaining, close to a thousand were transported to a kind of slavery in the West Indies.

An Act of Attainder (19 Geo II c.46) against leading Jacobites who had escaped the net was passed in the June of 1746. It was superceded a year later, by an Act of Indemnity (29 Geo II c.52) which extended a general pardon, excepting however eighty-four named Jacobite gentlemen who were skulking at home or in exile abroad.

The Disarming Act of 1746 (19 Geo II c.39) had redoubled the efforts of legislation of thirty years past to demilitarise the clans. The use of Highland dress, associated as it was in southern minds with the highlanders' method of fighting, was forbidden. To attack what was seen as the root cause of rebellion, the power of the chiefs over their clansmen, ward-holding, which was an ancient system of landholding involving military service as the superior required, was abolished and the whole system of heritable jurisdictions, giving judicial power to landowners, which was widespread in Lowlands as in Highlands was swept away by the Heritable Jurisdiction Act (20 Geo II c.53). Lord Chancellor Hardwicke would have gone much further. He pressed hard for the application of English law and judicial system in its entirety to Scotland, which would have reduced her to the status of an English county. (The post of Secretary of State for Scotland was already a casualty of the '45). Only adroit manoeuvring at Westminster by the 3rd Duke of Argyll thwarted Hardwicke in this.

(i) *The Act of Indemnity* (20 Geo II c.52)

Act for the King's Most Gracious
General and Free Pardon

The King, having already showed his Royal Inclination to Mercy by many particular instances of grace to such as had rendered themselves obnoxious to the Law and subject to the highest penalties—has resolved to grant his General and free Pardon in a large and bountiful manner, not doubting but that—it will raise a due sense of gratitude in all who have been artfully misled into treasonable practices against his person and government.— Therefore he desires it to be enacted by this Parliament that all his subjects—be acquitted, pardoned, etc. of all manner of treasons, felonies, seditious words, seditions, etc., all riots, offences, contempts etc. committed before 15th June 1747—with the exception of those excepted.—

—Excepting and foreprized all persons—who have been in the service of, or any ways employed by the King of Spain since the

nineteenth day of December in the year one thousand, seven
hundred and thirty-nine—or who have been in the service of or
employed by the French King, since the twenty-ninth Day of April
in the year one thousand seven hundred and forty-four, being one
month after the French King's Declaration of War against his
Majesty.

VII. And also excepted out of this Pardon, all Offences of levying
the War against His Majesty which began in this Realm in the Year
one thousand, seven hundred and forty-five by any Person or
Persons who has, or have been, or shall be beyond the Seas, at any
time between the twentieth Day of July, one thousand seven hundred
and forty-five, and the said fifteenth Day of June one thousand seven
hundred and forty-seven—

XXX. Excepted also out of this pardon, all and every Person and
Persons of the name and Clan of MacGregour—

—LX. Also excepted out of this Act of Pardon [eighty-three names
of Jacobite-minded nobility and gentlemen, almost all Scottish, from
"Peter Barry, Doctor in Physic" to" Alexander White the younger, of
Ardlehill"].

(ii) *The Heritable Jurisdiction Act* (20 Geo II c.43)

An Act for taking away and abolishing the Heretable
Jurisdictions in that Part of Great Britain called Scotland; and for
making Satisfaction to the Proprietors thereof; and for restoring such
Jurisdictions to the Crown; and for making more effectual Provision
for the Administration of Justice throughout that Part of the United
Kingdom, by the King's Courts and Judges there—and for rendering
the Union of the Two Kingdoms more complete.

For remedying the inconveniences that have arisen and may arise
from the multiplicity and extent of heretable jurisdictions in that part
of Great Britain called Scotland, for making satisfaction to the
proprietors thereof, for restoring to the crown the powers of
jurisdiction originally and properly belonging thereto, according to
the constitution, and for extending the influence, benefit, and
protection of the King's laws and courts of justice to all his
Majesty's subjects in Scotland, and for rendering the union more
complete, Be it enacted by the King's most excellent Majesty, by
and with the advice and consent of the lords spiritual and temporal,
and commons, in this present Parliament assembled, and by the

authority of the same, that all heretable jurisdictions of justiciary, and all regalities and heretable baillieries, and all heretable constabularies, other than the office of high constable of Scotland, and all stewartries, being parts only of shires or counties, and all sheriffships and deputy sheriffships of districts, being parts only of shires or counties within that part of Great Britain called Scotland, belonging unto or possessed or claimed by any subject or subjects, and all jurisdictions, powers, authorities, and privileges thereunto appurtenant or annexed or dependant thereupon, shall be and they are hereby, from and after the twenty-fifth day of March in the year of our Lord one thousand seven hundred and forty-eight, abrogated, taken away, and totally dissolved and extinguished—

II: Bitter Feelings among the Scots

There was a deep feeling of national humiliation as word spread of the brutal conduct of the Duke of Cumberland's army at Culloden and in the succeeding months. In London the Scots novelist Tobias Smollett, already a writer of distinction, expressed this in verse. In the highlands the indignity to the Gael of denying him his traditional dress was bitterly resented. Even the Heritable Jurisidctions Act, aimed at breaking the hold of the chiefs over their clansmen (and who could blame Westminster for this?) was strongly opposed as a contravention of the terms of the Treaty of Union of 1707. However an enlightened approach to the perennial highland problem did indeed emerge with the legislation for the administration of the forfeited Jacobite estates. As a proto-Highlands and Islands Development Board the Commissioners for Forfeited Estates may have been ineffective but their approach in keeping with the thinking of the Scottish Enlightenment, was the reverse of that of the authors of the Massacre of Glencoe of 1692, or the Duke of Cumberland in 1746.

(i) *Tobias Smollet: "The Tears of Scotland" (1746)*

Mourn, hapless Caledonia, mourn
Thy banish'd peace, thy laurels torn!
Thy sons, for valour long renown'd,
Lie slaughter'd on their native ground;
Thy hospitable roofs no more
Invite the stranger to the door;

In smoky ruins sunk they lie,
The monuments of cruelty.

The wretched owner sees afar
His all become the prey of war;
Bethinks him of his babes and wife,
Then smites his breast and curses life.
Thy swains are famish'd on the rocks,
Where once they fed their wanton flocks;
Thy ravish'd virgins shriek in vain;
Thy infants perish on the plain.

What boots it then, in every clime,
Through the wide spreading waste of time,
Thy martial glory, crown'd with praise,
Still shone with undiminish'd blaze?
Thy tow'ring spirit now is broke,
Thy neck is bended to the yoke.
What foreign arms could never quell,
By civil rage and rancour fell.—

(ii) *The Ban on the Wearing of Highland Dress*

20 Geo II c.39, 'An Act for the more effectual disarming of the Highlands' stipulated inter alia that none but the Army were to wear Highland dress.

—XVII And be it further enacted—That from and after the first Day of August one thousand seven hundred and forty-seven, no Man or Boy within that part of Great Britain called Scotland other than such as shall be employed as Officers and Soldiers in His Majesty's Forces shall, on any pretence whatsoever, wear or put on the clothes commonly called Highland Clothes (that is to say) the Plaid, Philabeg or little kilt, Trowse, Shoulder Belts—and that no Tartan or party-coloured Plaid or stuff shall be used for Great Coats or for Upper Coats; and if any such person shall presume—to wear or put on the aforesaid Garments or any part of them, every such person so offending—shall suffer imprisonment without bail during the space of six months—and being convicted for a second offence—shall be liable to be transported to any of His Majesty's Plantations beyond the Seas, there to remain for the Space of seven yers.

(iii) *Enforcement by the Military*

Station.
Head of Loch Rannoch.
July 20th.

Two Orderly Men with Reports from about Strathfillan, Apprehended two Highlanders in kilts, And were bringing them to Loch Rannoch, But in passing near a Village call'd Clifton, the Inhabitants mostly Women, got hold of one of the Soldiers, and the Prisoner made his escape. The other Soldier with the Man he had taken, got some Miles farther on his way, when the Inhabitants of another Village, assisted by two disbanded Highlanders, arm'd with sticks, rescued the other. The disbanded Soldiers were extremely abusive and Insolent, And threatened the Soldier very much (who had only his Side Arms) if ever he molested their Neighbours again, I thought Insults of this Nature were not to be pass'd over, for which reason I have sent a party Back, with the Orderly Men, who in their patroling, have had opportunities, of knowing where the disbanded Highlanders, and those whom they had taken live, to endeavour to secure them all, And if they are successfull, I shall send them before Clark Millan at Perth, who I hope will punish them, for insulting the soldiers in the execution of their Duty.

From Major Crawford, Perth.
Augt. 7th, 1749.

The Detachment of Genl. Pulteney's Regmt in Rannoch sent in to this place, on friday Night five Highlanders, taken up for wearing the Highland Dress Contrary to Law; they were Carried next Morning before Mr. Richardson, one of the Sheriffs Depute for this County, who acquitted one, as having a Blue upper Coat, but the other four, were Committed to Goal, in terms of the Act of Parliament, Viz.: one for wearing Trouse, And three for having Plaid upper Coats, They are Tenants to Sr. Robt. Menzies, and from the Parish of Fothrington.

Capt. Powell of Lord Ancram's Regmt.
Under His Command, 2 Sub.
Station. Inversnade Barracks.
Report. July 23, 1749.

Yesterday was sevennight, I apprehended a fellow for wearing the kilt, But upon my examining him found that he was one of the Thieves of this Country, On which I immediately acquainted the duke of Montrose of it, His Grace Immediately sent one of His Gentlemen to this place who desires me, to keep the Man, untill a Warrant is obtained for his Committment to Stirling, they being determined to prosecute him.

Capt. Scot of Genl. Guises' Regmt.
Under His Command, 2 Sub.
Station. Braemar Barracks.
Report.
Augst 4.

I have apprehended a Man for wearing the Plaid Contrary to Act
of Parliament, he had not only a Plaid on, But had under it carrying
a party colour'd great Coat, I immediately sent Him in that dress
over to Invercald, who is a Justice of the Peace, and used to give
orders for Quartering, of any parties that came here, Invercald told
the Sergt. that he did not now act as a Justice of peace, nor had not
done for some time past; therefore desired him to go to some other
Justice, As I cannot hear of any one in the Neighbourhood, I have
sent the Man to Aberdeen, to be punished as the Law directs. The
country people have good news, as they call it amongst them; this
fellow came past the Castle in his Plaid with all the assurance
Imaginable. Since the 23d of July Nothing has happened at any of
the out parties, and all is well.

Note. — The Ridiculous News amongst them is that the
Pretender, is Landed, in Long Island[1] with 20000 Men, which Spirits
them up greatly.

[1] By which was meant the Outer Hebrides.

Capt. Price of Col. Herbert's Regmt.
Under His Command, 1 Sub.
Station. Lagan Ach: Adrom.
Report. Augt. 17th, 1749.

—The Sergt. at Glencoe reports that on Sunday the 7 Inst. as two
of his party were going with his report to the Corpl. at Loch Leven,
they saw Duncan Cameron of Kinlochbegg wearing a Highland
Plaid And when he saw the soldiers he gave the Plaid to his Servant
Maid and made of as fast as he could, the men persued him But
could not overtake him, so returned Back and took the Plaid from
his Servant, the Serjt. has been in search of him two or three times,
but to no purpose, as he is a Man of some fortune And was in the
late Rebellion, think him a proper person to make him an example
of, so have sent a description of Him to all the parties, and Don't
Doubt but I shall soon have him prisoner.

Capt. Hughes of Gl. Pulteney's Regmt.
Under His Command, 2 Sub.

Station. Head of Loch Rannoch.
Report. August 12th, 1749.

Since last report, the Patroles took up in the Neighbourhood of
Rannoch, Duncan McGregor, Donald Mcgregor, Donald McGregor,
John Cameron, Alex. Robinson and John Cameron, I sent them to
Perth, and four of them were committed for wearing cloaths contrary
to Act of Parliament.

This week the patroles between here and Killin took up Ten men,
some of them dress'd in Tartan Trowyes and petticoats, short coats
and shoulder straps and one Man Compleatly Dress in Tartan
Cloaths and Trowyer, But Mr. Campbell the Sheriff Depute, at that
place dismissed them all. We also recovered the two Men, who had
been rescued at Clifton in Kilts, without any alteration to their
Dress, than Just Sewing the Kilt close before, in that manner they
were sent before Mr. Campbell who also dismiss'd them, tho the
Soldiers offer'd to Swear they were open when first apprehended,
The two disbanded Highlanders have absconded ever since, I must
be oblig'd to send my Prisoners for the future to Perth, as that
Gentleman seems Resolved to commit none of them.

Sept. 1st, 1749.

*Historical Papers relating to the Jacobite Period
1699-1750,* Vol.2, ed. Col. James Allardyce,
New Spalding Club (Aberdeen, 1894), pp. 516-21.

(iv) *Scottish Jacobites in Exile: Lochiel to James on a possible re-
run of the '45.*

Sir,

I most humbly beg leave to renew my duty and respect to your
Majesty in the beginning of the year, which I pray God may prove
more prosperous to your Royall Family and cause than the present
face of things give reason to expect. By what I took the liberty to
write on the twenty-sixth of last month, and what Yr. M. must have
from other hands, it will appear that the present misfortunes tho'
very great are not irretrievable; but at such a distance I fear Yr. M.
cannot be so fully informed as would be necessary to form a
judgement of the reall state of affairs, and the true disposition of Yr.
Ms. friends both here and Britain, for which reason I am grieved it is

not in my power to enable Lord Sempil to waite on Yr. M. at this
critical juncture, because I am persuaded his informations would
determine Yr. M. to accept of the succours that can be obtained,
rather than expose your faithful Highlanders to utter destruction, and
your whole kingdom of Scotland to the slavery with which it is
threatened. I even flatter myself that upon such lights as we are now
able to transmitt in this manner, Yr. M. may be graciously pleased to
send instructions and directions, since it is visible that the ruin of Yr.
M's. friends in Scotland would very much discourage, and perhaps
totally disspirit your friends in England, by which means the
Restoration would become impracticable, at least so difficult that it
could only be effected with an army superior to all the forces of the
Government, whereas the landing ten Regiments in Scotland before
the Highlands are depopulated, will not only unite all the
Highlanders but all other Scotsmen of spirit in Yr. M's. cause, and
give so much employment to the troops of the Government, that Yr.
M's loyal subjects in England may with small assistance be in a
condition to shake off the yoke, and compleat their own deliverance
and ours by a happy restoration.—I hope Yr. M. will approve of the
resolution I have taken to share in the fate of the people I have
undone, and, if they must be sacrificed, to fall along with them. It is
the only way I can free myself from the reproach of their blood, and
shew the disinterested zeal with which I have lived and shall dye.

Sir,
Your Majesty's most humble, most obedient, and most faithfull
Subject and servant,
DONALD CAMERON.
PARIS, January 16th, 1747.

Browne, op. cit., I, pp. 476-77.

III: Samuel Johnson gives the epilogue to Jacobitism in England

—To such a degree of unrestrained frankness had he now
accustomed me, that in the course of this evening I talked of the
numerouus reflections which had been thrown out against him, on
account of his having accepted a pension from his present Majesty.
"Why, Sir," said he, with a hearty laugh, "it is a mighty foolish noise
that they make.* I have accepted of a pension as a reward which has
been thought due to my literary merit; and now that I have this

247

pension, I am the same man in every respect that I have ever been; I retain the same principles. It is true, that I cannot now curse (smiling) the house of Hanover; nor would it be decent for me to drink King James's health in the wine that King George gives me money to pay for. But, Sir, I think that the pleasure of cursing the House of Hanover, and drinking King James's health, are amply overbalanced by three hundred pounds a year."

There was here, most certainly, an affectation of more Jacobitism than he really had; and indeed an intention of admitting, for the moment, in a much greater extent than it really existed, the charge of disaffection imputed to him by the world, merely for the purpose of showing how dexterously he could repel an attack, even though he were placed in the most disadvantageous position; for I have heard him declare, that if holding up his right hand would have secured victory at Culloden to Prince Charles's army, he was not sure he would have held it up; so little confidence had he in the right claimed by the House of Stuart, and so fearful was he of the consequences of another revolution on the throne of Great Britain; and Mr Topham Beauclerk assured me, he had heard him say this before he had his pension. At another time he said to Mr Langton, "Nothing has ever offered, that has made it worth my while to consider the question fully." He, however, also said to the same gentleman, talking of King James the Second, "It was become impossible for him to reign any longer in this country." He no doubt had an early attachment to the House of Stuart; but his zeal had cooled as his reason strengthened. Indeed I heard him once say, "that after the death of a violent Whig, with whom he used to contend with great eagerness, he felt his Toryism much abated.—"

*When I mentioned the same idle clamour to him several years afterwards, he said, with a smile, "I wish my pension were twice as large, that they might make twice as much noise."

James Boswell, *The Life of Samuel Johnson LLD,*
(entry for July 9th 1763).

IV: The Aftermath in France

In their anxiety to end the European war Louis and his ministers ignored Jacobite agitation for a re-run of the '45. Peace, when it came with the Treaty of Aix-la-Chapelle of October 1748, expressly required Charles Edward to quit France. His inability to force Louis to ignore this provision and his subsequent arrest (albeit with silken ropes) and expulsion from France was felt by the Prince as an even greater reverse than Culloden, and by the French nation with its reverence for legitimate monarchy as something of a national disgrace. Louis' standing with his own people was somewhat damaged thereby.

But the Gallic dream of getting the better of Britain by transporting French military superiority to the shores of Scotland and England continued undimmed. It was only Admiral Hawke's great victory at Quiberon Bay in 1759 which averted a two-pronged invasion attempt; a diversionary descent on the Ayrshire coast to be followed by cross-Channel invasion. Choiseul, Louis' chief minister thought of involving Charles Edward in this, but the latter's growing addiction to drink caused him to be discarded.

There was however to be one link, albeit a slender one between the Jacobite century and what was to come in France in the revolutionary years that lay ahead. The romantic story of Charles Edward's five months of danger and narrow escapes from his pursuers in the summer of 1746 appealed to the French. Diderot, the great French *philosophe* would cite the refusal of the Scottish highlanders to betray their Prince in the months after Culloden as evidence of the fundamental goodness of human nature; and it was this optimistic view of mankind and its potential which was to be the underlying faith of France's revolutionaries.

(i) *The Treaty of Aix-la-Chapelle, 1748*

The Definitive Treaty of Peace and Friendship, between his Britannick Majesty, the most Christian King, and the States General of the United Provinces. Concluded at Aix la Chapelle the 18th Day of October N.S. 1748.

In the Name of the most holy and undivided Trinity, the Father, Son, and Holy Ghost.

Be it known to all those, whom it shall or may concern, in any manner whatsoever. Europe sees the day, which Divine Providence had pointed out for the re-establishment of its repose. A general peace succeeds to the long and bloody war,—

XIX. The 5th article of the treaty of the Quadruple Alliance, concluded at London the 2d of August, 1718; containing the guaranty of the succession to the kingdom of Great Britain in the house of his Britannick Majesty now reigning, and by which every thing has been provided for, that can relate to the person who has taken the title of King of Great Britain, and to his descendents of both sexes, is expressly confirmed and renewed by the present article, as if it were here inserted in its full extent.

(The 5th article of the Treaty of the Quadruple Alliance of 1718 was as follows).

V. His sacred Imperial royal and Catholic Majesty, as also his royal most Christian Majesty, and the States General of the United Provinces do bind themselves, their heirs, and successors, to maintain and guarantee the succession in the kingdom of Great Britain, as established by the laws of that kingdom in the house of his Britannic Majesty now reigning, as likewise to defend all the dominions and provinces possessed by his Majesty. And they shall not give or grant any protection or refuge in any part of their dominions to the person, or his descendents, if he should have any, who during the life of James II. took on him the title of Prince of Wales, and since the death of that king, assumed the royal title of King of Great Britain. Promising alike for themselves, their heirs, and successors, that they will not give to the said person or his descendents, directly or indirectly, by sea or by land, any succour, council or assistance whatsoever, either in money, arms, military stores, ships, soldiers, mariners, or any other manner whatsoever. The same they shall observe with regard to those who may be ordered or commissioned by the said person or his descendents, to disturb the government of his Britannic Majesty, or the tranquillity of his kingdom, whether by open war or clandestine conspiracies, by raising seditions and rebellions, or by exercising piracy on his Britannic Majesty's subjects.—

A Collection of all the Treaties—between Great Britain
and Other Powers,
Vol.II, (London, 1785).

(ii) *Diderot's "Optimism"*

Letter to Sophie Vollard, November 1760.

"No, my dear friend, nature has not made us wicked. It is bad education, bad example, bad laws which have corrupted us—

"The Pretender, on whose head the English had put a price and whom they hunted for several months from mountain to mountain as a savage beast is hunted, found safety in the caves of these unfortunate highlanders who could have gone from wretched poverty to opulence by handing him over. But they never thought of doing so. Here is another proof of the natural goodness of man.

"*Le père Hoop* had a friend in a battle between the Scottish highlanders led by the Pretender and the English. This friend was serving with the latter. He had a hand cut off by a stroke from a highlander's broadsword. One of his fingers had on it a diamond ring. The highlander sees something sparkling on the ground. He reaches down and thrusts the severed hand in his pocket — and carries on fighting. These fellows know very well the value of gold and silver. If they did not hand over the Pretender it was because they did not want wealth at that price."

Denis Diderot, *Correspondence,* ed. Roth,
(Paris, 1957), Vol.3, p.228.

CHAPTER 12:

EPILOGUE:
JACOBITISM'S SECOND COMING

In 1784, the annexed Jacobite estates were returned to their former owners (and the prohibition of highland dress, by then for long a dead letter, was formally rescinded). But now, in Scotland, Jacobitism was indeed to 'come back again' and by means of literature and song to become deeply engraven — down to the present day — on the nation's consciousness. The chief proponents of this were James Boswell, Robert Burns, Lady Nairne and Sir Walter Scott.

I: James Boswell: the Sentimental Jacobite

Boswell was born in 1740. Coming of a landed family, despite (perhaps because of) the ultra-Hanoverian Edinburgh judge his father, Boswell was ever the sentimental Jacobite, though like Dr Johnson he was warm in his loyalty to George III. In the *Journal of a Tour to the Hebrides with Samuel Johnson LLD*, published in 1785 he inserted a narrative of what he had learned from Flora MacDonald and others of the adventures on Skye and Raasay after Culloden of 'the grandson of King James II', as Boswell tactfully termed Prince Charles. Boswell's narrative, though it covered only two weeks of the Prince's five months ordeal of danger in the Highlands throughout the summer of 1746, did much to project a sympathetic view of Charles Edward. (As the facts of that five months ordeal emerged piecemeal during the 19th century, and indeed down to very recent years, it has come to be recognised as one of the world's great adventure stories. Today the Prince is perhaps remembered more for this than for his impossibly autocratic ways). Here is a sample of Boswell's style.

> Prince Charles Edward, after the battle of Culloden, was
> conveyed to what is called the Long Island, where he lay for some
> time concealed. But intelligence having been obtained where he was

and a number of troops having come in quest of him, it became absolutely necessary for him to quit that country without delay. Miss Flora Macdonald, then a young lady, animated by what she thought the sacred principle of loyalty, offered, with the magnanimity of a heroine, to accompany him in an open boat to Sky, though the coast they were to quit was guarded by ships. He dressed himself in women's clothes, and passed as her supposed maid, by the name of Betty Bourke, an Irish girl. They got off undiscovered, though several shots were fired to bring them to, and landed at Mugstot, the seat of Sir Alexander Macdonald. Sir Alexander was then at Fort Augustus, with the Duke of Cumberland; but his lady was at home. Prince Charles took his post upon a hill near the house. Flora Macdonald waited on Lady Margaret, and acquainted her of the enterprise in which she was engaged. Her ladyship, whose active benevolence was ever seconded by superior talents, showed a perfect presence of mind and readiness of invention, and at once settled that Prince Charles should be conducted to old Rasay, who was himself concealed with some select friends. The plan was instantly communicated to Kingsburgh, who was desptched to the hill to inform the Wanderer, and carry him refreshments.—

After dinner, Flora Macdonald on horseback, and her supposed maid, and Kingsburgh, with a servant carrying some linen, all on foot, proceeded towards that gentleman's house. Upon the road was a small rivulet which they were obliged to cross. The Wanderer, forgetting his assumed sex, that his clothes might not be wet, held them up a great deal too high. Kingsburgh mentioned this to him, observing, it might make a discovery. He said he would be more careful for the future. He was as good as his word; for the next brook they crossed, he did not hold up his clothes at all, but let them float upon the water. He was very awkward in his female dress. His size was so large, and his strides so great, that some women whom they met reported that they had seen a very big woman, who looked like a man in woman's clothes, and that perhaps it was (as they expressed themselves) the Prince, after whom so much search was making.

At Kingsburgh he met with a most cordial reception; seemed gay at supper, and after it indulged himself in a cheerful glass with his worthy host. As he had not had his clothes off for a long time, the comfort of a good bed was highly relished by him, and he slept soundly till next day at one o'clock.—

On the afternoon of that day, the Wanderer, still in the same dress, set out for Portree, with Flora Macdonald and a man servant.

His shoes being very bad Kingsburgh provided him with a new pair, and taking up the old ones, said, "I will faithfully keep them till you are safely settled at St James's. I will then introduce myself by shaking them at you, to put you in mind of your night's entertainment and protection under my roof." He smiled and said, "Be as good as your word!" Kingsburgh kept the shoes as long as he lived.—

Journal of a Tour to the Hebrides with Samuel Johnson LLD;
London, 1785.
(Narrative inserted after entry for 13th September 1773).

II: Robert Burns and the Relics of a Gallant Nation

Robert Burns (still, today, hailed as Scotland's national bard) wrote in several political veins including Whiggish ones, but towards the end of his too-short life produced an important block of Jacobite songs, some collected, some written by himself. These are marked by great variation in style, from partisan ballad to tender love-song; and great virtuosity in matching words to music.

Burns latter-day Jacobitism is deeply paradoxical. His native Ayrshire had no Jacobite tradition, but — as he was proud to claim (historians are not too sure about it) — his paternal grandfather from the north-east had been 'out' in the 'Fifteen and had suffered for it. However by the end of his life Burns was politically a supporter of the 'country' opposition to the younger Pitt's 'court' interest and to government. Though modern historians tend to call the younger Pitt a Tory, this is anachronistic nonsense: he was a 'court' Whig. At the same time Burns' inmost thoughts seem to have been radical-revolutionary. In Burns overt politically 'country' stance and frustrated radicalism probably lies the impulse for his Jacobite songs.

He was also a cultural nationalist, anxious like his friend and correspondent the Earl of Buchan to preserve Scottish identity by collecting and revitalising what was of value in the national heritage. Jacobite song was therefore a vehicle by which he could voice much more profound and disturbing thoughts than later manipulators of sentimental Jacobitism.

By identifying Stuart monarchy with Scottish independence and corporate well-being Burns is able to fiercely criticise the corruption of civic virtue under Westminster rule. The reference to thistles (thrissles) and roses is of course a reference to England and Scotland.

Awa, Whigs, awa!
   Awa, Whigs, awa!
Ye're but a pack o traitor louns,
   Ye'll do nae guid at a'.

Our thrissles flourish'd fresh and fair,
   And bonie bloom'd our roses;
But Whigs cam like a frost in June,
   An wither'd a our posies.

   Awa, Whigs, awa! etc.

Our ancient crown's fa'n in the dust—
   Deil blin' them wi the stoure* o't,
An write their names in the black beuk
   Wha gae the Whigs the power o't!

   Awa, Whigs, awa! etc.

Our sad decay in church and state
   Surpasses my descriving.
The Whigs cam o'er us for a curse,
   An we hae done wi thriving.

   Awa, Whigs, awa! etc.

Grim Vengeance lang has taen a nap,
   But we may see him waukin—
Gude** help the day when Royal heads
   Are hunted like a maukin!***

*stoure — dust;
**Gude — God;
***maukin — hare

(ii) "*It was a' for our rightfu King*"

Burns based this poem on a chap-book ballad dating from 1746, but telling the story of an episode during King William's Irish war of 1689-90. He transmutes it into a haunting elegy.

It was a' for our rightfu King
    We left fair Scotland's strand;
It was a' for our rightfu King
    We e'er saw Irish land, my dear—
    We e'er saw Irish land.

Now a' is done that men can do,
    And a' is done in vain,
My Love and Native Land fareweel,
    For I maun* cross the main, my dear—
    For I maun cross the main.

He turn'd him right and round about
    Upon the Irish shore,
And gae his bridle reins a shake,
    With adieu for evermore, my dear—
    And adieu for evermore!

The soger frae the war returns.
    The sailor frae the main,
But I hae parted frae my love,
    Never to meet again, my dear—
    Never to meet again.

When day is gane, and night is come,
And a' folk bound to sleep,
I think on him that's far awa
    The lee-lang night, and weep, my dear—
    The lee-lang night and weep.

*maun — must

(iii) *The Meaning of Jacobitism*

Appropriately it was to be the national bard who gave voice to the essential meaning of the nobler side of Jacobitism, as is shewn by this quotation from a letter of his of 16th December 1789 to Lady Winifred Maxwell Constable whose ancestor, the last Earl of Nithsdale had suffered for his part in the '15.

—with your Ladyship I have the honor to be connected by one of the strongest & most endearing ties in the whole Moral World — Common Sufferers in a Cause where even to be unfortunate is glorious, the Cause of Heroic Loyalty! — Though my Fathers had not illustrious Honors and vast properties to hazard in the contest; though they left their humble cottages only to add so many units more to the unnoted croud that followed their Leaders; yet, what they could they did, and what they had they lost: with unshaken firmness and unconcealed Political Attachments, they shook hands with Ruin for what they esteemed the cause of their King and their Country.—

III: Lady Nairne and 'Traditional' Jacobite Songs

Lady Nairne was born Carolina Oliphant in "the Auld Hoose" of Gask in Strathearn in south Perthshire, in 1766. Her family had been perhaps the most consistently and intransigently Jacobite family in Scotland. Lady Nairne was named for Charles, the Bonnie Prince Charlie of the '45. George III was in fact not the least offended by what he regarded, rightly, as the eccentric ultra-conservatism of the Oliphants, rather than as a serious threat to his thrones.

In 1806 Caroline Oliphant had married Major (later Lord) Nairne, then an Assistant Inspector General of Barracks in Scotland. He was of Jacobite lineage; his post and their home was for a number of years in Edinburgh. Her poems and songs were originally all written anonymously, as authorship scarcely became a respectable married lady of good family and unobstrusive but strongly Evangelical piety. She died aged 79 in 1845. Her Jacobite songs were therefore written in the third generation after the '45, from the very heart of the Hanoverian establishment, and they began to appear during its long struggle with Revolutionary and Napoleonic France. They are primarily a celebration of certain Jacobite sentiments, but not the critical or subversive ones. (They are also far removed in sentiment from the Gaelic poems of Alasdair Mac Mhaighstir Alasdair of the '45). With Lady Nairne's songs, a sentimental Jacobitism entered the drawing rooms of aristocratic and well-to-do Scotland.

(i) *"Charlie is My Darling"*

The strength of this theme in the era in which Lady Nairne lived is underlined by the fact that no fewer than four versions of it exist. They are by Robert Burns, James Hogg, Charles Gray, and this one, printed anonymously in *The Scottish Minstrel* by Lady Nairne.

'Twas on a Monday morning,
  Right early in the year,
When Charlie came to our toun,
  The young Chevalier.

    Oh, Charlie is my darling,
    My darling, my darling;
    Oh, Charlie is my darling,
      The young Chevalier.

As he came marching up the street,
  The pipes play'd loud and clear,
And a' the folk came running out
  To meet the Chevalier.

    Oh, Charlie is my darling, etc.—

(ii) *"Will ye no come back again"*

This is an outstanding example of the romantic invocation of the Lost Cause. No place here for Lord George Murray's strongly stated view after Culloden that the pity was he came at all!

Bonnie Charlie's noo awa',
  Safely owre the friendly main;
Mony a heart will break in twa,
  Should he ne'er come back again.

    Will ye no come back again?
    Will ye no come back again?
    Better lo'ed ye canna be,
    Will ye no come back again?

Ye trusted in your Hieland men,
  They trusted you, dear Charlie;
They kent you hiding in the glen,
  Your cleadin' was but barely.

Will ye no, etc....

English bribes were a' in vain,
  An' e'en tho' puirer we may be;
Siller canna buy the heart
  That beats aye for thine and thee.

  Will ye no, etc.

IV: Sir Walter Scott: Reconciler and Romantic

Scott's *Waverley*, published in 1813 went much further in establishing her Jacobite past deep in Scotland's consciousness where it may well be thought to remain to this day. Yet, the celebrated novel seems to have been written to some considerable extent for Hanoverian purposes. The French Revolution had intensified the attachment of the Scottish ruling classes to their Hanoverian-patriot monarch, George III, in the face of the radical threat. There was a need to accommodate the ugly fact that the rebellion of '45 had taken place and that its consequences had been a national affront. Hence *Waverley* with its astonishingly spurious plot in which a young English army officer with Jacobite antecedents goes over to the Prince Charles' Highland Army, but after the rebellion is over wins back the good graces of government by the intercession of an English colonel who is the epitome of sanity and urbanity.

  Scott in the introduction to *Waverley* cites as the original for this tale the friendship in the course of the '45 of an old highland laird of his acquaintance and a South of Scotland colonel whose life he had saved at Prestonpans. But had there been any officer of the British army who had deserted in this way it is certain that, had he escaped the gallows, he would have had, like Lord Elcho, to endure the life-long banishment and the unyielding animosity of government. (It is strange that this does not seem to have been remarked on before).

  Scott, indeed, is hard on Jacobites in *Waverley* as elsewhere (e.g. *The Black Dwarf*, *The Bride of Lammermoor*, *Rob Roy*). The Baron Bradwardine of *Waverley* is a prosy, pleasing old bore: his 'original', Lord Pitsligo, was a saintly character of great common-sense. The scheming Fergus McIvor, next to Edward Waverley, the novel's principal character, bears no relation to any of the chiefs. Lord George Murray, the Jacobite general, in many ways the most admirable of men, nowhere appears.

But there was also Scott the romantic, and in the memorable passage where Edward Waverley first meets the Prince at Holyroodhouse he gave the romanticism he felt full rein for "a Prince to live and die for".

The reconciliation to these two divergent attitudes is seen in *Redgauntlet*, Scott's great elegy for Jacobitism. In this impressive melange of fact and fancy he has a middle-aged Charles Edward come back twenty years after the '45, only to find that his support is no more, and that even the authorities, in the person of another British Army Colonel of marked urbanity and sanity, do not even wish to arrest him. The Prince's touching renunciation of ambition which follows in the novel is entirely at variance with the actuality of the Charles Edward Stuart of the late 1760s.

The Concluding Paragraphs of Redgauntlet
(slightly abridged)

The last heir of the Stuarts leant on Redgauntlet's arm as they walked towards the beach; for the ground was rough, and he no longer possessed the elasticity of limb and of spirit which had, twenty years before, carried him over many a Highland hill, as light as one of their native deer. His adherents followed, looking on the ground, their feelings struggling against the dictates of their reason.

General Campbell accompanied them with an air of apparent ease and indifference, but watching, at the same time, and no doubt with some anxiety, the changing features of those who acted in this extraordinary scene.—

They arrived at the place of embarkation. The Prince stood a moment with folded arms, and looked around him in deep silence. A paper was then slipped into his hands. He looked at it, and said, 'I find the two friends I have left at Fairladies are apprised of my destination and propose to embark from Bowness. I presume this will not be an infringement of the conditions under which you have acted?'

'Certainly not,' answered General Campbell; 'they shall have all facility to join you.'

'I wish, then,' said Charles, 'only another companion.

Redgauntlet, the air of this country is as hostile to you as it is to me. These gentlemen have made their peace, or rather they have done nothing to break it. But you, come you, and share my home where chance shall cast it. We shall never see these shores again; but we will talk of them, and of our disconcerted bull-fight.'

'I follow you, Sire, through life,' said Redgauntlet, 'as I would have followed you to death. Permit me one moment.'

The Prince then looked round, and seeing the abashed countenances of his other adherents bent upon the ground, he hastened to say, 'Do not think that you, gentlemen, have obliged me less because your zeal was mingled with prudence, entertained, I am sure, more on my own account, and on that of your country, than from selfish apprehensions.'

He stepped from one to another, and, amid sobs and bursting tears, received the adieus of the last remnant which had hitherto supported his lofty pretensions, and addressed them individually with accents of tenderness and affection.

The General drew a little aloof, and signed to Redgauntlet to speak with him while this scene proceeded. 'It is now all over,' he said, 'and Jacobite will be henceforward no longer a party name. When you tire of foreign parts, and wish to make your peace, let me know. Your restless zeal alone has impeded your pardon hitherto.'—

The unfortunate Charles Edward had now given his last adieus to his downcast adherents. He made a sign with his hand to Redgauntlet, who came to assist him into the skiff. General Campbell also offered his assistance; the rest appearing too much affected by the scene which had taken place to prevent him.

'You are not sorry, General, to do me this last act of courtesy,' said the Chevalier; 'and, on my part, I thank you for it. You have taught me the principle on which men on the scaffold feel forgiveness and kindness even for their executioner. Farewell!'

They were seated in the boat, which presently pulled off from the land. The Oxford divine broke out into a loud benediction, in terms which General Campbell was too generous to criticise at the time, or to remember afterwards; nay, it is said that, Whig and Campbell as he was, he could not help joining in the universal Amen! which resounded from the shore.

[But our criticism is beside the point. Scott's purpose was quasi-political, to effect reconciliation in the Scottish psyche; and in this he succeeded magnificently.]

INDEX

For subjects, see also Table of Contents